International Organization

International Organization
Theories and Institutions

Second Edition

J. Samuel Barkin

palgrave
macmillan

INTERNATIONAL ORGANIZATION: THEORIES AND INSTITUTIONS, SECOND EDITION
Copyright © J. Samuel Barkin, 2006, 2013.

First edition published in hardcover and paperback in 2006 by PALGRAVE MACMILLAN® in the United States—a division of St. Martin's Press LLC, 175 Fifth Avenue, New York, NY 10010.

Where this book is distributed in the UK, Europe and the rest of the world, this is by Palgrave Macmillan, a division of Macmillan Publishers Limited, registered in England, company number 785998, of Houndmills, Basingstoke, Hampshire RG21 6XS.

Palgrave Macmillan is the global academic imprint of the above companies and has companies and representatives throughout the world.

Palgrave® and Macmillan® are registered trademarks in the United States, the United Kingdom, Europe and other countries.

ISBN: 978–1–137–30240–3

The Library of Congress has cataloged the first edition hardcover and paperback as follows:

Barkin, J. Samuel, 1965–
     International organization : theories and institutions / J. Samuel Barkin
          p. cm.
     Includes bibliographical references and index.
     ISBN 1–4039–7248–6—ISBN 1–4039–7250–8 (pbk.)
     1. International organization. 2. International agencies. I. Title.

JZ1308.B37 2006
341.2—dc22   2005051247

A catalogue record of the book is available from the British Library.

Design by Macmillan India Ltd.

Second PALGRAVE MACMILLAN paperback edition: March 2013

10 9 8 7 6 5 4 3 2 1

Transferred to Digital Printing in 2013

Contents

Acronyms

ACCOBAMS	Agreement on the Conservation of Cetaceans of the Black Sea, Mediterranean Sea and Contiguous Atlantic Area
ADB	Asian Development Bank
AfDB	African Development Bank
AFNOR	Association Française de Normalisation
ANSI	American National Standards Institute
AU	African Union
BIRPI	United International Bureaux for the Protection of Intellectual Property
BIS	Bank for International Settlements
CBD	Convention on Biological Diversity
CCAMLR	Convention for the Conservation of Antarctic Marine Living Resources
CITES	Convention on International Trade in Endangered Species of Wild Fauna and Flora
COE	Council of Europe
CSCE	Conference on Security and Co-operation in Europe
DPKO	United Nations Department of Peacekeeping Operations
DSM	Dispute Settlement Mechanism
EBRD	European Bank for Reconstruction and Development
ECB	European Central Bank
ECOSOC	United Nations Economic and Social Council
ECOWAS	Economic Community of West African States
ECSC	European Coal and Steel Community
EEC	European Economic Community
EU	European Union
FAA	Federal Aviation Administration
FAO	Food and Agriculture Organization of the United Nations
FATF	Financial Action Task Force
G-77	Group of 77
GA	United Nations General Assembly
GATS	General Agreement on Trade in Services

GATT	General Agreement on Tariffs and Trade
GDP	gross domestic product
GEF	Global Environment Facility
GSTP	Global System of Trade Preferences among Developing Countries
IADB	Inter-American Development Bank
IAEA	International Atomic Energy Agency
IASB	International Accounting Standards Board
IATA	International Air Transport Association
IBRD	International Bank for Reconstruction and Development
ICANN	Internet Corporation for Assigned Names and Numbers
ICAO	International Civil Aviation Organization
ICC	International Criminal Court
ICJ	International Court of Justice
ICPO	International Criminal Police Organization (also INTERPOL)
ICRC	International Committee of the Red Cross
ICSID	International Centre for the Settlement of Investment Disputes
ICTR	International Criminal Tribunal for Rwanda
ICTY	International Criminal Tribunal for the Former Yugoslavia
IDA	International Development Association
IFC	International Finance Corporation
IFI	international financial institution
ILO	International Labour Organization
IMF	International Monetary Fund
IMO	International Maritime Organization
INTELSAT	International Telecommunications Satellite Organization (currently ITSO)
INTERPOL	International Criminal Police Organization (also ICPO)
IO	international organization
IOC	International Olympic Committee
IPCC	Intergovernmental Panel on Climate Change
ISA	International Seabed Authority
ISO	International Organization for Standardization
ITO	International Trade Organization
ITSO	International Telecommunications Satellite Organization (formerly INTELSAT)
IUCN	International Union for the Conservation of Nature
IWC	International Whaling Commission
LRTAP	Convention on Long-range Transboundary Air Pollution
MAI	Multilateral Agreement on Investment
MDG	UN Millennium Development Goals
MEA	multilateral environmental agreement
MIGA	Multilateral Investment Guarantee Agency
NAFO	Northwest Atlantic Fisheries Organization
NAFTA	North American Free Trade Agreement
NATO	North Atlantic Treaty Organization
NGO	nongovernmental organization

NIEO	New International Economic Order
NPT	Treaty on the Non-Proliferation of Nuclear Weapons
OAS	Organization of American States
OAU	Organization of African Unity
OECD	Organization for Economic Co-operation and Development
OEEC	Organization for European Economic Co-operation
OSCE	Organization for Security and Co-operation in Europe
PD	Prisoners' dilemma
R2P	responsibility to protect
SADC	Southern African Development Community
SARS	Severe Acute Respiratory Syndrome
SC	United Nations Security Council
SPS	Agreement on Sanitary and Phytosanitary Measures
TBT	Agreement on Technical Barriers to Trade
TNC	transnational corporation
TRIMs	Agreement on Trade-Related Investment Measures
UDHR	Universal Declaration of Human Rights
UN	United Nations
UNCED	United Nations Conference on Environment and Development
UNCHE	United Nations Conference on the Human Environment
UNCTAD	United Nations Conference on Trade and Development
UNDAF	United Nations Development Assistance Framework
UNDP	United Nations Development Programme
UNEP	United Nations Environment Programme
UNESCO	United Nations Educational, Scientific, and Cultural Organization
UNFCCC	United Nations Framework Convention on Climate Change
UNFICYP	United Nations Peacekeeping Force in Cyprus
UNHCHR	Office of the United Nations High Commissioner for Human Rights
UNHCR	Office of the United Nations High Commissioner for Refugees
UNICEF	United Nations Children's Fund
UNMIK	United Nations Interim Administration Mission in Kosovo
UNODC	United Nations Office on Drugs and Crime
UNRWA	United Nations Relief and Works Agency for Palestinian Refugees in the Near East
UPU	Universal Postal Union
USSR	Union of Soviet Socialist Republics
WFP	World Food Programme
WHO	World Health Organization
WIPO	World Intellectual Property Organization
WMO	World Meteorological Organization
WTO	World Trade Organization

Preface

This is not a book about international organizations (IOs). Nor is it a book about global governance. It is a book about IO theory, and about the use of this theory to understand international relations. It does not attempt to systematically review the world of IOs or to comprehensively describe the UN or any other particular organization. Its goal is to review IO theory, and to use particular IOs illustratively, to suggest ways in which the theories discussed can help us understand the role of IOs in international politics. Similarly, because its focus is exclusively on IO theory and the application of that theory to IOs, it does not attempt to deal with other aspects of global governance, such as the role of nongovernmental organizations (NGOs) and global civil society in international relations.

This book is written as a primer for upper-level undergraduate students and for graduate students, either for courses on IOs or for the IO component of courses on international relations theory. It is designed either as a supplement to textbooks on IOs, or as an introduction to primary sources on IO theory (or both). In particular, the goal of the book is to show students of IOs the analytic tools available to them to understand what IOs are designed to do, how they work, what effects they have, and how to design them better. It goes beyond simple questions of whether IOs matter, and looks at the ways in which the different analytical tools developed within the rubric of IO theory are useful for answering different questions about the role of IOs in international politics. This second edition is both updated from the first and expanded to include new issue-areas, such as environmental governance.

The book is intended to fill what I see as a gap in books on IOs and IO theory: a gap between introductory textbooks and primary sources of theory. There are a number of books that do a good job of presenting the UN system from a bureaucratic, organizational, or historical perspective, but they are largely atheoretical. There are a number of introductory textbooks that present IOs in a theoretical context, but this context is based on a distinction between realism and liberalism that does not do justice to the breadth and nuance of IO theory. Primary sources for IO theory provide this breadth and nuance, but they generally relate theory to very specific questions or organizations. Putting these sources together to arrive at a big picture of IO theory can be a challenge for students. This book is designed to provide a concise bridge among these other categories of readings.

Books, even when authored alone, are always collaborative projects, and in the process of writing this one I have accumulated some debts of thanks. I would like to thank Beth DeSombre for comments on several versions of this manuscript, and much else besides, and Chip Hauss and Craig Murphy for their support of the project. The publication and editorial staff at Palgrave are excellent people to work with. Thanks are due to the Political Science Department of the University of Florida for its support of this project in its first edition, and to the Conflict Resolution, Human Security, and Global Governance Department of the McCormack Graduate School at the University of Massachusetts Boston for support of the second. Several generations of students in INR 3502 and INR 6507 (the course number for International Organization at the undergraduate and graduate levels, respectively, at the University of Florida) contributed (intentionally or not) to my thinking about how to teach about IO and IOs. Finally, thanks to Jessica Peet, who compiled the index for the first edition and provided comments for the second, and to Yuliya Rashchupkina who updated the index for the second edition.

Introduction: The State and International Organizations

The traditional literature in international relations begins with, and focuses on, states. From a political perspective, states have power, both military and economic, that other institutions or individuals do not. From a legal perspective, states are sovereign. In international law, states are recognized as actors; other institutions (or, for that matter, individuals) are not. And yet, international organizations (IOs) are attracting increasing attention, both positive and negative. They are also increasingly becoming a focus of study by political scientists. This book is an introduction to the study of IOs in the field of international relations. It looks at the different ways in which IOs are studied, and then applies these different modes of study to a variety of specific issue areas and cases.

"International organizations" are understood in this book to be inclusive intergovernmental organizations. Intergovernmental organizations, as opposed to nongovernmental organizations (NGOs) and corporations, are organizations that are created by agreement among states rather than by private individuals. Amnesty International, Greenpeace, and the General Motors Corporation all operate across national boundaries, but they were not created by governments. These NGOs and transnational corporations (TNCs) are integral parts of the international political system, but they are not IOs. The United Nations (UN), the Northwest Atlantic Fisheries Organization (NAFO), and the World Bank, however, were all created by treaties signed by states and are thus intergovernmental institutions. This book is about the latter group. Some IOs are created by other IOs rather than by states directly. These are often referred to as "emanations," and they still count as IOs because their members are sovereign states: even though they were created by other IOs, they are ultimately answerable to their member states.[1]

Inclusive organizations are those that all interested parties can join, whereas exclusive organizations are those designed specifically to exclude some countries. The most common example of an exclusive intergovernmental organization is the military alliance. Military alliances are exclusive because some countries are inevitably kept out of them; that is the point of alliances. They are organizations designed to protect those in the group from those outside it. As such, military alliances, for example, the North Atlantic Treaty Organization (NATO), are not covered in depth in this book. In contrast, even though the UN deals with security issues, it is an inclusive organization because all states can join it. Rather than defending states in the UN from those outside it, the UN is designed to protect its members from other members who break the rules. It should be noted here that regional organizations can be inclusive even if only members of the region can join, as long as the organization is focused inward and is not intended to work against those outside the region. An organization such as the European Union (EU) is in a middle ground between inclusive and exclusive organizations; in principle, all the countries of Europe can become members, but only after extensive negotiation with, and approval by, existing members.

Restricting the discussion to inclusive intergovernmental organizations may seem at first to be too restrictive, but doing so still leaves us with tens of thousands of organizations to look at and allows us to focus on the specific attributes of those organizations as a class. And these organizations cover a wide scope, in a number of ways. They can have anywhere from 2 to more than 200 member states (the UN, at the time of writing, has 193 members). They can have budgets anywhere from the tens of thousands of dollars per year to the tens of billions. Some employ one staff member, others have thousands of people on the payroll. Some are relatively anonymous, with only people who work within the same arcane issue-area having heard of them; others, such as the UN or the World Bank, are household names. Finally, IOs cover a huge range of issue-areas. Some deal with issues of peace and security, others with human rights or international economic or environmental issues, and yet others with the coordination of international aviation or broadcast standards. In fact, there are few areas of contemporary life in which there are no IOs creating rules, monitoring behavior, or promoting cooperation.

Where does the study of IOs fit into the international relations literature? The traditional study of international relations focused, and much of the field still focuses, on relations among states. Other forms of organization, whether intergovernmental or nongovernmental, do not figure prominently in this view of global politics. The past two decades have seen the development of a field called global governance, which looks at the way in which global interactions are regulated. From this perspective, the source of governance is not assumed a priori, but is a question to be asked. Global governance as a field of study looks not only at formal mechanisms of government, but also at "governance without government,"[2] patterns of regulation of global activity that do not come from specific authoritative sources. International organization as a field of study fits somewhere between traditional international relations and global governance. It remains more focused on states than much of the global governance literature, inasmuch as IOs are intergovernmental and participate in formal modes of governance. But it captures elements of that governance that can elude the focus in the traditional international relations literature on states alone.

What about the institutions themselves? Do IOs matter? What are their effects on international relations? How can we study them? How do we know what they are accomplishing and whether they are working? This book begins to address these questions by looking at four distinctions to be found in the theoretical literature on IOs. These distinctions are reflected by the titles of Chapters 1–4: the distinction between sovereignty and globalization, between power and interdependence, between regimes and institutions, and between efficiency and ideas. Chapter 5 provides a general overview of the global system of IOs, focused on the UN system. The rest of the book is devoted to applying these distinctions, these sets of theoretical concepts, to a set of specific cases. Chapters 6–14 focus on particular IOs within each issue-area that are either representative or particularly central. The IOs discussed in the second half of the book are meant to be illustrative examples; these chapters do not provide comprehensive surveys of the organizations active in each issue-area. The EU is not covered in any of these chapters, both because it is in so many ways an outlier, different from other IOs, and because there is an extensive literature on the EU that is separate from the literature on IOs, one that is too large to cover comprehensively in one volume along with the general literature on IOs.

The first of the distinctions around which the first part of this book is organized is between sovereignty and globalization. Sovereignty is the starting point in traditional international relations theory, which sees world politics as a struggle for power among sovereign states. In the past two decades, however, globalization has become a buzzword both for those applauding and for those opposing trends toward policy convergence among states. Is globalization undermining the sovereign state system? If so, what role do IOs play in the process? International organizations can be seen as the agents through which states are promoting the forces of globalization, or they can be seen as the agents that states are using to protect themselves from the broader forces of globalization. If the former, they are helping to undermine the traditional state system. If the latter, they are helping to support it. Chapter 1 looks at the theoretical relationship between IOs and globalization.

The second distinction follows from the first, and is the distinction between power and interdependence. Globalization results from, among other things, changes in technology, communications, and economics that make states more interdependent. In other words, the policy options of states are becoming increasingly constrained by the policy choices made by other states. Many analysts of IOs argue that they are the most effective ways for states to deal with interdependence. In other words, that they are vehicles through which states cooperate to promote the best outcomes for everyone in an interdependent world. Others argue, however, that IOs are not neutral agents of cooperation, but that they represent the interests of particular states and are mechanisms through which powerful states control less-powerful ones. Chapter 2 examines both arguments.

The third distinction is less about the place of IOs in the world, and more about how we can study them. This is the distinction between institutions and what the IO literature calls regimes (the word has a somewhat different meaning in this context than the colloquial usage). The regimes literature studies the effects of IOs on other actors in international relations, particularly states.

It looks at IOs as if they were black boxes, and examines the inputs into and outputs from these boxes. The institutional literature looks within the organizations themselves, and asks how the structure of the organization as an institution, and the people within it, affects what the IO does. In other words, the regime approach looks at the effects of IOs on other actors, whereas the institutional approach looks at the organization itself as an actor. Chapter 3 looks at these two different approaches, and asks what sort of information can be had from which sort of analysis.

The fourth and final distinction relates to what it is that IOs actually accomplish. This distinction can best be represented as one between efficiency and ideas. Some analysts of IOs focus on their role in making relations among states as efficient as possible. They do this by submitting IOs to what is essentially an economic style of analysis. Other analysts focus on how IOs affect the way that states, national decision-makers, and global populations more broadly think. In other words, they examine the effects of IOs on norms of behavior in international politics. This calls for a more sociological mode of analysis. International organizations clearly affect both the efficiency of relations among states and the ideas underlying those relations, but the distinction is important in terms of how we study the effects of IOs. Chapter 4 discusses the methodologies of both approaches. Chapter 5 provides some background information on the UN system as a whole.

Chapters 6–14 examine particular organizations and issue-areas through the lenses of theories of international organization. Chapters 6, 7, and 8 look at issues of peace, and of both international and human security. Chapter 6 introduces the concepts of collective security and human security, and focuses specifically on the role of the UN Security Council in enforcing them. Chapter 7 looks at other organizations involved in the maintenance of international and human security, including the UN Secretariat, and regional collective security organizations such as the Organization for Security and Co-operation in Europe (OSCE) and the Organization of American States (OAS). It also looks at IOs involved in other aspects on international and human security, such as the International Atomic Energy Agency (IAEA), and the International Criminal Court (ICC). Chapter 8 focuses on issues of human rights and humanitarian aid. The institutions used as examples include the Office of the United Nations High Commissioner for Human Rights (UNHCHR), the Council of Europe (COE), the Office of the United Nations High Commissioner for Refugees (UNHCR), and the World Food Programme (WFP).

Chapters 9, 10, and 11 look at the governance of the international political economy. Chapter 9 deals primarily with issues of international trade. It focuses on the World Trade Organization (WTO), and discusses in less detail organizations such as the World Intellectual Property Organization (WIPO) and the Organization for Economic Co-operation and Development (OECD). Chapter 10 addresses issues of international finance, with a primary focus on the International Monetary Fund (IMF), and a secondary glance at the Bank for International Settlements (BIS) and the G-7/8/20. Chapter 11 focuses on international development issues, using as examples the World Bank, the United

Nations Development Programme (UNDP), and the United Nations Conference on Trade and Development (UNCTAD). Chapter 12 is about global environmental governance, and examines the United Nations Environment Programme (UNEP) and a wide range of Multilateral Environmental Agreements (MEAs).

Chapter 13 is organized around a discussion of IOs that deal with some of the more technical and mundane aspects of international life, but on which life in the modern world has come to depend. These are often referred to as functional organizations, and the examples discussed in this chapter include the International Civil Aviation Organization (ICAO), the Universal Postal Union (UPU), and the World Health Organization (WHO). Chapter 14 looks at some organizations that lie at the border of our definition of intergovernmental institutions. These organizations are either hybrids of IOs and NGOs, or are NGOs that play some official role in the international system. The examples discussed in the chapter include the International Organization for Standardization (ISO), the International Union for the Conservation of Nature (IUCN), the International Criminal Police Organization (ICPO, or Interpol), the International Telecommunications Satellite Organization (ITSO, formerly INTELSAT), the International Committee of the Red Cross (ICRC), and the International Olympic Committee (IOC). Finally, Chapter 15 revisits the basic questions underlying this book: Do international institutions matter, and how do we study them?

1

Sovereignty and Globalization

This chapter starts with the distinction between sovereignty and globalization as a way of getting at the big picture of international governance. What is the place of international organizations (IOs) in world politics? IOs, defined here as inclusive intergovernmental organizations, are a relatively new phenomenon in international relations. They first appeared on the scene a little more than a century ago, in a modern state system that had already been around for more than 200 years. Before the advent of inclusive IOs there had been exclusive intergovernmental organizations, such as military alliances, among sovereign states. Predating the state system altogether were important international non-state actors such as the Catholic Church and the Holy Roman Empire. But these actors were not intergovernmental—they were not created by states, but rather existed independently of them.

The first organizations created by treaties among states designed to deal with particular problems that a number of states faced in common appeared in the nineteenth century. At first they were designed to address very specific issues of an economic and technical nature, such as creating clear rules for navigation on the Rhine River, delivering international mail, or managing the Pacific fur seal fishery in a sustainable manner.[1] While these narrowly-focused organizations grew slowly in number, they were followed in the wake of World War I (1914–1918) by new organizations with broader remits. The best known of these organizations is the League of Nations, created to help its member nations to maintain international peace and security, and avoid a repeat of the horrors of the war. But other organizations with relatively broad mandates were created as well, such as the International Labour Organization (ILO), the charter of which allows the organization to deal with international labor issues, broadly defined.[2]

The ILO still exists, and still does roughly the same job envisioned by its creators. The League of Nations does not—it failed to prevent World War II and failed to survive it. In the aftermath of the war, the League was replaced by an even more ambitious organization, the United Nations (UN). A primary goal of the UN, as stated in its Charter, is to deal with the same sorts of issues of international peace and security that the League was supposed to deal with.[3] But the UN brings under its umbrella a broad range of organizations that run the gamut of international issues.[4] Since World War II, the number of IOs has proliferated, slowly at first, and more quickly in the past few decades. According to the Union of International Associations, the number of intergovernmental organizations crossed 1,000 in the early 1980s, and by the early twenty-first century there were more than 5,000 (although the number seems to have held relatively steady for the past decade).[5]

Does this proliferation of IOs fundamentally change the way in which international politics works? International relations scholarship has traditionally regarded the sovereign state as the central institution in international politics. Recently, particularly in the past fifteen years, the concept of globalization has begun to appear in the international relations literature. A key implication of globalization is that the state is losing its autonomy as the central locus of decision-making in international relations. The debate between those who see the sovereign state as the key institution in world politics and those who see the process of globalization as displacing states is a good place to start the discussion of the role of IOs in international relations.

Sovereignty

When we think about international relations, we think primarily about the system of sovereign states. There are two key parts to such a system, what we might call internal sovereignty and external sovereignty. Internal sovereignty refers to autonomy, the ability of the state to make and enforce its own rules domestically. External sovereignty refers to the recognition of the state by other states, the acceptance of the state by the international community.[6] States do not necessarily have equal levels of both kinds of sovereignty. Taiwan, for example, has a level of internal sovereignty that is equivalent to that of many other industrialized countries. But it does not have full external sovereignty, and as a result cannot participate in many UN activities that lead to the creation of international rules. The Democratic Republic of the Congo, by contrast, has full external sovereignty, and can thus participate more fully in international activities. But it has limited internal sovereignty because it has no control over what happens in much of its territory. Similarly, the government of Somaliland, a breakaway territory in the northwest of Somalia, governs far more effectively than the official government of Somalia, but is not recognized internationally as sovereign, whereas the government of Somalia, despite an almost complete lack of internal sovereignty, is.[7]

The sovereign state system has not always been the central organizing feature of international relations. Empires, rather than sovereign states, wrote much of the political history of ancient civilizations, and the feudal era in Europe featured overlapping and territorially indistinct patterns of political authority. The genesis of the current system of states has often been dated back to 1648, when the Peace of Westphalia ended the Thirty Years War by diminishing the political role of many tiers of the feudal nobility. While this is a simplification of history, much of the system of sovereign states as we know it emerged in seventeenth-century Europe.[8]

One important feature of sovereignty, however, changed fundamentally in the nineteenth century. In the seventeenth and eighteenth centuries, princes were sovereign. From the perspective of the international community, a country was the property of its ruler, and representatives of the country represented the interests of the ruler rather than of the population. Beginning in the nineteenth century, and even more so in the twentieth, citizens became sovereign. Rulers became representative of their populations, rather than the other way around.[9] In the twentieth century, even dictators usually claimed to be ruling in the interests of the people, rather than for their own gain. This meant that although countries still warred with their neighbors to increase their territory, they also became more likely to cooperate with their neighbors to maximize the welfare of their citizens. This helps to explain the genesis of intergovernmental cooperation through IOs in the nineteenth century.

Globalization

But is this cooperation, and the increased prevalence of IOs that results from it, undermining sovereignty? The most popular set of arguments that it is can be called the globalization approach.[10] This approach begins with the observation that a set of transnational forces, ranging from mobile investment capital to global environmental degradation, is limiting the ability of states to make independent policy decisions. There are two effects of these forces. The first is an increasing tendency to act multilaterally rather than unilaterally—in other words, to create and act through IOs.[11] The other effect is to mold policy to fit the dictates of international economic forces.[12] A combination of these effects can be seen in many issue-areas. In international trade issues, for example, many states participate in the World Trade Organization (WTO) for fear of being ignored by international investors and transnational corporations (TNCs) if they do not.

Globalization can undermine both internal and external sovereignty. It can undermine internal sovereignty by diminishing state autonomy. The more practical decision-making power is transferred from governments to both IOs and nongovernmental actors, the less ability states have to meaningfully make policy decisions. This can affect some states more than others. The United States, for example, has much more input into the making and changing of WTO rules than, say, Singapore, even though Singapore, being much more of a trading nation than the United States, is affected more by the rules. Critics of globalization also hold it responsible for what is called a regulatory "race to the bottom," in which governments compete to get rid of labor and environmental regulations in order to attract investment by internationally mobile capital.[13] Countries can avoid this phenomenon, goes the argument, but only at great economic cost.

Globalization can undermine external sovereignty by loosening the monopoly of the sovereign state system on international political activity. This argument suggests that the more decision-making autonomy that IOs get, the more scope private actors such as NGOs have to participate in international policy-making, and the weaker the traditional state system becomes. This would help to create a system of global governance beyond international politics, understood narrowly as the relations among states. Furthermore, the more that IOs are looked to as the arbiters of regulation internationally, the more TNCs may be able to avoid being subject to national regulations, further weakening the state system. Of those who see IOs as helping to undermine state autonomy, some see it as a good thing, others as a bad thing. Some human rights and environmental activists, for example, see internationalization as the only effective check on regulatory races to the bottom.[14] Others see IOs as contributing to the problem by forcing on countries international rules pertaining to issues such as trade, which are not sensitive to local conditions or problems.[15]

These sorts of arguments are not new. In the early days of the Cold War, proponents of world government saw it as the best way to avoid perhaps the ultimate transnational problem, large-scale nuclear war.[16] Opponents of world government saw it as akin to losing the Cold War, as a means of selling out our values to a global lowest common denominator. The language of the debate has changed from world government to globalization, and the idea of a centralized world government has given way to one of a more diffuse form of global governance. However, the basic issues being debated have not changed fundamentally. But are those who believe that globalization is undermining sovereignty right?

Realism, Internationalism, and Universalism

One organizational framework that might help us to address this question is provided by Hedley Bull in *The Anarchical Society: A Study of Order in World Politics*.[17] Bull speaks of three traditions of thought in understanding the problem of international order: the realist tradition, the internationalist tradition, and the universalist tradition. The realist tradition sees states in a situation of anarchy, with little to constrain them except the power of other states. The internationalist tradition sees international relations as taking place within a society of states: states are the primary actors, but they are bound by this society's rules of behavior. The universalist tradition looks not to international politics, understood as politics among states, but to a global politics, which represents people directly as individuals rather than through states. Each of these three traditions takes a very different view of IOs, and each view can be instructive in helping us to understand the role of these organizations in international relations.

Realism looks to the role of IOs in international relations with some skepticism. For realists, the ultimate arbiter of outcomes in international relations is power. Outcomes can be expected to favor those with the most power, or those who bring their power to bear most effectively. And for realists, in the contemporary world, states are the organizations with the most power. States control most of the planet's military power, have an ability to tax that is not shared by any other institution, and are the issuers of the world's currencies.[18] International organizations share none of these features. Having no independent military capability, they depend on states to enforce their rules. Having no ability to tax, they depend on states to fund them. Having no territory, they depend on states to host them. As such, IOs can only really succeed when backed by powerful states. For realists, then, it makes little sense to focus attention on IOs, because IOs reflect the existing balance of power and the interests of powerful states. As such, it makes more sense to understand IOs as tools in the power struggles of states, than as independent actors or independent effects.[19]

The internationalist tradition has roots in the study of international law rather than in the study of power politics. It sees states in international society as somewhat analogous to people in domestic society. Domestic society works because most people follow most of its rules most of the time. Similarly, analysts of the internationalist tradition argue that most states follow most international law most of the time.[20] At any given point in time, the argument goes, there are generally accepted rules about how states should relate to each other, and we cannot understand international politics without looking at those rules. Even during times of war, when we would expect international society to be at its weakest, states usually follow certain rules of acceptable conduct. They do not necessarily do this out of altruism, in the same way that people in domestic society do not necessarily follow laws out of altruism. Rather, they recognize that they all benefit from a society that is rule-governed, and are therefore willing to accept rules if those rules bind others as well. From this perspective, IOs become the expressions of the rules that govern international society. Whether or not IOs have an independent effect as actors in international relations depends on whether they create the rules, or simply oversee rules created by agreement among states. But in either case, IOs are important because they regulate relations among states. It is important to note here, though, that from this perspective, states are still seen as the primary actors in international relations.

The universalist tradition differs fundamentally from both the realist and internationalist traditions in that it is not state-centric. Whereas the internationalist tradition sees states as constrained by the norms of a society of states, the universalist tradition sees states as increasingly irrelevant in the face of a developing global society, a society of people rather than of states. This tradition shares with the internationalist tradition the presupposition that domestic society works as much because its population accepts its rules as because the state enforces them. The difference is that the internationalist tradition applies this by analogy to states, whereas the universalist tradition applies it to people globally.[21] The greater the extent to which global civil society comes to be governed by a set of rules and behavioral norms shared across different peoples and cultures, the greater the extent to which it is this civil society, rather than the society of states, that guides global politics. In this tradition, IOs are more important as expressions of, and creators of, global civil society than they are as regulators of relations among states.[22] Accordingly, IOs should be studied as partial replacements for states rather than as mediators among states.

Approaching the sovereignty/globalization debate from the perspective of these three traditions, we get three different answers to what is happening. The pure realist answer to the question of the future of sovereignty is that the sovereign state system is continuing much the same as always. States remain the locus of power in the international system. Therefore, external sovereignty can be expected to remain as strong as ever, because states, the organizations with the power, have an interest in keeping it that way. In this view, states' degree of internal sovereignty is also not changing. Larger states are not losing autonomy to IOs, because those same large states are creating the rules of those organizations. Smaller, weaker states, it is true, do lack autonomy in the face of some IOs, but these states were always subject to a similar degree to the preferences of the larger, more powerful states.[23]

The pure universalist answer to the question of the future of sovereignty is that globalization is undermining it. The greater the extent to which IOs make rules that reflect global civil society, the less autonomy states have to make rules domestically that are incongruent with international norms. By the same logic, globalization also undermines external sovereignty, as IOs, NGOs, and other representatives of global civil society begin to replace states as the legitimate representatives of the global citizenry.[24] A system of truly global governance, to this view, is coming to replace international relations, understood as governance provided predominantly through cooperation among sovereign states.

The internationalist answer to the future of sovereignty in the face of globalization depends on whether one is asking about internal or external sovereignty. The internationalist tradition agrees with the universalist that globalization is eroding internal sovereignty, the autonomy of states to make rules domestically as they see fit. As international society, as represented by IOs, becomes stronger, states are increasingly bound to make rules collectively rather than individually. For example, as states participate increasingly in international trade, they gain a greater stake in trade rules that everyone shares, because trade would be hurt by the absence of such rules. This leaves states with less autonomy to make rules that conflict with those embodied in IOs. At the same time, however, the internationalist tradition agrees with the realist that the sovereign state system remains strong in the face of globalization. Rules are being made by states collectively rather than individually, but they are still being made by states.

This increasing tendency of states to make rules collectively is often labeled multilateralism and is the basis of a school of analysis located within the internationalist tradition. Unilateralism refers to a state acting alone, bilateralism to two states acting together. Multilateralism refers to a system in which it is expected that states will act as a group, through negotiation and IOs. The multilateralist school of analysis argues that multilateralism has, in the past half-century or so, become the expected way of doing business internationally.[25] States, multilateralists argue, still sometimes act alone, but this has become the exception rather than the rule. As such, multilateralism is a concept that will reappear regularly throughout this book.

Multilateralism can be seen as a form of globalization. In fact, antiglobalization protestors often point to multilateral organizations, such as the WTO and the IMF, as undermining national autonomy, the ability of countries to make trade and monetary policy to suit local conditions.[26] In other words, antiglobalization protestors are often opposed to some of the ways in which multilateralism undermines internal sovereignty. But it is also possible to argue that the state system as a whole, and with it external sovereignty, is actually made stronger when IOs are responsible for international decision-making. Multilateralism, and internationalist logic more generally, sees states, as opposed to other political actors or other potential representatives of global civil society, as the key decision-makers and policy-makers in global politics. To the extent that only states have votes in IOs and that only states participate in multilateral decision-making, multilateralism reinforces the role of the state. In other words, rather than undermining sovereignty, the multilateralist system is creating a new kind of sovereignty.

A good example of the tension between the internationalist and the universalist impulses in the creation of IOs can be found in the European Union (EU). The EU is an IO whose members share a common market for international trade and common legislation on a wide variety of issues ranging from social policy to environmental policy. The EU also has its own legal and foreign policy–making institutions. This makes the EU the most wide-ranging and comprehensive IO. It has twenty-seven members from throughout Europe, including twelve countries from central and eastern Europe and the Mediterranean that became members between 2004 and 2007.

There are three central bodies that participate in making EU policy and legislation. The first is the European Commission, which is a bureaucracy made up of commissioners who come from all the member countries, but who are meant to represent the EU rather than the country that appointed them. The second is the European Parliament, which is made up of members directly elected by the populations of the member countries. Conversely, the third body, the Council of Ministers, is made up of national politicians whose job is to represent their countries in making EU policy. The Commission and the Parliament can be seen as exercises in universalism. They are pan-European bodies that are supposed to both represent and develop a pan-European political consciousness. The Council, on the other hand, is more straightforwardly internationalist. It is an intergovernmental body in which participants representing individual countries act in the name of member governments to promote the national interest of those countries. The evolution of the EU, and its current politics, reflects this institutional compromise between a universalist EU and an internationalist EU. Either way, members of the EU have given up broad swathes of their decision-making autonomy—they are committed to enact regulations decided upon at the EU level. But individual states remain much more important actors in the Council, where they are directly involved in decision-making, than they are in the Commission and Parliament, where they are not.[27]

Globalization and Democracy

There are two ways to look at the realist, internationalist, and universalist traditions. One way is as descriptions of what is actually happening in the world of IOs. Each tradition allows us to look at an institution from a different perspective and thereby learn different things about it. Looking, for example, at the WTO, an internationalist lens allows us to observe the ways in which states are cooperating for their collective benefit. A realist lens allows us to observe the ways in which the more powerful states can achieve rules closer to their interests than to the interests of weaker states. A universalist lens allows us to observe the ways in which the WTO as an organization, and the idea of a rules-based trade system as a norm, are replacing states as the locus of real decision-making in issues of international trade. The balance among these three perspectives may well differ from organization to organization. Some IOs, for example, might offer greater scope for power politics than others, and some might engage in more universalist, rather than intergovernmental, decision-making than others. But we can address this balance empirically, by studying individual IOs and what they do. This balance will be discussed in more detail in the next chapter.

The other way to look at the three traditions is normatively. Looked at this way, each tradition describes not the way in which IOs do work, but the way in which they should work. Many realists believe that the state should represent the interests of its citizens rather than pursue a global common good. Universalists often see direct global governance, rather than a competitive state system, as an ultimate goal. And to internationalists, a society of states regulated by IOs combines the best of both the realist and the universalist traditions. And these traditions can also be used as sources of moral arguments about what international politics should look like. One illustrative line of moral argumentation concerns the relationship between IOs and democracy. The effects of IOs on democratic governance are important parts of both the anti- and proglobalization arguments, and a different perspective on these effects is offered by each of the three traditions. None of these perspectives is inherently more or less right than the others, and all provide perspectives worth considering.

Realism

There is a tendency to see the realist tradition as amoral, as simply a practical acceptance of the reality of power politics. But there is a democratic argument to be made for retaining state autonomy in matters of decision-making. Allowing nation-states to make their own rules allows different cultures to govern themselves as they see fit. Autonomy also fosters competition among states for better governance. (World government, its critics might argue, is no more than a lowest common denominator, and encounters little pressure to improve.)[28] Under the heading of the realist tradition here could be included nationalists, both cultural and economic, who feel that the role of the state is to represent the interests of its citizens and of its culture. If the state defers to a global good while other states pursue their own interests, then the state, and its citizens, lose.

There are three key empirical arguments against this realist perspective on the morality and democratic legitimacy of power politics. The first is that because of power disparities among states, only the interests of those who happen to live in powerful states determine international outcomes. Realism thus looks very different from the perspective of the United States than it does from the perspective of the Central African Republic. The second is that as the issues facing states are increasingly global in nature, global rather than national solutions are needed. Attempts to deal with issues such as climate change, air traffic control, or the international financial architecture through purely national policy are futile. The third argument against the realist perspective that state decision-making autonomy is preferable to collective decision-making is that competition among states can do much more harm than good. Competition can lead to stable balances of power, and it can lead to policy innovation. But it can also lead to hostility and war, in a way that multilateral or universalist cooperation are unlikely to.[29]

Internationalism

The moral claim made in this context by proponents of an internationalist perspective is that a multilateralist state system is more democratic than a competitive state system. Because multilateralism is a process in which all concerned states can participate, both the more powerful ones and the weaker ones, it allows all peoples to be represented in the making of international rules. In IOs such as the UN General Assembly (GA), this equal representation is formalized by a one-country, one-vote system. To the extent that the trend internationally is for more states to become democratic, the link between representative government at the domestic level and representative government at the international level is even stronger. IOs then become representative bodies of states, which are themselves representative bodies of citizens. As is the case with domestic legislatures, decisions are made by elected representatives of the people.

This internationalist perspective is itself, however, open to criticism. Where internationalists see democratic representation, some critics perceive it as decision-making behind closed doors by an international elite. Others see the process of negotiation leading up to the creation of IOs and the modification of their rules as an exercise in the finding of lowest common denominators that often please no one. Universalists see negotiations among states as favoring existing national elites, and as freezing out the institutions of international civil society, such as NGOs. Antiglobalization protestors at meetings of the WTO or of the international financial institutions (IFIs, primarily the IMF and World Bank) indeed attack these multilateral negotiating forums from both perspectives; economic nationalists argue that these IOs themselves need to be governed by tighter rules, while universalists demand more direct participation for NGOs that represent human rights or environmental issues.

Universalism

Universalists argue that it is only through the direct representation of global civil society that international relations can become more democratic. As such, any effort to improve direct representation by separating IOs from direct control by member states is a positive development. At present, the two most common ways of ensuring that this happens are increasing the autonomy of IOs and increasing NGO participation in them.

But both independent IO decision-making and NGO participation can also be criticized as antidemocratic. Nongovernmental organizations may well be expressions of global civil society, but they are not elected, and they represent the interests of their members, not of the population at large. Critics of NGO participation in IOs also point out that NGO membership is disproportionately biased toward middle-class, white citizens of Western states. In this sense, NGOs can be criticized as being neocolonial, as a mechanism for reintroducing rule by the West over the South through nonmilitary means.[30] Independent IO decision-making can similarly be criticized as being neocolonial, because the secretariats of IOs tend to be made up of "professionals," people trained in Western techniques for managing their issue-areas.[31] Even if they are acting from the best of intentions, they may focus on what they think they should do rather than what the population at large wants them to do.

Conclusion

Most of this book looks at IOs at the micro level, at the workings of particular IOs and their effects within their issue-areas. This chapter, focusing on the sovereignty/globalization distinction, looks at the macro level, at the effects of IOs in general, and individual IOs in particular, on patterns of global governance in general. Of the four distinctions discussed in the introduction, that between sovereignty and globalization is the only one that focuses broadly on the effects of IOs on governance patterns, rather than on governance outcomes within particular issue-areas. This broad focus provides both an opportunity and a potential pitfall. The pitfall is getting stuck at the general level. This can be seen in some discussions about globalization: arguments that globalization is good or bad miss the complexity of the issue. The distinction between sovereignty and globalization is nonetheless both a good starting point for discussions of IOs, and something worth keeping in mind when looking at IOs at the micro level. In particular, it is worth asking, as one looks at the effectiveness of an IO in dealing with a particular issue-area, does this present a good model of the way the world should be governed?

2

Power and Interdependence

Another of the distinctions that provide the theoretical focus for this book is that between power and interdependence. This distinction is related to that between sovereignty and globalization. The realist tradition assumes that power is the ultimate arbiter of outcomes in international relations. Both the internationalist and the universalist traditions take interdependence as a basic assumption. Dependence refers to a situation in which a state cannot effectively make and enforce policy on its own, but can do so only in cooperation with another country or countries. Interdependence is when these other countries, in turn, also find themselves dependent on the first country. A key part of the concept of interdependence, then, is reciprocity.[1] The internationalist response to interdependence is cooperation among states. The universalist response is the replacement of states by global, rather than international, decision-making.

One interpretation of the internationalist tradition would be that with multilateral cooperation in decision-making, cooperation would replace power as the focus of international politics. The debate between the pure cooperation position and the pure power position has often taken place using the language of absolute and relative gains.[2] Absolute gains are gains that states make compared with what would have been the case otherwise. For example, if a bilateral free trade agreement increases gross economic output of the two countries that have signed it by 3 percent over what would have been the case without the agreement, and both countries share in that increase equally, then both countries would have absolute gains of 3 percent in their GDPs. Relative gains are gains that a state makes in comparison with its rivals. For example, if two rival states increase their military force levels by 3 percent each, neither will have made a relative gain, because their force levels would have stayed the same relative to each other. If, however, one state's force level stays the same and that of its rival increases by one division, the first state's relative force level would have declined by a division, even though its absolute force level stayed the same.

If one state makes a gain of 4 percent and the other a gain of 2 percent, both states would have gained in absolute terms, but in relative terms, one state would have gained and the other would have lost. Whether a state in this situation perceives itself as gaining or losing depends on how that state defines its interests. Realists, who tend to see issues of national security as paramount, argue that in measures of military capabilities only relative gains matter, because military capabilities are measured against the capabilities of other states. Economists, for whom trade issues are paramount, usually focus on absolute gains, because what matters to them is the ability of individuals to consume. Therefore, they focus on the amount available to individuals with international cooperation compared with the amount available to the same individuals without cooperation.[3]

Despite the relative/absolute gains debate, most students of international organizations (IOs) would agree that states care about both. In multilateral negotiations, states generally care about both a good overall outcome and an outcome that reflects their own particular national interests, although the balance between the two can vary.[4] States that participate in trade negotiations, for example, are likely to care both that the agreement maximizes global economic output and that they benefit individually as much as possible from the increase in output. In other words, both interdependence and power matter. The question then for students of IOs is as follows: How do we study and contrast these two phenomena?

The phrase "power and interdependence" is familiar to most students of international relations theory from a book of the same title by Robert Keohane and Joseph Nye, first published in 1977.[5] Keohane and Nye argue that the traditional focus by students of power politics on force in international affairs is becoming obsolete. In some parts of the world, such as between India and Pakistan, military power still matters. But, argue Keohane and Nye, in other parts of the world, such as between the United States and Canada, the military balance is largely irrelevant, because neither country considers the use of force to settle bilateral disputes. They call the pattern of international relations in these latter parts of the world "complex interdependence."[6]

Complex interdependence has three key characteristics. As already mentioned, one of these characteristics is that military force plays a minor role in settling disputes. A second characteristic is that states have multiple channels of communication with each other. In essence, this means that national bureaucracies negotiate directly with each other. For example, if the United States and Canada are negotiating a fisheries agreement, it will probably be negotiated between officials of the National Marine Fisheries Service and the Department of Fisheries and Oceans, rather than by the Secretary of State and the Foreign Minister. On other issues, other sets of bureaucrats in different bureaucratic hierarchies negotiate with each other, often without much central coordination. The third characteristic is that there is no clear hierarchy of issues. In a traditional realist world, national security issues matter more than other issues. In a complex interdependent world, states do not clearly prioritize issues. A diverse array of issue-areas, ranging from security to trade, finance, the environment, human rights, telecommunications policy, and health policy may find their way onto the international agenda, but states do not clearly prioritize among them.

This complex interdependent world is similar to the globalized world, with cooperation among states, envisioned by internationalists, as discussed in Chapter 1. States generally deal with global issues multilaterally, without clearly prioritizing some issues over others, and with a focus on finding the best technical solutions rather than on political gain. Keohane and Nye do not conclude from this, however, that power has become irrelevant. Military power continues to be important in those parts of the world that are less involved in complex interdependent multilateralism. And even in the core of the complex interdependent world, power remains relevant. The difference is that power in a multilateralist world no longer comes primarily from the threat of military force, because such threats are rarely credible. Rather, in these contexts, power comes from asymmetries in interdependence.[7]

In a dependent relationship, State A depends on State B, but State B does not depend on State A. This should give State B power over State A, because State B can threaten to terminate their relationship. Should the relationship be terminated, it would hurt State A much more than State B. As an example, during the oil crisis of 1973–1974, many Western states depended on Persian Gulf states for petroleum, but the Gulf states did not depend on Western states for anything as critical in the short term. This gave the Gulf states (after an embargo of a few months, to show that their threat of terminating the relationship was credible) the power to dictate oil prices to Western states and contract terms to Western oil companies.[8]

In a perfectly interdependent relationship, State A and State B depend on each other equally. As such, neither state can credibly threaten to terminate or impede their relationship, because everyone knows that this would be equally costly to both states. This means that neither state can gain an advantage in bargaining power from the level of dependence of the other. To continue with the example used above, in the 1980s, most Western countries reduced their dependence on petroleum from the Persian Gulf by improving their energy efficiency and by finding other sources of supply. At the same time, many of the states in the Gulf became more dependent on the West for trade, services, and security. These trends reduced asymmetries in dependence to the point where the Gulf states could no longer credibly expect that the threat of an embargo would allow them to dictate prices.

Perfectly interdependent relationships, however, are not the norm in international relations, even in a complex interdependent world. In between pure dependence and perfect interdependence, there are asymmetries in interdependence. This is when all countries depend on each other, but some more than others. For example, both the United States and Singapore would suffer if the WTO, and with it, multilateral rules on international trade, collapsed. But the Singaporean economy is much more dependent on trade than the U.S. economy, so Singapore would suffer proportionally more.[9] Singapore's greater dependence on trade gives the United States greater bargaining power than Singapore in negotiations on WTO rules. As a general rule, the greater the asymmetry of interdependence, the greater the relative power of the less-dependent country.

Keohane and Nye look at these issues from a primarily internationalist perspective. A complex interdependent world is one in which states are still the primary agents of governance internationally, but in which they approach this governance multilaterally rather than unilaterally. From this perspective, the primary question of the role of power in the study of IOs is how state power manifests itself in the creation and management of IOs. From a universalist perspective, the question is different. A universalist would look less at the power of states as it affects IOs than at the power of IOs themselves and at the relationship between their power and the power of states.

Power in IOs

Beginning with the internationalist perspective, there are a number of sources of state power and a number of ways in which the power of particular states can be expressed in the creation and management of IOs. Power can be expressed in negotiations, in the setting of agendas, and in the creation of institutional bureaucracies and procedures. Sources of power include asymmetries of interdependence among countries, asymmetrical dependence of IOs on particular countries, structural power, and ideology.

The most straightforward expression of state power in the creation of IOs and multilateral rules is negotiating power. When an issue comes up, and State A favors one outcome and State B another, and in the end State B accedes to the preferred outcome of State A, then State A can be said to have greater negotiating power than State B. In practice, it can be a little more difficult to identify negotiating power. State A might have made a concession on some other issue, or State B might simply have cared less about this particular issue than State A. But on the whole, it is clear that some states, such as the United States, have more overall negotiating power in multilateral forums than others, such as Monaco or Burundi.[10]

Negotiating power can be thought of as the direct use of power by a state in managing an IO. But there is also what has been called the "second face of power,"[11] that is, the ability to set the agenda. Negotiating power looks at who gets their way on an issue that comes up for discussion. The second face of power looks at who gets to set the negotiating agenda in the first place, or, who gets to decide what gets talked about and what does not. Agenda-setting power can be more difficult to study than negotiating power, because it involves looking at what does not happen, rather than at what does. In other words, it involves asking about the things that did not make it onto an IO's agenda, which is an inherently more open-ended question than looking at the outcomes of issues that did make it onto the agenda.

As an example of agenda-setting power, consider the negotiations leading up to the Kyoto Protocol to the United Nations Framework Convention on Climate Change (UNFCCC). The negotiations were based on the idea that each state would cut back greenhouse gas emissions a certain amount from their existing emission levels. As a result, the states that polluted the most before the negotiations could continue to pollute the most under the terms of the Protocol. This approach can be seen as favoring states that came into the negotiations as particularly heavy polluters, and as penalizing both countries that were more environmentally responsible in the past and countries that were too poor to have polluted much at that point. Other pollution baselines, such as one based on national population, are conceivable, but were not on the negotiating agenda. Does this mean that no states were interested in talking about this possibility, or that some states had an interest in keeping this possibility off the agenda and had the power to do so? Arriving at an answer requires looking in considerable detail at the prenegotiation process, the process through which the agenda was decided.[12]

One can also speak of a third face of power, the power to shape the way people think about issues.[13] Take, for example, the preference shown by the United States since the 1980s for the use of market mechanisms in dealing with pollution issues. As a result of this, many IOs have included market mechanisms in their issue-areas, even though the United States has made no active effort to put them on the agenda. Joseph Nye, while discussing U.S. foreign policy, calls this "soft power."[14] The third face of power is thus the ability to set general terms of discourse. The third face of power is even more difficult to identify empirically than the second. Do IOs use market mechanisms more than they used to because of U.S. power, or because market mechanisms have worked well in the past? It can be very difficult to tell.

Related to the third face of power is what critical theorists call structural power. The other forms of power discussed here can be thought of as relational or interactive power, the power of one actor over other actors. Structural power refers to the power of institutions to "define what kinds of social beings actors are."[15] For example, people who work for the International Monetary Fund (IMF) think like economists in doing their jobs, because that is what the institution expects of them. This generates and reinforces patterns of institutional behavior even if that is not the specific intention of the individuals involved. Among other things, structural power helps to drive some of the pathologies of IOs discussed in the next chapter.

The final entry on the list of ways in which states can express power with respect to IOs is through the creation of institutional bureaucracies and procedures. This can be called institutional power. It refers to the ability of particular states to put their own people into positions of power in IO bureaucracies, and the ability of particular states to affect the structures of those bureaucracies in ways that suit their interests. This can vary from institution to institution. For example, the President of the World Bank and the Managing Director of the IMF are always an American and a European, respectively, but since 1982, the Secretary-General of the UN has been from neither. This reflects the different levels of relative institutional power of the North and South in these two institutions.

There are thus a variety of ways in which state power can be expressed in the creation and management of IOs. But what is the source of this power? The answer that Keohane and Nye provide us with is asymmetries of interdependence.[16] When one country needs an IO less than another, it will have relatively more power in creating and managing it. In the case of the World Bank, for example, some countries primarily put money into the organization, and others primarily borrow from it. The borrowers, for the most part, need the organization more than the investors. This means that investors are more willing to walk away from the organization than the borrowers, which gives the investors bargaining leverage with respect to the borrowers, a leverage that in effect gives them relative power within the organization. This allows the investors to maintain, and freeze borrowers from, direct control of the World Bank.

Asymmetries of interdependence can be less straightforward. Sometimes, wealthier countries need an agreement more, or faster, than poorer ones, which undermines their negotiating power.[17] In negotiations over geosynchronous satellite spots, for example, countries that had no ability to build or launch such satellites received concessions from those that did, because the latter needed an agreement relatively quickly, and the former did not.[18] In environmental negotiations, states that are recipients of other states' pollution need the biggest polluters to participate in IOs in order for those IOs to usefully address the problem. This gives big polluters, or even potential big polluters, negotiating power, because the recipients of pollution are asymmetrically dependent on them to solve the problem.[19] Asymmetries of interdependence, in short, need to be established on a case-by-case basis, and are not always obvious.

Asymmetries of interdependence not only affect states in their relationships with each other and with IOs, but also affect IOs in their relationships with states. For example, when the United States started withholding dues in an attempt to force the UN to reform its administration and budgeting, the UN reacted by undertaking reforms in an attempt to appease the United States and get it to pay its dues.[20] Had Nauru withheld its dues for the same reason, it is unlikely that the UN would have reacted at all. This difference is probably caused by relative levels of UN financial dependence—it receives 22 percent of its budget from the United States, and 0.001 percent of its budget from Nauru.[21] The UN's financial dependence on the United States has given the latter substantial power to force change in the former.

An additional source of power for some states with respect to others in the forum of IOs is institutional. This refers to elements in the institutional structure of particular IOs that confer power to particular states or groups of states at the expense of others. These structural elements can be constitutional, enshrined in the treaty that gave rise to the organization. They can also stem from such factors as personnel or location.

There are several constitutional elements of an IO that can confer relative power to some states rather than others. One of the most straightforward of these elements is voting structure. A majority of IOs work on a one-country, one-vote basis. But not all do. In the UN, for example, each country has the same one vote in the General Assembly (GA) and most of its subsidiary bodies. But in the Security Council, five specific countries (the United States, China, Russia, France, and the United Kingdom) have a special voting category that allows them to singlehandedly veto resolutions, an ability not shared by the other ten members of the Security Council. Structurally, this veto power gives those five states significantly more power than the non-veto states in the central security organ of the contemporary multilateral system. Most countries have no vote at all in the Council at any given point in time, and many have never had the opportunity to serve on the Council at all.

There are other examples of IOs that do not have a one-country, one-vote rule. Both the World Bank and the IMF, for example, have voting structures based on what is called historical subscription. This means that a country's proportion of the total vote in those institutions is equal to the proportion of capital that the country has put into the organization over its history. In practice, in the IMF, the United States has almost 17 percent of the vote, and Japan and Germany each have around 6 percent. Several dozen countries, meanwhile, have less than 0.05 percent of the vote.[22] Of IOs that operate on a one-member, one-vote basis, there are some in which the European Union (EU), rather than its constituent countries, is a member, meaning that it gets one vote rather than the twenty-seven it would get if its constituent countries voted separately.[23]

Even the one-country, one-vote rule is not power-neutral. China, with more than 1.3 billion people, gets the same one vote as Palau, with fewer than 100,000 people. This has the effect of empowering less-populous countries. And within one-country, one-vote systems, different levels of majority are needed for a vote to carry. Sometimes, a simple majority suffices, as is the case with most GA resolutions. At other times, a two-thirds or three-quarters majority, or even consensus, is needed. For example, decisions by the GA on "important issues," including the admission of new members and the apportioning of budgetary dues, require a two-thirds majority.[24] The Convention for the Conservation of Antarctic Marine Living Resources (CCAMLR) requires consensus for "matters of substance," but simple majorities for other matters.[25] The higher the voting threshold, the greater the power of individual disaffected countries to block agreement. Simple majority systems empower the median state, the country with the average opinion, because that country is needed to carry a majority either way. Consensus systems empower those states whose preferences are farthest from average, because they have the ability to hold up agreement until they are appeased.

Beyond institutional elements such as voting rules, other constitutional elements of international relations such as problem definition and bureaucratic structure can convey structural power to specific states. The effects of these elements on relative state power are often less clear than those of voting structure, but they are real nonetheless. Both problem definition and bureaucratic structure play a role in influencing the way in which an IO is set up to deal with a particular issue. The closer problem definition is to a country's own interest in that issue, the more empowered that country is likely to be by the IO. Bureaucratic structure often follows from problem definition, reinforcing the effect.

Take two examples, fisheries and narcotics. The Northwest Atlantic Fisheries Organization (NAFO) was created by the countries that account for most of the fishing in the international waters of the northwest Atlantic, with a mandate to maximize long-term potential fishing yields of individual species. The structure of NAFO includes a scientific committee, the job of which is to provide scientific estimates of how much of each species fished commercially in the region can be fished in any given year without depleting the breeding stock and undermining the long-term viability of the fishery. This problem definition and bureaucratic structure has the effect of favoring the interests of coastal states (primarily Canada and Greenland) over noncoastal states with long-range fleets that fish in the region. It does so because the coastal states tend to be more interested in long-term viability of the stock, which is an issue best determined scientifically, whereas countries with long-range fleets tend to be more interested in maximizing returns in the medium term, which is a less technical and more political issue.[26]

In the case of narcotics, IOs that are involved in international narcotics issues, such as the United Nations Office on Drugs and Crime (UNODC), tend to focus on drugs as a crime problem rather than a public health problem.[27] This problem definition tends to favor major consumer countries, such as the United States, over major producer countries, such as Colombia. A problem definition that focuses on crime puts the onus on producing and exporting countries to change their behavior, but does not require a similar change in behavior in importing and consuming countries. In short, the problem is defined internationally as being the fault of the exporters more than the importers, and there is more pressure on the former to combat production than on the latter to combat consumption.

In addition to constitutional elements, matters such as location and personnel can also influence the distribution of national power in international institutions. It is no accident, for example, that both the IMF and the World Bank are headquartered in Washington, DC.[28] The location of the GA and Security Council in New York may also empower the United States.[29] It is not clear whether the location of other IOs, particularly those with a primarily technical rather than political function, matters. For example, it is unlikely that Canada gains any political advantage at all from hosting the ICAO in Montreal. Geneva served as a second home for the UN and as the headquarters for a range of UN subsidiary organizations for over half a century before Switzerland even joined the UN in 2002. Kenya may gain some slight political advantage from hosting the United Nations Environment Programme (UNEP) in Nairobi, but no more than that. Kenya did, however, gain significant international prestige from being the first developing country to host the secretariat of a major IO. A headquarters in Nairobi, however, can be a mixed blessing from the perspective of the effectiveness of the organization, as will be discussed in Chapter 12. It makes UNEP a less appealing draw for experts, and keeps it farther from the centers of the multilateral system than would be the case if its secretariat were located in Geneva.

Personnel issues are often more the result of relative national power than its cause. For example, South Africa holds the presidency of the Security Organ of the Southern African Development Community (SADC) more than any other member country. But this is a reflection of, rather than any real source of, the central role that South Africa plays in southern African security issues. Personnel issues can matter in IO bureaucracies below the top level as well. Many positions throughout IO bureaucracies require "professional" qualifications and university degrees. A much higher proportion of citizens of developed countries than developing countries have these sorts of qualifications, meaning that a disproportionate number of the middle managers of IOs are often from developed countries. Furthermore, many of the managers from developing countries received their qualifications from universities in developed countries. Even if IO bureaucrats do not consciously represent the interests of their home countries or regions in their professional capacities, they can nonetheless imbue their organizations with values and mindsets that were learned in or reflect the interests of the developed rather than developing world.[30]

This observation leads to the final category of sources of relative national power in the creation and management of IOs: ideology. The notion that the ideology underlying IOs can empower some states over others is more contentious than the notion that different voting structures can be differentially empowering. Ideology is a form of the third face of power; its effects can be very difficult to measure. But it is an issue worth taking seriously, for both research design and empirical reasons. In terms of research design, the difficulty of measurement should not determine what social scientists do and do not study. Empirically, IOs are often charged by their detractors with ideologically empowering some states over others. If students of IOs are to weigh these charges, they must be able to determine whether there is any substance to them.

Examples of these sorts of charges come from across the ideological spectrum. During the latter half of the Cold War, the UN as a whole, along with particular organizations within it, such as the GA and UNESCO (the United Nations Educational, Scientific, and Cultural Organization), was deemed by many U.S. politicians to be too sympathetic to socialism, thus empowering the Soviet Bloc in the Cold War.[31] This charge contributed to the U.S. withdrawal from UNESCO, and to the gradual decline of American enthusiasm for the UN from its peak in the early post–World War II era.[32] Meanwhile, both critics of IOs from developing countries and critics of globalization from developed countries have charged that much of the IO system, particularly those institutions dealing with economic issues, favors neoliberal economics and capitalism. This has the effect, they say, of empowering the West—since the IOs focus on Western ways of doing business, they legitimize neoliberal economics and delegitimize other forms of economic organization.[33] These criticisms will be discussed in more detail in Chapters 9–11.

These charges merit examination, both on their own merits and because, if they are believed, they can undermine the potential of IOs to offer cooperative solutions to global issues. Other charges of ideological empowerment are more straightforward. The IO system, for example, as well as several particular IOs, defines and promotes human rights in a way that is more compatible with Anglo-American tradition than with other cultural traditions. This empowers Western countries, where these rights tend to be respected, at the expense of those countries where non-rights-based traditions predominate. This is so because the bias of the IO system toward human rights legitimizes Western countries' use of human rights as a political weapon. Many readers will find this perfectly reasonable on the grounds that human rights are ideologically progressive (although cultural relativists may well disagree). It nonetheless remains the case, however, that human rights norms, as adopted by the IO community, have an effect on both relative state power and structural power in global governance.

The Power of IOs

So far, the discussion of the relative effects of IOs on state power has been from an internationalist perspective, on the basis of the assumption that the primary role of IOs is to mediate among states. From a universalist perspective, the next step is to ask, Do IOs themselves have power? There is no question that IOs, as a whole, are asymmetrically dependent on states. They are created by states, depend on them for their funding, and can be terminated by states. But this does not necessarily mean that IOs are entirely dependent on states. This leaves us with a question: To what extent do IOs, as actors in international relations, have power distinct from the power of the states that support them?

International organizations do not have the traditional sine qua non of power in international relations, military force.[34] Some IOs, however, have some policing and juridical powers. They can, for example, employ independent means for monitoring whether or not states are complying with international rules, although it is more often the case that they rely on states for this information. It is more frequent that IOs have the power to adjudicate. Examples of organizations with this power include the International Court of Justice (ICJ) and the Dispute Settlement Mechanism (DSM) of the WTO. But realists might respond that IOs can play judicial roles in the absence of independent enforcement capabilities, not because they have independent power, but because they are backed by the power of states. Universalists might argue in response, however, that to the extent that these judicial bodies adjudicate agreements and create authoritative interpretations of international law, they do, in effect, have the power to affect international law, and international norms of behavior, in ways that states cannot precisely control.[35]

There are two primary sources of independent power for IOs: moral authority and information. Moral authority is the power of an IO to legitimately speak as the official voice of the international community with respect to its issue-area in order to get both people and states to pay attention to it, even when it does not have material resources. Moral authority in turn provides two routes through which IOs are empowered.[36] The first is the ability to shame.[37] Most states accept principles of multilateralism, and IOs represent sets of rules and procedures that the member states have already explicitly agreed to. Because of this, states do not want to be seen, either by other states or by their own populations, as breaking IO rules any more than necessary. During the 1990s, for example, Guatemala and Honduras improved their human rights records significantly. This change of behavior was partly in response to the activities of human rights IOs, which had no powers of enforcement per se but did have significant powers of international embarrassment.[38] In the late 1990s, Canada changed the development standards for its national parks under pressure from the International Union for the Conservation of Nature (IUCN). The IUCN had no powers of enforcement, but the Canadian government found the charge of environmental irresponsibility, coming from the IO that oversees the system of international natural heritage sites, to be an unacceptable embarrassment to a domestic population that thinks of itself as relatively environmentally responsible.[39]

The other way in which IOs can use moral authority as a source of power is through political entrepreneurship. Political entrepreneurship is the use of structures of governance by individuals or organizations to advance particular political positions or to put particular issues on the political agenda. Leaders of IOs, in their official capacities, speak with the authority of their organizations and can use that authority to put things onto the international agenda that might not otherwise be there. For example, when the Secretary-General of the UN (at the time of writing, Ban Ki-moon) makes a major pronouncement, it almost as a matter of course gets widely reported in news media throughout the world. There are few other people who can claim this sort of automatic media exposure. Similarly, the World Health Organization (WHO) declared a focus on mental health for World Health Day 2001.[40] This had the effect of putting mental health issues on the domestic healthcare agendas of countries where these issues might otherwise not have been discussed.

Along with moral authority, the other primary source of independent IO power in international politics is control over, and ability to create, information. One way in which IOs exercise this control is through the agency of what some scholars call "epistemic communities." Peter Haas, who popularized the phrase in the context of IO theory, defines an epistemic community as "a network of professionals with recognized expertise and competence in a particular domain and an authoritative claim to policy-relevant knowledge within that domain or issue-area."[41] In other words, an epistemic community can be said to exist when all of the technical experts on an issue agree. Particular IOs can come to represent epistemic communities. For example, when all of the scientists dealing with the issue of pollution in the Mediterranean Sea agree on a particular plan of action, it can be very difficult for states in the Mediterranean basin to disagree with that plan.[42] Similarly, the Intergovernmental Panel on Climate Change (IPCC) is a more or less conscious attempt by the World Meteorological Organization (WMO) and UNEP to create an epistemic community on the subject of climate change. This is starting to work: fewer and fewer governments now attempt to argue that global climate change is not happening, in part because the epistemic community of the IPCC is making such arguments less and less credible.

Along with epistemic communities, IOs can create standards that affect the ways in which both governments and countries do business. A concrete example of such standards can be found in the International Civil Aviation

Organization (ICAO). Because all current international commercial airline flights use ICAO standards, any attempt to change international civil aviation standards has to go through the ICAO. Otherwise, the change would either be pointless (because no one would subscribe to it), or it would require both creating a new organization and luring a critical mass of countries away from the ICAO, which would be a major political challenge. This gives the ICAO a pivotal position in all discussions of international civil aviation standards. A different sort of example is provided by the creation, under the auspices of the UN, of the concept of sustainable development. Once the concept became generally accepted within the UN, it began to find its way into the constitutional documents of other IOs as well. Gradually, it became the accepted concept within which international discussions of issues that affect both environment and development were discussed. The UN, by creating the idea of sustainable development as a standard, has thus created a language within which a whole range of issues is discussed.[43]

Conclusion

Does interdependence generate more cooperative international relations, or are IOs simply a new forum for traditional power politics? The answer, of course, lies somewhere between these two categorical statements. But what the interrelationships are between IOs and power in international relations is a question to which the answer is likely to vary across different issue-areas and different IOs. Unfortunately, there is no clear way to measure power. Sometimes we can get at questions of power by looking at negotiations, at other times by looking at outcomes, and at still other times by looking at institutional structures. The one key thing to take from this chapter is to remember to look, and to remember to look beyond the obvious, at all of the potential sources and forms of power.

3
—

Regimes and Institutions

What do we look at when we study IOs? There are two general approaches to this question in the field of IO theory: the regime approach and the institutional approach. Regimes, as used in this context, refer to the behavioral effects of IOs on other actors, principally on states. They have been defined as "sets of principles, norms, rules, and decision-making procedures around which actor expectations converge in a given issue-area."[1] This definition will be unpacked below. For the moment, the key element of the regime approach is the focus on actor expectations; the definition does not even mention IOs per se. In contrast, the institutional approach looks at what happens within particular IOs, rather than at the effects of IOs on other actors.

An analogy can be made here to an approach to the study of political institutions more generally called the "black box" approach. Some approaches to the study of politics look at political institutions as if they were black boxes, where we can see what goes in and what comes out, but not what happens within the box itself.[2] A pluralist approach to the study of national politics, for example, looks at the pressures on government from various domestic political groups (the inputs), and the resultant government policy (the output).[3] It does not, however, look at what happens within the government to turn pressures into policy. Rather, it usually assumes some sort of decision rule. Other approaches, conversely, focus on what happens within the "black box" of government, on, perhaps, the relationship between the executive and legislative branches or on the mechanics of party politics. Regime analysis is a black box approach to the study of IOs. Institutional analysis looks inside the black box. In addition to discussing the theoretical implications of these two approaches, this chapter will focus primarily on the mechanics of the institutional approach. The mechanics of the regime approach will be discussed in more detail in Chapter 4.

Institutional Approaches

Many of the earliest studies of IOs fit into a category that has been called formal institutional analysis.[4] This approach looks at the formal structure, organization, and bureaucratic hierarchy of IOs. The starting point for this sort of analysis is the organization's charter, which is in turn usually the text of an international treaty. The charter specifies when and why an IO will come into being, what it is called, and which countries (or other actors) can be members. It also specifies what the bureaucratic structure of the organization will be, and what powers it will have. It often discusses decision-making procedures within the organization, and its voting structure. Finally, it indicates how the organization will be financed, often provides a process for countries to leave the IO, and sometimes, though infrequently, provides a mechanism for the organization to be terminated once its function has been fulfilled.[5]

Formal institutional analysis is an important starting point for institutional research into IOs. The previous chapter discussed the importance of such things as voting structure to questions of relative power in IOs. One cannot, for example, understand the politics of the UN Security Council without understanding the mechanics of the veto power of the five permanent members. Similarly, one cannot understand the lending patterns of the IMF and World Bank without knowing about the strong voting position of the United States and its allies. International organizations that work on a unanimity or consensus basis, such as the Convention for the Conservation of Antarctic Marine Living Resources (CCAMLR),[6] generate different patterns of cooperation than those that work on a majority vote basis.

Understanding the bureaucratic structure of an IO is similarly important in understanding what the organization can and cannot do. This involves looking at the size, composition, and components of the structure of a given organization.[7] The issue of size is a relatively straightforward one. A bureaucracy with a thousand full-time employees will operate differently from a bureaucracy with two. For example, the IMF, with a staff of roughly 2,400 people, can track, research, publish extensive reports on, and make policy toward the economies of over 100 countries simultaneously.[8] In contrast, the Agreement on the Conservation of Cetaceans of the Black Sea, Mediterranean Sea and Contiguous Atlantic Area (ACCOBAMS), headquartered in Monaco, has only a handful of staff, and is thus far more limited than the IMF, both in the range of activities it can monitor and in the depth in which it can report on them.[9]

When looking at the composition of an IO's bureaucracy, a key distinction to keep in mind is the difference between administrative employees and political appointees. Most IOs have both an administrative and a political element. Administrative employees work for the organization itself, and their primary loyalty is presumably to the organization and its goals. Political appointees work with the IO, but work for their home governments, with which their primary loyalty is supposed to lie. For example, a specialist on the economy of a particular country at the IMF will be an administrative employee of the IMF. Irrespective of the country the analyst came from, she or he is employed by, paid by, and ultimately answerable to the IMF as an institution. A member of the Board of Governors of the IMF, on the other hand, will be an appointee of a particular member country, and will be expected to represent the interests of that country in the making of IMF policy. As a general rule, the bodies that act as the equivalents of legislatures for IOs and make broad policy (such as general assemblies) are composed of political appointees, whereas executive bodies such as secretariats, the bureaucracies that implement the policies, are staffed with administrative employees. The relative balance of power between these two groups, however, can vary from organization to organization. An organization with a strong secretariat can influence policy-making, whereas when the secretariat is relatively weak member states can end up micro-managing implementation.[10]

Different IOs can also have different components in their bureaucratic structure. Almost all IOs will have some sort of secretariat, which is the central administrative organ of the organization. These, as has already been mentioned, can vary greatly in size and scope. Some IOs will piggyback on the secretariats of larger IOs rather than create a wholly new bureaucratic structure. This can save resources when an IO is starting up, and allows smaller IOs to use their limited budgets and resources more efficiently. A good example of this sort of setup is the United Nations Environment Programme (UNEP), which provides secretariat functions for several different treaty organizations, ranging from the Montreal Protocol on Substances that Deplete the Ozone Layer to the Convention on Migratory Species of Wild Animals.

Beyond the strictly administrative functions of the secretariat, IOs can have bodies that deal with scientific research, technical standards, adjudicating disputes, and interactions with member countries. These bodies can be either subsidiary to or separate from the secretariat. Many IOs that deal with environmental issues, for example, have separate scientific bodies. These bodies are tasked with developing programs of research on the relevant environmental phenomena that are separate from the research undertaken by national research communities. There are two reasons for an IO to have this sort of research capability. The first is to provide research in areas where such research does not already exist. The Intergovernmental Panel on Climate Change (IPCC), for example, was authorized by the UN General Assembly (GA) explicitly to provide the sort of overview of climate science and the issue of climate change that did not exist at the time. The IPCC issues reports every five or six years that remain significantly more extensive than any other overviews available on the issue.[11]

The second reason that some IOs have separate research capabilities is to create a body of scientific expertise that is seen by the member states of the organization as being politically neutral, and thus independent of the interests of other states. This allows states to have a common body of accepted facts on which to base discussion of rules and national obligations. For example, in many IOs that deal with international fisheries issues, states often suspect the scientific reports of other states of being designed to maximize those states' fisheries quotas, rather than to accurately portray the health of fish stocks. An independent scientific council associated with the IO can allay those fears and generate a body of estimates of stock health that all participants will be willing to use as a basis for negotiating quotas. It is often through these scientific bodies, whether designed to provide impartial research or create new knowledge, that IOs develop the epistemic communities discussed in the previous chapter.[12]

Bodies that deal with technical standards are similar to scientific committees, except that they focus on setting specific operational standards rather than on independent research. For example, the secretariat of the International Civil Aviation Organization (ICAO) includes the Air Navigation Bureau and the Air Transportation Bureau. These bureaus employ technical experts on the subject of air navigation and civilian air transportation, who then propose international standards for the airline industry. These standards are then accepted or rejected by the ICAO Council, the governing body made up of member country political appointees. Technical bodies tend mainly to employ people with specific professional expertise in the relevant issue-areas. These also often work with representatives both of national standard-setting bodies, and of the relevant industries. The technical bureaus of the ICAO would thus create new standards in consultation with national airline regulators (such as the Federal Aviation Administration [FAA] in the United States) and representatives of both the airline industry and the major manufacturers of commercial jets.[13]

Another category of administrative function to be found in many IOs is juridical, or legal. This function can consist of offering legal advice and adjudicating the settlement of disputes among states. Many IOs have a legal department or bureau that provides advice both to the secretariat and to member states on legal issues related to the IO's remit. To continue with the example from the last paragraph, the ICAO secretariat includes a legal bureau, the job of which is to provide advice "to the Secretary General and through him to the various bodies of the Organization and to ICAO Member States on constitutional, administrative and procedural matters, on problems of international law, air law, commercial law, labour law and related matters."[14]

There is one IO that deals almost exclusively with adjudication: the International Court of Justice (ICJ). There are also a few bodies that deal with the enforcement of international law with respect to individuals, such as the special tribunals set up to deal with war crimes in the former Yugoslavia and Rwanda, and the International Criminal Court (ICC).[15] Many treaties call for the creation of ad hoc panels to settle specific disputes relating to their rules. A few IOs have full-time dispute settlement bodies as part of their organizational structure. The best-known example is the WTO's Dispute Settlement Mechanism (DSM), which adjudicates trade disputes among WTO member states. Judges from a variety of member states who are generally accepted as experts in international trade law preside at hearings at which states are represented by their lawyers. International adjudicative bodies such as the DSM, whether permanent or ad hoc, tend to behave very much like domestic courts.

The final major category of administrative function to be found in the secretariats of many IOs is what might be called direct implementation. Many IOs, particularly those that deal with development and humanitarian issues, have employees on the ground in member countries, either assisting governments or taking on activities that governments might normally undertake. Not all IOs that deal with humanitarian issues do all of their own direct implementation. Many subcontract with NGOs for some or all of this work. But for many IOs, direct implementation is their primary raison d'être.

A good example of this latter sort of IO is the Office of the United Nations High Commissioner for Refugees (UNHCR). The UNHCR secretariat fulfills all of the standard administrative functions of bureaucracies, and plays an active role in publicizing refugee issues, lobbying for the rights of refugees, monitoring member country behavior with respect to refugees, and fundraising. But the bulk of its efforts are aimed at giving direct relief to refugees on the ground, through more than 400 offices in more than 120 countries. The UNHCR works in concert with more than 700 NGOs, so it does engage in some subcontracting of its efforts. But it does much of the work itself, as suggested by its in-house staff of close to 8,000 employees, 87 percent of whom work in the field rather than at the head office in Geneva.[16]

Several other IOs focus on direct implementation. Many of these, like the UNHCR, are UN agencies, including the United Nations Children's Fund (UNICEF) and the United Nations Relief and Works Agency (UNRWA). For other IOs, such as the World Health Organization (WHO) and the Food and Agriculture Organization (FAO), direct implementation is a major but not predominant function. Some IOs that focus on implementing specific projects in member countries, such as UNICEF, the World Bank, and the United Nations Development Programme (UNDP), maintain representation in many countries, but implement projects primarily through grants to governments and NGOs, rather than through in-house staff.

Many IOs that one might not normally think of as dealing with direct implementation do in fact have administrative components that focus on this task. To return to an example used above, the ICAO has a Technical Cooperation Bureau that sends experts to assist developing countries in improving their civil aviation technical standards. The Bureau's job is to provide expertise, rather than funding. Funding for the Bureau's programs comes from either other IOs, such as the UNDP, or the governments being assisted.[17] Other IOs have different approaches to direct implementation. The International Maritime Organization (IMO), for example, runs the World Maritime University in Mälmo, Sweden, which offers courses and degrees on issues and techniques related to maritime and shipping safety.[18]

A final administrative function, noted above with respect to the UNHCR, is fund-raising. International organizations are generally thought of as being funded by member states, and this is usually the case to a significant degree. The constitutional documents of most IOs specify either the funding mechanism or rules for arriving at a funding mechanism for the IO. Assessments are sometimes based on a flat rate per country, but more often require that larger and wealthier countries pay more. For example, the structure of UN dues is based on the concept of ability to pay. This results in the United States paying 22 percent of the UN's basic budget, and several small, poor countries paying the minimum level of dues, 0.001 percent.[19] Many IOs set their dues structure based on the UN structure.

But not all funding for IOs comes from mandatory dues from member states. Many IOs raise funds, both voluntary contributions from member states and donations from private individuals. The largest single pledge by a private individual to an IO was $1 billion, by Ted Turner to the UN.[20] There are a number of IOs that depend on a constant stream of smaller donations in order to maintain their programs. The UNHCR, for example, has a Donor Relations and Resource Mobilization Service in the Division of External Relations in its Secretariat. UNICEF runs a network of thirty-six national committees, each of which is registered as an NGO in a developed country, to raise funds for it. These national committees contribute roughly a third of UNICEF's annual budget of about $3.7 billion.[21]

Neofunctionalism

Formal institutional analysis is based on the premise that we can learn about what an IO does from the way it is set up, and the way in which it is organized at any given point in time. This is certainly a good, perhaps even a necessary, starting point in understanding IOs. It is, however, static: it can paint for us a picture of where an IO is at a particular point in time, but cannot tell us anything about how and when an organization will change. And IOs do change. Sometimes, they disappear when their function has become obsolete. But they can grow and acquire new roles. What started off as the European Coal and Steel Community (ECSC), a relatively narrow and limited organization, has become the European Union (EU), an organization that affects almost all aspects of life in its member states. The IMF was designed to oversee a system of fixed exchange rates. That system collapsed in the early 1970s, and yet the IMF still exists, having found new roles for itself.

The inability of formal institutional analysis to deal with functional change in IOs led, in the 1950s, to the development of an approach to the study of IOs known as functionalism. This approach suggested that as the problems facing both states and IOs were becoming more international, the scope for global governance was expanding. This meant that the functions of IOs had to continuously expand to keep apace. Functionalists saw IOs themselves as important drivers of this process, by identifying new areas where international governance was needed and by proposing ways of dealing with these new demands. This approach developed to a large extent with reference to the process of European integration through the European Economic Community (EEC, a precursor to the EU), although one of the seminal works of the functionalist approach focused on the International Labour Organization (ILO).[22]

The functionalist approach focused on technical demands for international governance. The ICAO provides a good example of this process: as international civil air transport expanded, the complexity of the rules needed to keep the industry operating smoothly grew as well. This change generated a technical need for greater international cooperation, and helps to explain the gradual expansion of the ICAO. The increased technical need also had the effect of empowering the ICAO as an agenda setter in its area of expertise, allowing it an active role in moving the process of functional integration forward.

By the 1960s, it was becoming clear, however, that much of the increase in international cooperation through IOs was political rather than purely technical.[23] The UNHCR, for example, grew much faster than the number of refugees in the world in the second half of the twentieth century. The UNHCR's growth, then, could not have been fueled exclusively by the technical demands imposed by a greater refugee population. It was fueled as well (perhaps primarily) by an increasing political consensus among states that they had an ethical responsibility to ameliorate the plight of refugees. This consensus was helped along to a significant degree by the UNHCR itself, by both its successes in helping refugees and its lobbying on their behalf. A variant of functionalism, called neofunctionalism, developed in the 1960s to account for political as well as technical demands for increased global governance.[24]

A neofunctionalist approach, then, looks at the political, as well as technical, processes of integration of governance functions globally. It looks more at the evolution of governance patterns within an existing institutional and organizational structure than at the creation of new forms of organization.[25] It would, for example, look at why the WHO declared a focus on mental health for World Health Day in 2001, thus putting an issue that had existed longer than the organization on the global health agenda. No new institution was created, but political leadership made a global issue out of something that had previously been entirely within the purview of national governments.

The political leadership that leads to neofunctionalist integration can come either from states or from IOs. Neofunctionalism thus spans the distinction made at the beginning of this chapter between institutional approaches and regime approaches. To the extent that the political leadership comes from states, or, for that matter, from any actors other than IOs, neofunctionalism is a precursor of regime approaches.[26] The evolution in IO theory from neofunctionalism to regime theory is discussed in the next chapter. To the extent that the political leadership comes from within IOs, neofunctionalism takes an institutionalist perspective. It looks at the way IOs, as actors, are changing global governance. It has the advantage over formal institutional approaches that it directly addresses the issue of change, be it change of structure, change of mission, change of scope, or change of scale, in IOs. It has the advantage over earlier functionalist approaches that it can cope with the broad array of issue-areas in international governance that are political rather than purely technical. In other words, it allows us to ask why IOs push some issues rather than others onto the international agenda.

Neoinstitutionalism

Neofunctionalism served to bring politics back into the study of IOs, in a way that classical functionalism or formal institutionalism did not allow for. But it shares one major limitation of its two predecessors. It can address the question of what IOs do, but not of how well they do it. It can look at the place an IO holds on the international agenda, and the way in which it changes that agenda, but it cannot really look at the overall effect that the organization has on world politics. By the 1980s, this common limitation of institutionalist approaches led to a focus within the IO theory community on regime approaches.[27]

By the late 1990s, however, some students of IOs began to feel that the pendulum had swung too far in the direction of regime analysis.[28] Since regime analysis black boxes IOs as institutions, it cannot address the effects of what goes on inside those boxes on international politics. If IOs in fact operate as they are designed, and work efficiently to deal with the problems they are designed to deal with, then treating them as opaque black boxes should not be a problem. But this assumes both that IOs are efficient organizations that deal with the problems they are designed to deal with, and that they have little independent power separate from states to redefine their missions and their internal organization. A rejuvenation of institutionalist approaches was driven by the observation that these assumptions were not entirely reasonable.[29]

But both formal institutionalism and neofunctionalism are also limited in the extent to which they can capture the politics internal to IOs, and the political power of IOs. Formal institutionalism looks at how IOs are designed on paper. This is a necessary step in understanding the internal politics of IOs, but not a sufficient step because organizations do not always function in the way they are designed and laid out. Formal institutionalism can also capture the power resources that IOs are formally given in their constitutional documents, but not those that they develop informally. Neofunctionalism, meanwhile, recognizes that IOs both have significant agenda-setting power in international politics, and have some autonomy in deciding what to put on those agendas. But neofunctionalism is nonetheless limited by the assumptions that IOs set agendas to further international governance in the issue-areas that they were designed to deal with, and that they will ultimately act to represent the broader interests of the states that created them.[30]

A response to these limitations is neoinstitutionalism, also called sociological institutionalism.[31] Rather than taking as a starting point the structure and purpose of an organization as defined by outside actors, neoinstitutionalism looks at the actual organizational dynamics within institutions.[32] It borrows from fields outside of international relations theory, such as the study of bureaucratic politics in political science and the study of institutions in sociology, that look at the way bureaucracies behave and at the effects of these broader patterns of behavior.[33]

As applied to IOs, this means looking at bureaucratic and institutional rules and politics within the IOs, rather than at constitutional documents or the demands of the issue-area. This can be done in a number of ways. Historical institutionalism looks at the ways in which norms and procedures within particular institutions have developed over time. This approach tends to understand institutional histories as path-dependent, limiting the extent to which the analyst can generalize across institutions. Functional institutionalism focuses on the rules and procedures within organizations, and looks at how these rules and procedures shape the behavior both of the organization and of the people within it.[34] Analysts using this approach to the neoinstitutionalist study of IOs have often concluded that IOs exhibit a strong tendency to be as committed to their own internal rules and procedures as they are to their formal mission, and a tendency to be committed to their own survival as institutions.

There are two ways to look at an IO's commitment to its own rules and procedures. The first is as an empowering mechanism. States create IOs to serve a particular purpose, and create their structure to further that purpose. But it is the IOs themselves, once they have been created, that create their own norms and operating procedures over time. To the extent that they are committed to these procedures, and to the extent to which the IO makes a difference in international politics, the creation and maintenance of procedures allows the IO to dictate how things will be done within its issue-area. When combined with effective claims by IOs to both impartiality (they serve the international community, rather than the interests of particular states) and expertise, this functional autonomy allows IOs to operate as independent actors with considerable freedom of action.

The IMF is a good example of this process. This organization is limited in what it can do by its charter and by its member states. Within these limitations, it is supposed "to promote international monetary cooperation, exchange stability, and orderly exchange arrangements; to foster economic growth and high levels of employment; and to provide temporary financial assistance to countries to help ease balance of payments adjustment."[35] One of the main ways in which it does this is to lend money on condition that the borrower state adopts certain policies. But the organization has considerable leeway in deciding which conditions to impose. There is little oversight of the conditions imposed on certain loans, which are determined within the bureaucratic structure of the IMF, and which can have a major effect on the economic health of individual countries. Understanding which conditions are to be imposed requires looking in some detail at rules, procedures, and politics internal to the IMF.

The second way to look at an IO's commitment to its own rules and procedures is as a "pathology."[36] A pathology in this context is when the bureaucratic empowering mechanisms discussed above lead to organizational dysfunction. This can mean behavior that is at odds with the organization's mission, that is internally contradictory, or that simply does not make sense.[37] An example of such a pathology can be found in the World Bank. The staff in the World Bank's bureaucracy who are in charge of making loans to developing countries are judged by the volume of loans that they make. They are not judged by whether the project for which the money was loaned is ultimately a success. This gives them an incentive to approve loans that are of dubious development value in order to maximize their loan portfolio and increase their profile within the World Bank bureaucracy.[38]

Another example of organizational pathology can be found at the UNHCR. The High Commission's Protection Division, located primarily at the organization's headquarters in Geneva, is the UNHCR's legal arm. It is responsible for protecting the rights of refugees under international law, and tends to approach this mission in a narrow legalistic sense. The regional bureaus, on the other hand, are more interested in the ultimate causes of refugee flows. This can lead to internal dispute within the organization on issues such as the repatriation of refugees. The Protection Division will concern itself primarily with the individual rights of refugees, including the right not to be repatriated without consent. The regional office, on the other hand, may well be more concerned with figuring out what course of action will stop the flow of refugees in the first place, whether or not that course of action is in strict compliance either with international law or with the official institutional norms of the UNHCR.[39]

More broadly, an organization as large and as wide-ranging as the UN will inevitably find itself in situations where different parts of the organization are trying to do incompatible things. In late 2001, for example, some parts of the UN sympathized with the bombing of Afghanistan,[40] while other parts were attempting to engage in supplying humanitarian aid. This resulted in an unclear message as to where the UN stood, and what role it played, with respect to governance in Afghanistan.

A final observation of neoinstitutionalist analysis is that bureaucracies will often have a great commitment at minimum to their own self-preservation and at maximum to institutional growth. For example, the system of fixed international exchange rates, known as the Bretton Woods system, fell apart in the early 1970s. The organization designed to manage the system, the IMF, might have been expected to go out of business as a result, and perhaps be replaced by a new IO designed to meet the needs of the system of floating exchange rates that replaced the Bretton Woods system. But the IMF did not go out of business. Instead, it created a new role for itself based on the concept of conditionality, a role that was never really envisioned for it.[41] Several IOs, not least among them the UN and the EU, are constantly expanding the range of issues over which they have authority. Most new IOs these days are created by existing organizations, rather than by states; in other words, IOs are not only expanding, but are also reproducing.[42] A neofunctionalist may ascribe this to the demands of global governance in an increasingly globalized world. A neoinstitutionalist would want to find out if it was the result of institutional pathologies. Only empirical research could resolve this dispute.

A relatively new attempt to bridge the gap between traditional institutionalism (in which IOs do what they are designed to do) and neoinstitutionalism (in which IOs do what is in their institutional interest) has been through the use of the principal–agent model. This model, developed in microeconomics and brought into the study of IOs, sees states (principals) as creating IOs (agents) to undertake specific tasks for them. As long as the agents undertake those tasks reasonably well, the principals will leave them alone, because extensive oversight is expensive. But when the behavior of the agents strays too far from the goals of the principals, the principals must act to rein the agents in. This theoretical approach can be useful for explaining both why states give IOs some autonomy, and when states will act to limit that autonomy, and has been applied to a wide range of IOs.[43]

Regime Analysis

While institutional analysis was the predominant approach used for studying IOs in the 1950s and 1960s, and has been making something of a comeback recently, the predominant approach for studying IOs in the 1980s and 1990s was regime analysis. Arguably, it is still the predominant approach.

The key difference between a regime approach and an institutional approach lies in whom the different approaches look to as actors. Institutionalists look to the IOs themselves as actors, and ask what it is that the organizations do. Regime analysts, on the other hand, look to other actors, primarily states, as the source of outcomes in international politics, and ask what effects the various principles, norms, rules, and decision-making procedures associated with IOs have on the expectations and behaviors of states. Institutionalists study IOs by looking at what happens within the organizations. Regime analysts study IOs by looking at the behavior of states and at the effects of the norms and rules that the organizations embody on that behavior.

Regime analysis, as suggested above, arose out of a frustration with the limitations of institutional analysis. Primary among these limitations is the inability of institutional analysis to address the bigger picture of the effect of IOs on patterns of behavior in international relations more broadly. It can tell us what IOs do, but not what difference they make. Regime analysis provides a corrective to this by allowing us to question both where IOs come from and how effective they are.

Some students of IO theory have suggested that regime theory is an evolutionary development from early formal institutionalism, through neofunctionalism.[44] But it is perhaps more useful to think of a pendulum, with institutionalist analysis at one end and regime analysis at the other. A broad understanding of the role of IOs in international relations requires both approaches: it requires that we understand both how IOs work and what effects they have on other actors in international politics. The pendulum occasionally swings too far in one direction, but after a while, the gravitational pull toward understanding IOs pulls it back into balance. Unfortunately, it often then gets pulled too far, and swings out of balance in the other direction. This is what happened in the 1980s, when the balance swung in the direction of regime theory. It remains to be seen whether the pendulum has been pulled back into equilibrium by neoinstitutionalism.

Meanwhile, one approach that has become popular in the field in the past few years that can be seen as pulling the pendulum back toward regime theory is network analysis. This approach does not look at the behaviors of individual actors, be they states or IOs, but rather at relationships, at the networks that connect actors. These networks can include IOs and states, and can also include other sorts of actors in international politics, such as NGOs. By mapping the networks, and both identifying key nodes (actors or institutions with the most links in the network) and the relative density of connections in different parts of the network, scholars hope to identify patterns that result in more effective governance. This approach has been applied to issue-areas as varied as international trade, environmental cooperation, and arms control.[45] Network analysis can be seen as a form of regime theory because it looks at the relationships among institutional actors, rather than at the inner workings of those actors.

There are a few observations worth mentioning at this point about the definition of regimes. The first is that they are issue-area specific; the systems for repatriating refugees or for allocating national fishing quotas are regimes, the international system as a whole is not. The second is that regime analysis specifies a range of things to look at, such as principles, norms and rules, and decision-making procedures. This covers the gamut from the very general (principles) to the very specific (decision-making procedures), and from the explicit (rules) to the implicit (norms). Different schools of thought within regime theory tend to focus on different parts of this definition. In particular, there is a rationalist approach to regime theory that focuses mostly on rules and procedures and asks how we can make regimes as efficient as possible in solving the problems they are created to solve. There is also what has been called a reflectivist approach,[46] which focuses on principles and norms. Proponents of this approach tend to ask questions about the effects of IOs on the ways in which actors in international politics think and on the ideas that drive international relations. This tension between efficiency and ideas is the fourth distinction around which the theoretical section of this book is constructed, and provides the focus of Chapter 4.

4

—

Efficiency and Ideas

The tension between efficiency and ideas, between rationalist and reflectivist methodologies, affects both the institutional and regime approaches to the study of international organizations (IOs). But the effects of this tension are most evident in the latter, which, as we have already noted, looks not at IOs themselves, but at their effects on the patterns of international politics more broadly. The regime approach first caught on in the early 1980s, and has since then remained the predominant framework in political science for studying IOs. Both the rationalist (often called neoliberal institutionalist) approach and the reflectivist (often called constructivist) approach can trace their lineage back to the early days of the literature on regimes.[1]

Rationalism and Transparency

The rationalist approach to the study of international regimes is essentially an attempt to apply some of the concepts and tools of economics to the study of IOs. It looks at states the way most economists look at people—as unitary, rational, utility-maximizing actors. Unitary in this context means that states have an identifiable national interest and a single identifiable voice, rather than being a collection of individual decision-makers and domestic interest groups. Rational and utility-maximizing mean that states make cost–benefit calculations of the behavioral options open to them and make decisions on the basis of what will maximize their interests. Rationalists recognize that these assumptions are gross simplifications of the way state decision-making works, but argue that they are useful approximations of the way that international politics works.

The starting point for the rationalist analysis of international regimes is what has been called the rational cooperation literature.[2] This literature begins with the premise of the collective action problem, a situation where everyone would be better off if everyone cooperates, but each actor has an individual incentive to free ride and have everyone else cooperate. The classic example of a collective action problem is union membership.[3] All individual workers want the benefits that collective bargaining can give but would just as soon avoid paying union dues as their individual dues will have very little impact on how good a job the union can do in contract negotiations. An international example of this problem is the case of free trade. Economists tell us that all countries in aggregate will be best off if they all adopt free trade policies. But individual countries can benefit by judicious use of tariffs as long as other countries remain free traders. The problem, though, is that if all countries choose tariffs (as they may if given a choice) everyone is worse off.[4]

A collective action problem with two participants is often called a prisoners' dilemma (PD). This dilemma is often used in international relations theory as a metaphor for collective action problems more broadly. In a PD situation, the first choice of each actor is to cheat while the other cooperates, the second choice is to cooperate while other actors cooperate as well, the third choice is to cheat while other actors cheat as well, and the least preferred outcome for each actor is to cooperate while the other actor cheats. In this situation, the best collective outcome is for the actors to cooperate. But each actor individually has a strategic incentive to cheat, because each actor does better cheating than cooperating regardless of what the other actor does, if each actor cannot affect the actions of the other. In a perfect world, the two states would cooperate, but left to their own devices, they will probably cheat. Each state will thus get its third rather than second choice. One way in which they can get from the third choice to the second is to sign a contract that commits them both to mutual cooperation.[5]

Why do people enter into long-term contracts that constrain their behavior in the future? Economic theory tells us that the market is the most efficient way of allocating resources. Long-term contracts have the effect of taking goods and services off the market by committing them to a single buyer or seller for some time in the future. The economic rationale for doing this is a concept known as market failure. Markets are only completely efficient when they work perfectly, which they can only do in theory. In practice, there are always market imperfections, and the more imperfect markets are, the less efficient they are. There are three kinds of market imperfections: imperfect information, transaction costs, and imperfect property rights. Contracts are a way of dealing with these imperfections.

Imperfect information is when one or both of the parties to a transaction do not know enough to be fully informed about what they are doing. This is the reason, for example, that we are willing to pay more for a doctor's opinion about our health than for the opinion of someone with no medical training. We do not have enough information to make a fully informed decision about our health, and are willing to pay someone with the appropriate qualifications a premium to help us do so.

Transaction costs are the costs of doing business. When we walk to the store to pick up some milk, for example, the transaction costs include the time spent walking to the store. This is why we usually buy enough milk to last awhile, even at the risk of some of it going bad, rather than going to the store for fresh milk every day. One of the reasons most employment contracts are only renegotiated every year or more is that it would be hopelessly inefficient to negotiate salary terms with employers before starting work each day: the transaction costs, the time spent negotiating, would be too high.

Property rights specify who owns what and who is responsible for what costs. For example, it would be hard to sell a piece of polluted land if no one knew who was responsible for cleaning up the pollution. People are generally not willing to invest as much in property for which they do not hold clear title as they are when they do, because without clear title the investor cannot know the extent to which he or she will benefit from the investment. This need for clear property rights provides the explanation for a wide range of government activity, from basic criminal law to specific regulations on issues such as pollution standards. For economists, in fact, it is a basic role of government to create as perfect a market structure as possible domestically by creating a legal and physical infrastructure that maximizes the clarity of property rights and information flows and minimizes transaction costs.[6]

Rationalists have applied these insights to the study of international regimes. Having assumed that states are rational unitary actors, rationalists then go on to look at international relations as a sort of marketplace. States transact in this marketplace for policies rather than for goods and services, but the rationalist's starting point is that the logic of the marketplace operates nonetheless. In this view, treaties and agreements among states are like contracts among people and corporations.[7] People enter into contracts in order to maximize their interests in whatever situation they find themselves. States sign treaties and agreements for the same reason.

The seminal works in the rationalist approach to the study of international regimes have focused on the demand for regimes: When will states want to form regimes, and for what purposes?[8] The answer these analyses give is that states will want to create regimes when faced with collective action problems that result from highly imperfect markets in the international political marketplace. When states are unable to maximize their interests because of poor international flows of information, high transaction costs in international politics, and inadequately defined international property rights, they will attempt to create regimes to improve information flows, reduce transaction costs, and specify property rights. These goals are sometimes lumped together under the broader heading of the "transparency" function of international regimes.[9]

A regime can improve the international flow of information in a number of ways. It can create new information, act as a repository for existing information, or create standards that improve the comparability of different sources of information. The scientific bodies often created by multilateral environmental agreements (MEAs) are an example of the first category. Examples of the second category include the Intergovernmental Panel on Climate Change (IPCC), which is tasked with providing an overview of existing science on the subject of climate change,[10] and the International Whaling Commission (IWC), which requires that member states submit the statistics that they generate to the IWC so that all of the available statistics can be found together in one place.[11] Examples of the third category (creating standards that improve comparability) include the IMF, which creates standards for reporting national accounts statistics so that these statistics will be comparable across states, and the International Organization for Standardization (ISO), which creates product standards that companies are free to adopt or not, as they choose.[12]

A regime can reduce transaction costs by providing a forum for discussing issues, by creating standard rules and procedures for dealing with issues, and by creating administrative structures. A good example of a regime that has implemented these strategies is the UN Security Council. The logic behind the Council is that when threats to international security occur, an authoritative international body should discuss them. But to set up such a body each time there is a new threat to international security would take weeks or even months, when the response time required is often measured in hours. The Security Council is thus in part an exercise in reducing transaction costs. It is the accepted forum for discussing threats to international security, so when such a threat occurs, states do not have to waste time figuring out where to discuss it. Furthermore, the members of the Council have representatives in residence, so they can get to a meeting in a matter of hours, rather than days. It has standard rules of procedure, so that state representatives can get straight to the business at hand rather than having to discuss how to proceed. And it has an administrative structure to deal with things such as record-keeping, translation, etcetera, so that the representatives can get directly to the point without having to worry about these functions.[13] The same logic can apply to most international regimes, and the more often the parties to a regime need to deal with new issues, the greater the need to reduce transaction costs.

A regime can specify property rights by creating specific rules that demarcate who owns what and who is responsible for what, and by enforcing them, or at least adjudicating disputes relating to them. The term "property rights" as used here should be understood broadly, to mean any rule that affects who has the right to benefit from an economic good. It refers as well to the right to be compensated for exposure to an economic "bad," such as pollution, caused by others. The WTO, which is almost entirely about the specification of property rights, provides an example of this function. Most WTO rules are about what countries are and are not allowed to do with their borders with respect to trade. A basic rule of the WTO is that a country must treat foreign goods the same way it treats domestic goods.[14] This gives countries the right to have their goods treated fairly by the countries that import them. The general acceptance of this right should then encourage countries to participate more fully in international trade. The WTO also has a Dispute Settlement Mechanism (DSM), which is in effect an international trade court that adjudicates disputes and sets clear rules as to what countries are allowed to do in retaliation (punishment) for breaches in the rules. The WTO, in short, is designed to increase international trade by specifying and enforcing national property rights with respect to international trade issues.

This example does not mean, however, that specifying property rights is only useful for IOs that focus on economic issues. It can help promote international cooperation in a variety of issue-areas. In the issue-area of international security, for example, the most basic rule that the Security Council is supposed to enforce is the prohibition against invading the territory of another state. This rule defines a property right—states have the right to their territorial integrity unless they fail to meet specific conditions of behavior set by international law. In the area of international environmental management, fisheries agreements often specify precise quotas of particular fish species for national fleets. This is also a property right, because ships from a given country have the right to fish up to the quota, and no more. Property rights in this context should be understood broadly as including any rule about who can do what with respect to anything that countries might want to own or control.

Rationalism and Efficiency

From the rationalist perspective, states create regimes and agree to be bound by the rules of those regimes in order to minimize market imperfections in the international political marketplace. Looked at another way, this is the same thing as saying that states create regimes to maximize the efficiency of their interactions with each other. The rationalist approach can explain the creation of a wide range of international regimes in a variety of issue-areas where states focus on minimizing costs and maximizing benefits, such as international security, economic cooperation, and even human rights.

The rationalist regime literature, as we have seen, began with a focus on the demand for regimes. But the concept of efficiency, which is a fundamental part of this approach, allows analysts to do other things as well. Efficiency gives us a goal to focus on when designing regimes as well as a tool for evaluating how successful the regimes are. There are two questions to keep in mind with respect to both of these tasks: Does this regime make states better off than they were without it? Can it be designed, or redesigned, to make them better off still?

In the case of economic regimes, the answer to these questions is sometimes relatively straightforward, at other times less so. Trade economists, for example, can create estimates of the extent to which a specific trade agreement is beneficial. The World Bank, for example, estimated in 2001 that the results of a new round of trade talks could add \$2.8 trillion to the global economy by 2015.[15] The effect of the IMF's activities in response to the Asian economic crisis of 1997, however, is harder to assess, because we do not know what would have happened without the IMF.

Similarly, in the case of environmental regimes, the answer can often be specified quite precisely. International environmental regimes are usually created to deal with situations where environmental problems are happening at a larger scale than can be contained effectively within the borders of individual states. Regulation by individual states would therefore lead to suboptimal management—either overuse or underprotection—of environmental resources. The effects of regimes on the management of these resources can often be measured fairly accurately.[16] For example, many fish species on the high seas are overfished because no single country is in a position to impose quotas on the amount fished, as they might do were the fish within national waters. This results in a classic collective action problem, where the incentives for individual countries match those of a PD game. The efficiency of an international fisheries regime can be measured by looking at how well its quota system works to maintain fish stocks.

In the case of regimes in issue-areas such as human rights or international security, the efficiency of regimes can be harder to measure, because we know less about what would be happening without the regimes. For example, most people who look at security issues agree that the UN Security Council works better than the League of Nations at improving international security. But it is very hard to know how much difference this makes, because the international contexts of the 1920s and the early twenty-first century are so different. Even in the unlikely event that we could eliminate the Security Council for a year as a control experiment, it would be hard to tell how much difference its absence was making, because each security crisis is different.

The discussion to this point has looked at the question of regime efficiency inductively, by asking how much difference a regime has made once it has been created. But rationalist scholars of international regimes have also used their approach to study regimes deductively, by asking how what we know about market failure and efficiency can be applied to create more efficient regimes. With respect to reducing transaction costs, this can be fairly straightforward, and involves creating forums for interaction, administrative structures, and sets of rules and procedures that make repeated interactions on the issue less costly. With respect to improving information flows and specifying property rights, it can be more complicated.

The literature on maximizing efficiency with respect to information flows and property rights has tended to focus on two issues, monitoring and enforcement. Monitoring is important both to improving information flows and to improving property rights. It is important to improving information flows because it generates information that states need in order to handle the issue-area in question effectively. In international fisheries agreements, for example, states cannot decide on reasonable quotas until they know who is fishing how much, how many fish are out there, and how quickly they can reproduce. Monitoring the behavior both of fishers and of fish thus generates information that is necessary to the proper functioning of the regime. But monitoring is also important to improving property rights, because in order to enforce property rights, participants must first know who is trying to breach the rights of other states. In both cases, monitoring is a necessary first step to enforcement, because enforcement requires knowledge of who is breaking the rules.

Successful monitoring can be hampered by inadequate technology and by excessive cost. Monitoring activity in support of the international whaling regime is hampered by the fact that we do not have the technology to track the movements of populations of whales at sea.[17] Many treaties require countries to report on domestic conditions, either economic or environmental. Examples of this include national accounts statistics gathered by the IMF, or information on atmospheric carbon emissions gathered for the United Nations Framework Convention on Climate Change (UNFCCC). Generating such reports is generally not an onerous burden for developed countries, which often gather these statistics for domestic purposes anyway. But many smaller, poorer countries do not have the resources, either fiscal or human, to collect these statistics effectively. The cost of self-monitoring in these cases, even given the best of intentions, can hamper the transparency of the regime.[18]

The greatest obstacle to successful monitoring, however, is the unwillingness of states to cede too much authority to representatives of international regimes. The various international regimes on nonconventional weapons (nuclear, biological, and chemical) provide good examples here. In order for these treaties to be fully enforceable, the regimes would have to allow for on-site monitoring both of weapons sites and of industrial sites, either by other states or by the treaty secretariat. The relevant treaties allow some of this, but the amount of on-site inspection to which countries will acquiesce is limited by their fears both of having military secrets compromised and of industrial espionage.

Often, the obstacles generated by inadequate technology, high costs, and sovereignty concerns work together. In international fisheries cooperation, for example, monitoring can be made more accurate by putting third-party observers on all boats that fish in international waters. But many states object to this on the grounds of both cost and sovereignty, with the result that monitoring cannot be carried out at an adequate level. One of the objections that the United States has to proposed amendments to the Biological Weapons Convention, to take another example, is that the monitoring is inadequate.[19] This inadequacy is due to a combination of sovereignty issues (not all states will allow sufficiently intrusive monitoring) and dual-use issues (it can be difficult, particularly at the early stages of research, to distinguish between the development of biotechnology for civilian uses and for military uses).

Technological innovation can help to overcome some of the problems in monitoring. Satellite tracking, for example, can accomplish much of the monitoring that used to require on-site or on-vessel inspection, at a fraction of the cost and without raising many of the sovereignty issues.[20] So new technologies are worth looking at for solutions to monitoring issues. They are not, however, a panacea; sometimes technological solutions can be found, but at other times they cannot. Figuring out the most effective point at which to regulate behavior can also make monitoring easier. For example, agreements to control pollution from ships at sea can work well when they focus on equipment standards, which can be inspected at any port. But they do not work as well when they focus on behavior standards, because ships usually violate the standards when they are in the middle of the ocean, where it is difficult for them to be caught.[21] Careful thought to what sorts of regulations can most easily be monitored effectively will often yield regimes that are more effective.

Successful monitoring can by itself help to increase compliance with international regimes.[22] Countries are less likely to cheat on their obligations the more likely they are to be caught. This is true because states do not want to undermine either the agreements they have entered into (assuming that they considered the agreement to be beneficial in the first place) or their credibility as negotiating partners in the negotiation of future agreements. But in many cases, monitoring is only a first step toward getting countries to fully comply with their obligations to international regimes. An often-necessary second step is enforcement.

How do we punish states and force them to change their behavior when they cheat? There are four main avenues for enforcement of international regimes: juridical, political, economic, and (for want of a better term) ethical. The juridical avenue involves the use of international courts or tribunals. The political avenue allows individual states to enforce the regime through the traditional mechanisms of state power. The economic avenue builds incentives into agreements that make compliant behavior economically beneficial and noncompliant behavior costly. The ethical avenue uses shaming as a technique to embarrass states into complying with their international commitments. In practice, these four avenues of enforcement often overlap, but they are still useful theoretical concepts.

The juridical avenue is perhaps more an exercise in transparency than in enforcement per se. Political realists in fact often deride international law, the result of international juridical activity, as futile because it lacks direct enforcement powers. But the role that courts and tribunals play in maintaining the property rights of states in international interactions is nonetheless important, as it makes clear, in a forum seen to be impartial, who is in the right and who is in the wrong in any particular dispute. An example of an international regime focused on juridical enforcement is the International Court of Justice (ICJ). By the logic of realism, the ICJ should be irrelevant. But states continue to make use of it anyway.[23]

Much of the actual enforcing of international regimes is done by states rather than by international organizations, through diplomatic, military, or economic means. A good example here is the Security Council. This is a political, rather than juridical, body; the representatives to the Security Council who decide who is in the right and who is in the wrong with respect to a threat to international security are diplomats and politicians, not jurists. And when the Security Council makes a decision that requires enforcing, it does not have the ability to do the enforcing itself. For that, it relies on the military (and other) capabilities of its member countries. Forces may intervene in disputes under the banner of the UN, but the soldiers themselves are part of national armies.

Some regimes include facilities for distributing funds, which can be used as avenues of economic enforcement. Money can be withheld or increased in response to state compliance with the regime. A classic example of this approach to enforcement can be found in IMF conditionality. The regime of which the IMF is the institutional anchor requires states to engage in certain sorts of fiscal and macroeconomic behavior. The IMF makes adhering to these behaviors a condition for providing loans, and often gives loans in multiple segments (which in the financial world are called "tranches") in order to have something to withhold should states cease complying with the regime after they have got some money. Other research indicates that this sort of economic enforcement only works well when funds are withheld until after states have demonstrated regime-compliant behavior.[24]

An example of a combination of enforcement tools can be found in the WTO. Disputes concerning the international trade regime can be taken to a juridical body, the WTO's DSM, which decides whether states have violated the rules of the regime. If the juridical body finds that a state is in breach of the rules, it authorizes the complainant to take retaliatory action through its own trade policy. So there is a juridical element (the DSM), a political element (enforcement through state trade and tariff policy), and an economic element (WTO rules clearly specify the economic magnitude of allowable retaliation in any given case).[25]

Finally, there is ethical enforcement, or shaming. Sometimes states, as is often the case with people, are simply embarrassed when caught cheating. As was discussed in Chapter 2, this is a source of power for IOs. But it is not only IOs that can enforce a regime through shaming. Shaming can be done by states, by nongovernmental organizations (NGOs), or by other civil society actors, such as news media. Whatever the source, as long as it embarrasses governments sufficiently that they change their behavior in a way that brings them more in line with the regime, shaming has the effect of enforcing the regime. Unlike juridical, political, and economic enforcement, however, shaming does not fit well into a rationalist logic. It relies on decision-makers thinking in terms of the appropriateness of behaviors, rather than in terms of cost–benefit analysis. This logic of appropriateness has less to do with transparency than with legitimacy. And legitimacy, in turn, is something generally discussed in the literature from a reflectivist, rather than a rationalist, perspective.

Reflectivism and Legitimacy

Regimes are about the effects of IOs and international cooperation on state behavior. These effects can take two broad forms, regulative and constitutive. A regulative effect is one in which actors accept, and abide by, certain rules of the game. A constitutive effect is one that creates a new game for the actors to play. Rationalist methodologies focus exclusively on regulative effects. Reflectivist methodologies address both kinds of effects, but tend to emphasize the constitutive ones.[26]

Take, as a metaphor, a game of chess. In order to play chess, one must understand the regulative rules: knights can move only on the vertical and horizontal, bishops only on the diagonal, pawns only one square at a time, and so on. One could presumably change the regulative rules, if both players agreed, and still be playing chess, just a slightly different form of chess. There are also, however, constitutive rules that are often not clearly stated, but that are fundamental to the game. For example, you cannot dump the board if you are losing. If you make a habit of this, no one will play with you. This is a constitutive rule because the basic concept of chess does not work unless the players are willing to accept a loss when the regulative rules indicate that they have lost.

Two examples from the world of IOs might help to clarify this distinction. The first is from the international trade regime. This system abounds in regulative minutiae—the final document from the Uruguay round of negotiations, which created the WTO, ran to approximately 550 pages of regulative detail.[27] But all of this detail depends on the norm of nondiscrimination, the idea that countries treat all other countries equally. Nondiscrimination has regulative effects, but it is also a constitutive norm: if countries do not accept the basic principle, the entire system falls apart. Nondiscrimination is not the only principle available upon which one could base international trade,[28] but it is the one that the current system is built on. The entire superstructure of international trade rules requires that participating countries accept it.

A second example is from the rules of war. One of these rules is that a country is not allowed to target civilians in war.[29] This rule certainly has regulative effects; for example, it strongly affected NATO targeting choices in Libya in 2011, and U.S. targeting choices in its air campaigns in Iraq in 2003 and Afghanistan in 2001. But it depends on the idea that belligerents, soldiers, are in principle different from civilians. When military efforts require support, funding, etcetera, from national communities, this distinction can be weak, both in practice and in principle. Why, for example, is a janitor working at a military base (and working there because it was the only job available) a legitimate target, while a journalist who is not in uniform but who argues loudly in favor of the war not a legitimate target? The answer is that this is a constitutive distinction that has been accepted by the international community. It is one of the ideas on which the rules are based, rather than being one of the rules.[30]

In the same way that the object of rationalist study in regime theory can be summed up as transparency, the object of reflectivist study can be summed up as legitimacy.[31] Most people obey most laws most of the time not because of specific calculations of interest or fear of punishment, but because they accept the law as legitimate.[32] For instance, most people do not resort to murder as a method of dispute settlement, because they accept the idea that murder is morally wrong. Constitutive rules help us to determine what constitutes legitimate behavior and what does not. For example, most moral systems see human life as having value in and of itself. This makes taking such a life, in the absence of a good reason for doing so (e.g., self-defense) illegitimate. Underpinning regulative law (no murder) with generally accepted constitutive rules (human life has moral value) makes the specific law more likely to be widely accepted. A regulative law that does not have accepted constitutive underpinnings can be much more difficult to enforce, as the United States discovered during prohibition.

The reflectivist approach to the study of international institutions, then, tends to focus on ideas about what constitutes legitimate behavior, by looking at both the regulative and constitutive elements of international regimes. Whereas the rationalist approach assumes that human behavior will be based on maximizing utility, the reflectivist approach assumes that people will pay attention to the appropriateness of behavior. Applied to the international level, this approach argues that states will want to behave in ways that are seen as appropriate, given accepted international norms. These norms, in other words, legitimate state behavior.

Arguably the most basic constitutive norm in contemporary international relations is the idea of sovereignty.[33] Sovereignty gives rights to states, primarily the right to noninterference by other states. But sovereignty requires legitimacy, and legitimacy can only be granted by the international community, the community of states.[34] As an example, the Taliban were never recognized by the UN as the legitimate government of Afghanistan, even though they controlled most of the country. Diplomatically, this made it relatively easy for the United States to use force to remove the Taliban from power in 2001. The United States may well have done the same thing anyway, but one of the reasons that no other country even questioned U.S. interference in Afghanistan was that even though the international community recognized Afghanistan as a country, it did not recognize the Taliban as a legitimate government.

Another increasingly important norm in international politics is respect for human rights. This is a much newer constitutive norm than sovereignty; it did not really enter the international relations discourse until after World War II. There are several international organizations and international agreements that focus on human rights, which together can be thought of as the international human rights regime.[35] This regime is so strong that most of the world's countries have signed most of the agreements. Skeptics would argue, however, that these agreements have no teeth, that countries sign them in order to avoid international opprobrium, but that they do not go on to reform their human rights behavior, as required by the agreements.[36] Optimists say that on the whole, respect for human rights is increasing globally and that these agreements have played a role in bringing about this improvement.[37] How do we know who is right? How can we tell if a constitutive norm, an international regime understood reflectively, is working?

Reflectivism and Effectiveness

The question of the effectiveness of international regimes is more complicated from a reflectivist perspective than from a rationalist one. From the rationalist perspective, effectiveness can be reduced to efficiency, the extent to which the regime changes the behavior of states and other actors in international relations. The rationalist approach focuses on regulative rules that clearly specify how actors are expected to behave, and those same rules can be used as a metric for effectiveness. States either follow them or they do not.

Approached from a reflectivist perspective, this same metric is less useful for measuring the effectiveness of a regime. This is the case for three reasons. First, the reflectivist approach tends to focus on patterns of behavior in general rather than on compliance specifically. A good analogy can be drawn here with speed limits. From a rationalist perspective, speed limits, as rules of behavior, are often failures; they are more often broken than obeyed. But from a more sociological perspective, they can be seen as successful, as they provide a baseline for behavior. People will generally drive at a different speed on a road with a 30 mph limit than on a road with a 70 mph limit. People may not be strictly obeying the rule, but the rule is still affecting their behavior. Similarly, states often cheat at the margins of their obligations under the WTO system. From a rationalist perspective, this suggests a weak regime with inadequate enforcement. From a reflectivist perspective, however, the fact that the international trade regime provides the behavioral baseline of expectations from which states cheat only at the margins suggests that the regime has been effective in establishing multilateralism, nondiscrimination, and other criteria as legitimate standards of behavior.

The second reason why adhesion to rules is less useful as a metric for determining regime effectiveness from a reflectivist perspective is that constitutive regimes do not always specify clear rules for behavior. For example, as previously suggested, a core constitutive regime in the contemporary practice of international relations is sovereignty. Some actors in world politics can be thought of, for a variety of reasons, as semisovereign.[38] One instance of such an actor is Taiwan, which although in many ways is like a normal state, is not considered by the international system to be fully sovereign. This status affects Taiwan in a variety of ways. It cannot join the UN. It can join the WTO, but as a "separate customs territory," not as a state.[39] The Taiwanese government gives generous aid to countries that allow it diplomatic representation, because such representation makes it seem more legitimately sovereign. None of this is governed by explicit rules, but the actions both of the Taiwanese government and of other governments toward Taiwan suggest that these fuzzy rules about sovereignty still matter.

The third reason why adherence to specific rules does not necessarily tell us about the effectiveness of a regime from a reflectivist perspective is that there is no clear hierarchy of norms. Norms of human rights, for example, often come into conflict with norms against interference in the affairs of other states. Sometimes one norm will predominate, sometimes the other, and sometimes there will be some sort of compromise. This does not make either norm more or less effective than the other, or one necessarily preeminent. The answer to questions of effectiveness in this context is provided by the degree to which each norm affects actor behavior overall.

So what does this tell us about the question that led into this section, whether or not the international human rights regime is effective? It tells us to look at human rights as a norm rather than as a rule, as a baseline for expectations of state behavior, and as a legitimator of sovereignty. There are a number of ways of going about doing this. We can compare the behavior of states in general, or of less rights-respecting states in particular, with their behavior in the past and see if overall patterns with respect to human rights have changed. This can tell us the extent to which respect for human rights has become the norm in world politics.

We can also look at instances in which human rights norms are clearly being broken and observe the responses both of the states breaking the norms and of other states. When a state does something that it knows to be illegitimate, and either has been or expects to be caught doing it, it often responds by justifying its behavior either as supported by a different norm, or as a justifiable exception. When looking at the behavior of states breaking a norm, then, a good indicator of regime strength is to look at the extent of the "yes, but..." response. For example, Russia often responded to criticism of the extent of its use of force in Chechnya by labeling the Chechens as terrorists. China has responded to criticisms that it lacks democracy at the national level by attempting to create democratic processes at the local level. To use a different norm as an example, since the end of the Cold War, the United States has been careful to nest all of its uses of force internationally (which break a general norm against the use of force) in multilateral settings, thus drawing legitimacy from the norms of multilateralism and collective security. This is true, for example, even of the case against Iraq in 2003. The weapons of mass destruction issue provided leverage in part because that issue could draw on a decade of Security Council resolutions.

The responses of other states are also good indicators of the strength of a regime. When other states protest a behavior, it suggests that the international community as a whole sees the behavior as illegitimate. This does not mean that states cannot engage in illegitimate behavior, but it does make such behavior costly. To use an example of an extreme breach of human rights norms, the Rwandan genocide suggested that the genocide regime was real, but weak. It was sufficiently effective that the perpetrators of the genocide were no longer accepted as legitimate participants in international politics. But it was not sufficiently effective to motivate states or the international community to do anything to stop the genocide while it was in progress.[40]

A third way of looking at the effectiveness of regimes, understood reflectively, is to look at patterns of discourse in international politics. The extent to which actors in international politics—both representatives of states and representatives of NGOs—speak about a norm, and speak in the terms of a norm, the more the norm is likely to serve as a baseline for expectations. This form of analysis begins with the assumption that language matters, that the terms we use to communicate with each other about an issue affect how we think about the issue.[41] If, for example, we find that the leaders of China speak often about human rights, when they did not twenty years ago, we can conclude that human rights norms are stronger than they used to be.

Conclusions

The rationalist and reflectivist approaches to the study of international regimes look at different kinds of regime effects. The rationalist approach is best for studying issue-specific cooperation among states. It is useful for designing regimes that make such cooperation work efficiently. The reflectivist approach is best for studying conceptually how the international system, how international organization, works more broadly. It is useful for studying the general rules of the game, rather than specific regulations.

Regimes will have both rationalist and reflectivist effects. In some regimes, particularly the more functional ones, the rationalist effects may predominate.

In other regimes the reflectivist effects may predominate. The international regime literature tends to divide the field into camps—you are either on one side or the other.[42] The rationalist/reflectivist distinction might be more usefully understood, however, as different methodologies appropriate for addressing different questions. A full understanding of any given regime, one that addresses both regulative and constitutive effects, requires that both approaches be used.

5

The United Nations and Its System

The first half of this book discusses theoretical approaches to the study of international organizations (IOs). The second half examines the role of IOs in particular issue-areas. This chapter acts as a bridge between these two halves by looking at the overall structure of IOs in the international system. A great number of multilateral IOs in today's world are related in some way or other to the UN, and therefore, the UN provides a good focal point for a discussion of the IO system as a whole. The UN is also the focus of many of the debates on the role of IOs in contemporary global governance, particularly those discussed in Chapters 1 and 2. This chapter will thus both lay out the institutional background for the issue-specific chapters to follow and show how some of the theoretical discussions in the study of IOs apply to the UN system.

The Structure of the UN

To speak simply of the UN can be misleading, because the term can refer to a number of different things. It can refer to a set of countries, to a specific set of institutional structures located in New York City, or to the entire set of institutional structures that come under the administrative purview of the UN headquarters. More broadly, it can refer to what is known as the "UN system," which encompasses a large group of IOs, many of which are not in any way within the administrative hierarchy of the UN headquarters. A good place to start any discussion of the UN, therefore, is with an explanation of how the various institutions that are a part of the UN system relate to one another.

At its most basic, the UN refers to a set of member countries (currently 193), a constitutional document (the Charter of the UN), and five basic organs: the General Assembly (GA), the Security Council, the Secretariat, the International Court of Justice (ICJ), and the Economic and Social Council (ECOSOC). A sixth basic organ, the Trusteeship Council, suspended its operations in 1994. These organs are directly mandated by the Charter. Some of the organs, particularly the GA and ECOSOC, have in turn created subsidiary agencies, and the Secretariat and Security Council have various kinds of subsidiary bodies, offices, and departments. There are also a number of autonomous agencies that are part of the UN system but these are not administratively subsidiary to the central organs of the UN.[1] And finally, there are regional organizations designed to provide some of the functions of the central organs for regional issues. As with autonomous agencies, these regional organizations are generally not administratively subsidiary to the central organs, but are encouraged within the UN system as regional mini-UNs. For an up-to-date overview of the administrative structure of this system (which includes all of these parts except for the regional organizations), see the UN's organizational chart, which can be found online at http://www.un.org/en/aboutun/structure/org_chart.shtml.

The subsidiary agencies, which are often thought of as major IOs in their own right, have in common that they have been created by, are in principle overseen by, and can be disbanded by their superior organizations. In other words, they are answerable to the central organs of the UN. They usually draw at least a portion of their budgets from UN funds as well. Apart from these similarities, subsidiary agencies can be quite different in focus, scope, and scale. Their foci run the gamut from international security (such as specific peacekeeping operations), to economics and development (e.g., the United Nations Conference on Trade and Development [UNCTAD] and the Regional Economic Commissions), to human rights and humanitarian intervention (including the United Nations High Commissioner for Refugees [UNHCHR] and United Nations High Commissioner for Human Rights [UNHCR]). Some are run from within the UN Secretariat (e.g., the Office of the UN Security Coordinator); others have their own secretariats, headquarters, and bureaucratic structures (such as the United Nations Children's Fund [UNICEF]). Some focus on research and monitoring, while others are active on the ground in implementing the goals of the UN. Some employ a handful of people, others employ thousands. Some are fairly actively overseen by the UN organ that created them, and others operate almost independently of the central UN bureaucracy.

The autonomous agencies (some of which predate the UN) and the regional organizations have much more tenuous administrative links with the UN proper. Autonomous agencies interact with and send reports to ECOSOC but are not answerable to it, and do not draw their funding from general UN funds. They have been brought into the UN system because they perform functions that are in keeping with the UN's general mission and with the UN's multilateral approach. But they would in all probability function in much the same way if all formal links with the UN proper were severed. Similarly, the UN is supportive of regional cooperation organizations as a sort of multilateralism of first resort for regional issues. This allows issues that are essentially of a regional nature to be dealt with in a way that is in keeping with that of the UN system, but without burdening the UN proper with issues that could be effectively dealt with in a more local forum.

The UN, Sovereignty, and Power

This book started with questions about the effects of IOs on state sovereignty, and the extent to which IOs have power in contemporary international relations. To the extent that it is the central IO in the system, the UN would seem to be a good place to begin answering these questions. But the answers depend on what we mean by the UN—whether we are speaking of the central organs, these organs plus their associated subsidiary organizations, or the UN system as a whole. This is particularly true when asking questions about agency, that is, about IOs as actors. One can certainly speak of particular institutions and agencies within the UN, whether the UN Secretariat or a particular subsidiary agency, as a corporate actor, in the same way that international relations scholars often speak of states as if they were individuals. Ascribing agency to the UN more broadly, including all of the subsidiary agencies, is more problematic. While all of the particular institutions within the UN are technically administratively interrelated, the links, both authoritative and operational, are often quite tenuous. In other words, the extent to which any one individual or office speaks for the UN, broadly defined, is not clear. And finally, ascribing agency to the UN system is, in most cases, inappropriate. The autonomous and regional agencies are simply not part of the authority structure of the UN proper, let alone its administrative structure. As such, the UN proper cannot authoritatively speak for them.

The questions with which this book began concerned the relationships between sovereignty and globalization, between power and interdependence, and the place of IOs in these relationships. Applied to the UN, these questions can be phrased as follows: To what extent is the UN replacing states as the primary locus for international and global governance? How powerful is the UN becoming relative to states? The answer depends on whether one is looking at the UN as an actor or the UN as a system. Looking at the UN as an actor, it does indeed have some power, but certainly not power of the sort that might threaten either the sovereignty of the core states in the system or the centrality of the sovereign state system itself in global governance. Looking at the UN as a system, it has little direct power, but at the same time, it plays a fundamental role not in undermining but in redefining the sovereign state system.

Looking at the UN, even narrowly defined, as an actor is, as was suggested above, problematic. It makes more sense to locate agency in the specific organs of the UN, which is what the next section of this chapter will do. The organs taken together speak neither with the same voice nor with the same sort of authority. One can draw a loose analogy between the various organs of the UN and the components of domestic governments (e.g., the GA being analogous to a legislature, the Security Council to an executive, the Secretariat to a permanent bureaucracy, and the ICJ to a supreme court). This analogy suggests the possibility of the UN as a whole as representative of an international community that itself has agency. But this agency is at best diffuse, and the agency of the international community tends to be expressed with respect to particular issues through the appropriate international institution.

Given the difficulty of ascribing agency to the UN in general, rather than to specific organs and institutions within it, it is also difficult to speak of the UN as a whole as a locus of power, rather than speaking of the specific institutions within it as individual loci of power. This suggests that those who view the UN as an actor and as a source of world government, rather than as a representative example of a mode of governance, are seriously overestimating its capabilities as an actor. This is true both of those who look forward to a UN-led world government and of those who fear it.[2] Those who hope for a UN-led world government think that the UN's various components cumulatively give it the potential to act as a global government. But these components do not make the UN an actor in the way that well-functioning national governments are. To speak of, say, the U.S. government as an actor with respect to the international community, despite its checks and balances, can be both meaningful and useful: however fractious the process of making foreign policy, the policy can be put into practice in a coherent and relatively unified way. In other words, the U.S. government may not think like a unitary actor, but it can act as one. The same cannot be said of the components of the UN.

When looked at as a system rather than as an actor, the UN has a different impact on sovereignty and a different sort of power. The UN as a system can be seen as redefining the way in which states habitually interact with each other, the basic way in which the state system operates. In other words, the UN system has in important ways redefined sovereignty. This is not to say that it has necessarily weakened sovereignty as an institution. Rather, it has changed the content of the set of rules, the international regime that we understand by the term sovereignty. The UN system has created this change by normalizing and routinizing the practices associated with multilateralism, a pattern of state interaction focused on inclusive negotiation aimed at the creation of rule-based solutions to issues that have the potential to create international conflict. Multilateralism is now the expected norm of state behavior in a way that was not true half a century ago.[3] States still act unilaterally on occasion, but when they do they are often seen as acting inappropriately.

Multilateralism can be, and often is, seen as a form of globalization. It is a pattern of collectively making rules that apply to all participant countries. In this sense, it can be seen as undermining state sovereignty, because it does decrease the autonomy of states to make domestic rules and regulations as they see fit. But at the same time, multilateralism reifies sovereignty, because it is states, and only those states recognized as sovereign by the community of states, that participate in the creation of common rules. Thus, multilateralism, the modus operandi of the UN system, simultaneously promotes a form of globalization and reifies a form of sovereignty.

Does the UN system have power? The answer to this question depends on how one defines power. If one defines power in terms of agency, the ability of an actor to get something done or to change an outcome, then the answer is no. The UN as a system has little independent agency. If one defines power in terms of the effects of structure, without requiring that it be the result of some conscious or active attempt to change outcomes, then the UN system does have some real power, through the regime of multilateralism. This regime has significant agenda-setting power and does help to define the way actors, both states and individuals, think about international politics and what constitutes appropriate political behavior in international relations. It has, in short, become habitual practice for states to think in terms of inclusive negotiation as a first resort when confronted with international issues, either political or technical. The regime of multilateralism also has some real power in constraining conscious state behavior.

An example of this structural power is the attempt by the two Bush administrations to work through the UN Security Council in dealing with Iraq in 1990 and 2003. Acting multilaterally became a goal in itself (although not necessarily a primary goal), even though the United States was perfectly capable of acting non-multilaterally, and even though the second Bush administration was rather more skeptical of the practice of multilateralism than the first. There are limits to the constraining power of the regime—the United States in the end acted without Security Council support in 2003, although it did undertake to assemble a large coalition to give the war some multilateral legitimacy. But the efforts made by the United States to gain this support suggest that the power is real.

The GA

Thus, the UN as a system has a significant amount of power, but a structural power, a power without agency. To find agency in the UN, one must look at its specific institutions. The remainder of this chapter examines the central organs of the UN both as institutions and as regimes. This discussion will illustrate some of the theoretical debates discussed in earlier chapters and provide some background to the examination of the role of IOs in particular issue-areas to be undertaken in later chapters.

The first of these organs is the GA, which is, in a way, the core organ of the UN in that it is the only organ in which all member countries are represented all of the time. Its primary activities are to pass resolutions and to create subsidiary agencies to deal with particular issues. The resolutions are not binding; they are indicative of the majority opinion of the community of nations, but they are not considered to be international law, nor are they enforceable. The GA works on a one-country one-vote basis. Resolutions on most issues can be passed by majority vote, although "important questions,"[4] including, among other things, those relating to membership in the UN and to budgetary issues, require a two-thirds majority. The GA includes both the plenary body (the GA proper) and several permanent committees, each of which, like the plenary GA, includes all countries that are members of the UN. It is in these committees that much of the actual negotiating and crafting of resolutions is done. The GA elects a new president and seventeen vice presidents each year from among the members of the national delegations. It thus has no senior bureaucrats of its own; its senior management is drawn from within the ranks of the national delegations.

The GA is therefore best seen as a forum, as a regime, rather than as an institutional actor. It is a place for the community of states to discuss issues of common concern, and is a creature of those states rather than an independent actor on the international stage. It does not have an executive function, although many of its subsidiary organizations do. It does, however, have significant budgetary powers (although in practice, it is the staff of the Secretariat that proposes budgets, subject to the approval of the GA). The structure of the GA, with its emphasis on equal representation and majority voting, yields a voting majority for developing countries, particularly the Group of 77 (G-77), a caucus of third-world countries.[5] This gives the G-77 effective control over the distribution of much of the UN's budget, when its members choose to act as a group. This control, however, only matters insofar as the countries with the biggest assessments of UN dues pay up. In practice, the largest donor countries, particularly the United States, have been able to restrain the growth of UN budgets and force a decline in the size of the UN's bureaucracy by threatening to (and, for much of the 1990s, actually proceeding to) withhold the payment of assessed dues. The GA, therefore, is in practice more democratic as a forum than as manager of the UN's budget.

From a regime perspective, it seems easy at first glance to dismiss the GA as a talking shop, where small countries with little power on the international stage vote on resolutions that in the end have little effect on outcomes in international politics. In fact, the report of a high-level panel sponsored by the previous Secretary-General, Kofi Annan, criticized the GA for an "inability to reach closure on issues" and an "unwieldy and static agenda."[6] From a rationalist perspective, a talking shop has some minor benefits in terms of transparency. It reduces transaction costs by providing a permanent structure and set of rules for communication within the community of states, and it can improve flows of information by making it easier for states to communicate their preferences effectively to the community of states as a whole. But given that the results of GA debates rarely include specific rules of behavior or decision-making procedures, skeptics can argue that this improved transparency does not really translate into an increased efficiency of meaningful international cooperation.

This rationalist skepticism overlooks the role of the GA in facilitating the creation and oversight of its subsidiary bodies, in which role it may not be particularly efficient but is certainly more efficient than such creation and oversight would be absent the Assembly. More importantly, a rationalist examination of the GA can miss perhaps its most important function: legitimation. It may not be able to enforce its resolutions, but it nonetheless speaks with some real moral authority simply because it is the core democratic organ of the UN, and, to some extent, the voice of the community of nations.[7] The Assembly helps to legitimate broad principles such as the sovereign equality of nations and the cooperative settlement of disputes, and can also be used to legitimate positions on specific issues.

For example, the signatory states of the Antipersonnel Mine Ban Convention (also known as the Ottawa Treaty)[8] faced a situation in which the world's major powers refused to join them, even though they constituted a large majority of the world's states. This threatened to make the convention pointless. The signatory states then made a conscious decision to launch the convention through a GA resolution, not a normal course of action with technical treaties. Furthermore, annual resolutions call for universal implementation of the Convention (interestingly, some non-signatories regularly vote for these resolutions). Clearly, they took this route in order to legitimize the campaign against antipersonnel landmines despite the refusal of some key major military powers to cooperate. This suggests that these states, the majority of the world's states, take the GA's legitimation role seriously.

The Security Council

The UN Security Council is both more specialized in its focus and more unusual in its design than the GA. The Security Council is designed to focus specifically on issues of international security, and is the body charged by the UN charter to authorize the use of force to maintain collective security. The question of collective security as such is discussed in the next chapter, but the design of the Security Council as an institution is discussed here.

The design of the Security Council is, at its core, a response to the failures of the collective security mechanisms of the League of Nations. From a regime perspective, the League's inefficiency at promoting transparency made it ineffective at contributing to collective security. The Security Council was designed specifically both to decrease the transaction costs inherent in the League model and to specify property rights much more clearly to promote more efficient cooperation.[9] The League failed, among other reasons, because its rules and decision-making procedures neither allowed for fast and detailed responses to threats to international security, nor clearly identified those responsible for enforcing the responses that had been agreed upon.

The Security Council was designed to overcome these shortcomings through the mechanisms of a limited membership and a clear connection between those states that make decisions about collective security and those charged with enforcing them. Membership in the Council is restricted to fifteen states.[10] The Council is permanently in session (unlike the GA), and the size of each national delegation is strictly limited. The effect of these organizational features is to limit transaction costs—the Council can debate an issue on very short notice, and the debate can proceed relatively efficiently because of the small number of states and people participating. The Security Council then has clear authority both to decide what issues constitute threats to international security and to mandate action—diplomatic, economic, and military—to combat those threats.

The Council's voting structure supports its ability to use this mandate effectively. A key problem with the League's attempts to deal with issues of collective security was a disjuncture between those who mandated action and those expected to actually undertake it. Action could be mandated by a group of small states that collectively constituted more than half of the membership, but that even collectively did not have any real enforcement capabilities. The

Security Council was designed to overcome this problem by giving the major military powers in the system permanent membership, a disproportionate share of the vote, and the ability to veto potential Council decisions. This improves the "property rights" of the enforcement system by giving those who will supply enforcement more direct and individual control over the assignment of enforcement. But the veto power innovation has not proved to be ideal. During the Cold War, Soviet and U.S. vetoes led to deadlock on the Council, resulting in a quarter century during which the Council did little.[11] The selection of veto powers has also become increasingly dissonant with actual distributions of power more than half a century after the end of World War II. But the innovation did nonetheless create an institution that is more effective, and certainly more long-lived, than the League.

Beyond efficiency, the Security Council is an effective legitimator in international politics, perhaps even more so than the GA. One might have expected the disproportionate voice given to the traditional major powers on the Council, in a UN that otherwise promotes the sovereign equality of states, to lead most other countries to view it as more representative of the international power structure than of international legitimacy. But this has not really turned out to be the case. The Security Council has an integral institutional role in determining the legitimacy of states, both through its authority to adjudicate questions of international security and its role in allowing countries to join the UN.[12] But the Security Council is also seen by much of the contemporary world as the only body that can legitimately authorize international violence. A good example of its role in political legitimation is the debate that preceded the invasion of Iraq in 2003. There was never any question that an invasion would be carried out overwhelmingly by U.S. forces. But much of the world was nonetheless willing to accept such an invasion only if the Security Council authorized it, despite a widespread recognition that such an authorization would in function be a matter of political horse-trading among the permanent members.

Having said this, and as the above comment about political horse-trading suggests, the Security Council is better viewed as a forum than as an actor. A number of features of its institutional structure militate against it functioning as an independent actor in international politics. It has no bureaucracy independent of its participating members. Its president is drawn from among the delegates representing its fifteen members, and the presidency rotates on a monthly basis,[13] suggesting that there is little vesting of interests in that office. And while the five permanent members lend continuity to the Council, the ten rotating members are elected for terms of two years and cannot be immediately reelected, meaning that the continuity is only partial. The Council also has no independent powers of enforcement. It is dependent for these on the capabilities of UN member countries, so that even were it to develop an interest separate from those of its member states, it could not do anything to promote that interest independently of them.

Nevertheless, the structure of the Security Council clearly has empowering effects. Its legal and treaty structure as the organ of the UN charged with the authority to legitimize the use of force internationally has clearly helped to make the international community into a reality to be taken into account by states making decisions relating to issues of international security. And the membership and voting structure has had the effect of empowering the five permanent members at the expense of the rest of the membership of the UN. In the contemporary world this is perhaps least true of the United States, which, as the world's predominant military power, is constrained by the legitimacy of the Security Council's authority as much as it is enabled by its veto on the Council. It is truer of the other four permanent members, which, through their veto power, have a greater individual say in matters of international security than their interests in the issue at hand, or their potential contribution to enforcement measures, may warrant. It can also give them a greater say than other countries that are more directly involved in an issue or that are in a position to contribute more to enforcement. As an aside, this voting structure also has the incidental effect of disempowering the European Union (EU) in matters of international security. Because two EU members (the United Kingdom and France) are permanent members of the Security Council, but the EU as an institution is not represented there (unlike at many IOs dealing with economic issues), these two countries have a vested interest in acting as individuals with respect to issues that the SC deals with, rather than as members of the EU.

The Secretariat

The UN Secretariat, much more than any of the other four organs of the UN, can reasonably be seen as an independent actor in international politics. The Secretariat is the UN's central bureaucracy, and in this sense it provides the institutional support for the transparency and legitimation functions of the other UN organs. But it is also the only one of the organs that can speak with a strong and (somewhat) independent voice about international politics. It can do so largely through the office of the Secretary-General. The Secretary-General is charged in the UN Charter to "be the chief administrative officer of the Organization,"[14] and as such deals with the everyday details of managing a large organization, but is not empowered to play an active role in international politics beyond bringing "to the attention of the Security Council any matter which in his opinion may threaten the maintenance of international peace and security."[15] The Secretary-General is also instructed by the Charter to remain politically neutral, to maintain an "international character."[16] Over the years, this combination of political neutrality and authority to raise issues on the international stage has increasingly given Secretaries-General a significant independent voice in international politics.

This voice is empowered by the moral authority of the UN system and by the position the UN, and the Secretariat, holds within that system. It is constrained, however, by the same factors. The UN charter gives the Secretary-General the ability to effectively put items on the Security Council's agenda. But perhaps more importantly, the moral authority of the UN gives the Secretary-General an effective bully pulpit from which to put issues on the international agenda, and an effective claim to neutrality from which to mediate in disputes. But in order to maintain this moral authority, the Secretary-General must remain within the bounds of the instructions of the Charter and must maintain a reputation both of internationalism and of political neutrality. In other words, the office empowers its occupant only insofar as he or she[17] acts in a manner in keeping (or generally perceived to be in keeping) with the office. Furthermore, since the Secretary-General has neither the ability to legislate nor the ability to enforce, the power and effective agency of the office depends on the ability to persuade. This in turn means that the effectiveness of any given Secretary-General as an independent actor in international politics depends greatly on political skill (and the skill levels of Secretaries-General has varied greatly).[18]

As an actor in international relations, the Secretary-General tends to play the role either of agenda-setter or of mediator. As agenda-setters, Secretaries-General can use the authority of the position, and the access to the media that goes with that authority, to raise or promote certain issues on the international agenda, and to embarrass states into changing their behavior. This can be done through either public or private diplomacy. As mediators, the Secretaries-General have often used the office proactively to defuse escalating crises, and to monitor potentially escalatory situations. They do this personally in some cases, and in others appoint special representatives to mediate in or monitor a variety of places at the same time; the current Secretary-General, Ban Ki-moon, has several dozen Special Representatives, Personal Representatives, and Envoys throughout the world.[19] One of these, his Special Envoy to Syria, is (at the time of writing) the immediately previous Secretary-General, Kofi Annan. These representatives and envoys act to a certain extent as a personal foreign service for the Secretariat.

In addition to the lack of legislative and enforcement powers, and the need to maintain the legitimacy of the office, the Secretary-General is also constrained as an independent actor in international politics by the need to administer the UN. This is a substantial task, involving a Secretariat staff of over 20,000 people.[20] Kofi Annan in fact devoted quite a bit of effort toward administrative reform within the Secretariat during his tenure as Secretary-General, an effort that is still underway.[21] Functionally, the need to successfully administer the UN also entails remaining on good terms with member countries in general, and major donor countries and permanent members of the Security Council in particular. It also entails restrained use of the Secretary-General's independent voice: A bully pulpit used too often dilutes its message, and too much activity on the part of the Secretariat would strain a limited budget. Secretaries-General tend also to be relatively moderate and centrist as a function of the way in which they are chosen. They are appointed by the GA on the recommendation of the Security Council. This means that they must first be approved by vote of the Security Council, without a veto being cast by any of the five permanent members, and then by two-thirds of the GA. In other words, they must be approved both by the Council veto powers and by the G-77, a process that generally leads to a compromise candidate.

ECOSOC, the ICJ, and the Trusteeship Council

The other three organs of the UN are dealt with here only briefly. The ICJ is a body designed to adjudicate disputes between countries and to interpret international law. Although those who view IOs as instruments of globalization might see the ICJ as such an instrument because its existence suggests an international law to which all states are subject, an equally strong, or perhaps stronger, argument can be made that the ICJ serves to reinforce the sovereign state and the international state system. This is the case both because only states have standing before the ICJ, and because acceptance of arbitration by the ICJ is voluntary. Only states have standing before the court because in international law, only states have legal personality; people do not. In effect this means that the ICJ is reinforcing the idea that states are the core actors in international relations. And states need only appear before the court when they agree to do so. In other words, the ICJ does not even infringe on national sovereignty to the point of requiring states to submit to international arbitration. Many states have committed themselves in advance to appearing before the ICJ when called upon to do so, a process called compulsory jurisdiction.[22] But many of these commitments are qualified: they do not apply in all circumstances, and states still retain the right to rescind their commitments.

The Trusteeship Council was created to oversee "the administration of territories whose peoples have not yet attained a full measure of self-government,"[23] the actual administration of which was to be undertaken by specific (usually colonial) states. The last territory that fell within the Council's mandate to become independent, Palau, did so in 1994, at which point it voted to suspend its activities indefinitely. In other words, even though the Trusteeship Council is officially still one of the UN's six central organs, it is for all practical purposes defunct.

The final organ is the Economic and Social Council, commonly known as ECOSOC. The responsibilities of this body include information gathering, the drafting of treaties, and coordination of UN functions within economic and social issue-areas, broadly defined. ECOSOC consists of fifty-four members, elected by the GA for three-year terms. Despite this limited membership, it functions in many ways like a committee of the GA. It is the focal point for liaison with a wide array of subsidiary IOs and is the main point of contact and coordination with the affiliated specialized agencies. It has also created a number of commissions, both functional and regional, designed both as coordinative and as information-gathering bodies. Many treaties and conventions, including those leading to the creation of new IOs in economic and social issue-areas, are first discussed and drafted here.

In terms both of the forum/actor distinction and the regime/institution distinction, it is reasonable to think of ECOSOC as a more constrained version of the GA. It has little agency, and is better understood as a forum, yet the organizations and commissions subsidiary to it often do have agency and are capable of putting issues on the international agenda independently of the actions of states. Its power lies mainly in the ability to set agendas and bestow legitimacy, a power both less broad and less deep than that of the GA, but significant none-theless. From a rationalist regime perspective, it has some success in improving information flows and decreasing transaction costs. From both a regime and an institutional perspective, it is subject to the same criticisms as the GA. The cumbersomeness of its procedures and the size and complexity of its organizational structure limit the effectiveness with which it can increase the efficiency of cooperation with respect to economic and social issues and legitimize new ways of thinking about and dealing with them.

6

From International to Human Security

The UN system is involved in the whole gamut of issue-areas in international politics. The second half of this book consists of chapters that focus on the role of specific international organizations (IOs) in these issue-areas. This chapter and the next look at collective security. There are two reasons to begin with collective security. One is that in many ways it provides the core design function of the UN, the IO at the heart of the contemporary multilateral system. It is the issue that features most prominently in the UN Charter, and is probably still the function most closely associated with the UN in the popular imagination. The second reason is that many students of international relations are more skeptical of the role of IOs in the realm of security than in other issue-areas, and those analysts who question most pointedly whether IOs matter at all tend to focus their skepticism on security issues.[1] Security thus constitutes at the same time a central function of IOs and a hard-case test of whether or not they matter in international relations.

The core security mechanism of a multilateralist world is the system of collective security. This is a system in which all participant states agree to forswear the use of force in the settlement of disputes, and furthermore agree to act collectively against any state that chooses to initiate the use of force. Such collective action must be authorized by a multilateral mechanism, in other words, by an IO that is responsible for defining breaches of international security. Collective security can be contrasted with more traditional security alliances in that it is inclusive, while alliances are exclusive. In other words, alliances are usually formed against an outside enemy (whether current or potential), while a collective security organization aims to include all states and provide each with security against all of the others. Having said this, the meaning of collective security itself has changed over time. It was originally primarily state-centric, focusing on the security of national borders. But it is increasingly coming to be associated with human security, the security of people rather than states, and with a responsibility to protect people whose security is systematically at risk.

This chapter focuses specifically on the Security Council. It begins with a general discussion of the concept of collective security and its development over time in the context of the UN generally and the Security Council specifically. It then discusses the institutional features of the organization, and analyses it in the context of the four theoretical distinctions discussed in the earlier chapters of this book. This chapter, in other words, focuses on the Security Council in the context of theories of IO more generally. It does not attempt to provide a comprehensive discussion of international peacekeeping and peacemaking, or a full history of the development of these functions.[2] The following two chapters examine other IOs that deal with international and human security, from both collective security and humanitarian perspectives.

The Security Council and Collective Security

That collective security is a core design feature of the UN is suggested by the Charter, the preamble of which begins with the words "We the peoples of the United Nations determined to save succeeding generations from the scourge of war," and the first article of which states: "The Purposes of the United Nations are: 1. To maintain international peace and security, and to that end: to take effective collective measures for the prevention and removal of threats to the peace, and for the suppression of acts of aggression and other breaches of the peace." Collective security here is defined as a mechanism to maintain international security, understood as the security of nations against other nations. This reflects the historical experience of World War II, of expansionist states violating the borders of other states. As the historical context has changed over time, both the focus of and the mechanisms for collective security have changed as well.

The Charter provides two mechanisms for maintaining international peace and security, both of which focus on the Security Council as the institutional mechanism for carrying out this task. Chapter VI, entitled "Pacific Settlement of Disputes," allows the Security Council to involve itself in any dispute that it sees as a threat to the international peace, and to investigate, arbitrate, and recommend solutions. Chapter VII, "Action with Respect to Threats to the Peace, Breaches of the Peace, and Acts of Aggression," gives the Security Council the authority to define threats to and breaches of the peace, and to define the appropriate response of the international community, ranging from diplomatic pressure, to economic sanctions, to the use of force.[3]

In practice, the extent to which the Security Council has used these two mechanisms has varied over time. The use of both mechanisms was limited during the Cold War by the U.S.–Soviet confrontation. A result of the Cold War confrontation was that many, if not most, local conflicts took on geopolitical implications, as one side in the local conflict aligned itself with one side in the Cold War, and the other local side aligned with the other geopolitical pole. Since any kind of action by the Security Council required the agreement of both superpowers (for reasons discussed below), many disputes generated stalemate rather than action from the Council.

There were, nonetheless, several occasions on which the United States and the Soviet Union could agree on language for a Security Council resolution, either because neither cared particularly about the conflict in question, or because they agreed that a conflict was getting out of hand and represented a genuine threat to international stability. One of the best known of these resolutions, and a good example of a Chapter VI action, is Security Council Resolution 242, passed at the end of the Arab–Israeli war in 1967. This resolution called, among other things, for a cease-fire and withdrawal from territories occupied during the war. Even though the resolution had little effect on the course of the war, it did have both short-term and long-term effects. In the short term, the resolution provided the basis for a cease-fire that both sides could agree to without having to negotiate with each other directly. In the long term, Resolution 242 still provides a starting point for most discussions of conflict resolution in that part of the world. The resolution thus provided both transparency and legitimacy in much the same way as was envisioned by the drafters of the UN Charter.

While the use of Chapter VI actions was constrained by the Cold War, the use of Chapter VII was, with one exception, eliminated entirely by the U.S.–Soviet confrontation. In the Korean War, the first major use of the UN system to authorize a collective use of force, it was the General Assembly (GA) rather than the Security Council that legitimated the use of force. The first large-scale military intervention authorized by the Security Council under Chapter VII, in the Belgian Congo in 1960, turned into a disaster for the UN, both politically and financially. UN forces spent four years in the Congo without a clear mandate, and the UN was not able to raise sufficient funds over and above its standard dues to cover the costs of the operation. The intervention went so badly that the Security Council did not authorize another full-scale Chapter VII intervention for the next three decades. The next Chapter VII action was in response to Iraq's invasion of Kuwait in 1990. This action, made possible by the end of the Cold War, differed from the intervention in the Congo in that there was a clear and achievable mission (removing Iraqi forces from Kuwait), and sufficient force and funding available to achieve it.

Between the failure of the Congo intervention and the success in Kuwait, the Security Council created a new mechanism for promoting international peace and security, called peacekeeping. This is the activity for which the Security Council was known best for many years. Often referred to as "chapter six-and-a-half" (because it involves the use of military forces, but only with the consent of all of the parties to a conflict), peacekeeping missions use UN-sponsored forces as buffers between combatants to help secure cease-fires that the combatants have already agreed to. Whereas Chapter VII is clearly talking about an enforcement mechanism, peacekeeping is really more of a transparency mechanism. It is a more limited tool, since it is only useful after the terms for cessation of hostilities have been agreed to; it is a less contentious tool because all parties agree to the presence of the peacekeepers, and the Security Council does not have to choose one side of a dispute over the other. In other words, peacekeeping is a mechanism through which the Security

Council can contribute to international peace and security without having to identify one particular party as responsible for breaching the international peace in the first place.

Peacekeeping, as a mission, was first created in response to the Suez Crisis in 1956. The crisis began when, in response to the nationalization of the Suez Canal by the government of Egypt, the United Kingdom and France invaded and occupied the area surrounding the Canal, supported by an attack by Israel on the Sinai Peninsula. The idea of a UN-sponsored force to replace British, French, and Israeli forces in Egypt, with the consent of all parties, was suggested by Lester Pearson, the Canadian Foreign Minister (a suggestion for which he later won the Nobel Peace Prize). The concept of peacekeeping caught on because it allowed the Security Council to play a less ambitious, less politically contentious, and less costly but still useful role in international dispute resolution at a time when the realities of the Cold War prevented full-fledged Chapter VII interventions. By 2011, the UN had listed fifteen ongoing peacekeeping operations, although some of these might be better described as statebuilding operations (see below). These missions involve over 98,000 uniformed personnel, and cost close to $8 billion annually. The longest running current operation, the United Nations Peacekeeping Force in Cyprus (UNFICYP), has been in continuous operation since 1964.[4]

The second new mechanism for the promotion of international peace and security that has evolved in Security Council practice more recently is often referred to as state-building or peace-building. This new mission, which the Security Council really got involved in only after the end of the Cold War, has UN forces oversee the administration of post-conflict areas and the building of local capacity for self-governance. State-building is thus a curative and preventive mechanism, rather than an enforcement mechanism per se. In helping areas that have been the sites of threats to international security to build viable self-governance structures, the hope is that they will not degenerate once again into security-threatening behavior. State-building missions have had considerable success in stabilizing several countries around the globe over the past decade, ranging from East Timor to Bosnia to Sierra Leone to Honduras. The missions have certainly not made any of these places model states, but conditions in all of them are significantly better than before the UN arrived, and probably much better than had the UN not arrived. Other missions, however, such as that in Haiti, have not been as successful.

The recent willingness of the Security Council to involve itself in state-building also often blurs the conceptual boundaries between the maintenance of international peace and security on the one hand, and humanitarian assistance on the other. This willingness to undertake missions that have a clear humanitarian element to them mirrors a trend in the UN community more broadly: the trend toward focusing on human security as much as on international security. Human security is focused on the well-being of individuals, rather than on the security of states, and thus encompasses security of the individual from her or his own state. The concept comes originally from the international development community, particularly the United

Nations Development Programme (UNDP), which will be discussed in more detail in Chapter 11. But it has increasingly featured in the IO discourse across issue-areas over the past two decades.

The clearest current manifestation of this idea in the context of collective security within the UN system is the responsibility to protect, often abbreviated as R2P. This is defined as the responsibility of each individual state "to protect its populations from genocide, war crimes, ethnic cleansing and crimes against humanity," and of the international community "to help to protect populations... on a case-by-case basis and in cooperation with relevant regional organizations as appropriate, should peaceful means be inadequate."[5] On the one hand, this language clearly identifies the rules of sovereignty as associated with the responsibility of states to maintain certain standards of behavior with respect to their own communities. In other words, it globalizes a definition of crimes against humanity that circumscribes sovereign right. On the other hand, the language on the role of the Security Council in enforcing R2P that is to be found in UN documents is relatively modest. It calls on the Security Council to act not in all instances but only when "appropriate."

While the origins of the concept of a responsibility to protect lie outside the Security Council, primarily in the academic community and in other organs of the UN, the Council has taken up the language of R2P in authorizing the use of force. For example, in authorizing the international air campaign in support of forces rebelling against the Gaddafi regime in Libya in 2011, Security Council Resolution 1973 explicitly invoked a responsibility to protect. However, the response to similar levels of violence in Syria the following year was different—the Security Council authorized observers, rather than bombers. R2P should therefore be seen as a concept that can enable international intervention when the circumstances are propitious, but not as one that is strong enough to drive intervention when circumstances are not. It does make a real difference—intervention in Libya would have been much less likely without a broad acceptance by the international community of such a concept. But it is unlikely to lead in the near future to a world in which all crimes against humanity trigger the mechanisms of collective security.

The creation of the two mechanisms of collective security that are not specified in the UN Charter, peacekeeping and state-building, reflected the ambitions of the Security Council with respect to authorizing the use of force at two particular points in time. These ambitions have varied significantly since the creation of the UN. While the language of the UN Charter suggests grand ambitions for the role of the Security Council in the maintenance of international peace and security, the reality of the Cold War quickly limited that role. Peacekeeping was a response to those limitations. The end of the Cold War created new hope that the Security Council would play an activist role, an optimism that was reinforced by the success of the first major post–Cold War test of the Council in response to the Iraqi invasion of Kuwait in 1990. The success of the Security Council immediately after the end of the Cold War allowed for the expansion of its activities into the area of state-building. This new optimism, however, has been brought into question by events ranging from the debacle in Somalia in 1993 to the second war with Iraq in 2003—this time without Security Council authorization. The concept of the responsibility to protect can be seen as an attempt to regain the sense of purpose in collective security that marked the immediate post–Cold War era.

The Structure of the Security Council

The reason that the end of the Cold War had such an effect on the ambitions of the Security Council has to do with its voting structure, one of two institutional particularities that have a major impact on the way in which it operates. As noted in Chapter 2, the Council has what is basically a two-tier or two-class membership and voting structure. The Council has at any given time fifteen members. Of these, ten are elected on a rotating basis for two-year terms (five new members are elected each year) from among the membership of the UN, in a way that ensures that all regions of the world are represented. These temporary members have one standard vote each. The other five members are permanent. These are the United States, Russia, China, France, and the United Kingdom. The five permanent members have special votes, often referred to as vetoes. A resolution in the Security Council needs nine votes to pass, but a vote against it by any one of the permanent members, even if all other fourteen members vote in favor, prevents the resolution from being adopted.[6]

This veto power prevented the Security Council from playing an active role in international politics during the Cold War because the superpowers tended to have conflicting interests to at least some extent in most international conflicts, threatening a veto by either the United States or USSR.[7] The voting structure was designed to give the countries that would necessarily play the greatest role in maintaining international security, by virtue of their size and military capabilities, the greatest role in determining where force would be used. The goal in designing the system like this was to avoid the dynamics of the League of Nations between the two world wars, when the League would call for military action to combat threats to the peace, but no countries with significant military forces would actually be willing to contribute the necessary forces. Somewhat coincidentally, the five veto powers are also the five major nuclear powers (although China and France were veto powers for two decades before they became nuclear powers, and India, Pakistan, and Israel also have significant nuclear weapons capabilities but no veto power).

But there are other countries that argue that the balance of power has changed since the end of World War II, and that the structure of the Security Council should change in response. Japan, Germany, and India have all campaigned for permanent seats on the Security Council. Japan in fact at one point announced that it was considering reductions in the funds it was willing to make available to the UN, and tied this explicitly to the fact that its attempts to get representation on the Security Council in the early 2000s were getting nowhere, although in the end it did not carry through with the threat.[8] At the same time, there is widespread support among a large majority of UN members who do not have permanent seats on the Security Council for the idea of expanding the number of countries on the Council, to achieve broader representation and a better balance between the traditional great powers and the rest of the world.[9] The 2005 World Summit, a meeting of world leaders hosted by the GA that was designed in part to deal with questions about the structure of the Security Council, supported in principle the idea of reform, but was unable to agree on any particular plan.[10]

An expansion of the number of rotating members is unlikely to happen soon, and any change in the veto mechanism is unlikely at all. The reason for this is simply that any change in the structure of the Security Council needs to be approved by the existing Council, meaning that any one of the five existing permanent members can veto any change. At minimum, the veto power means that none of the existing permanent members can be voted off without their consent. But it also means that it will be very difficult to expand the number of states with vetoes. Expansion would mean dilution of the institutional power accorded to the existing permanent members by their special position, and that makes them resistant to change.

The second institutional peculiarity of the Security Council that has a major impact on the way in which it operates is that it does not have its own secretariat. Its secretariat functions are performed by the UN Secretariat. In other words, there are no senior bureaucrats who work for the Security Council as an organization—they work either for the Secretariat or for member governments. This undermines the extent to which the Security Council as an institution can be an independent actor in international politics, as well as a regime. Each new mission that the Security Council authorizes requires the creation of a new organization, a new institution designed specifically for the task at hand, with coordination among the missions being provided by the UN Secretariat. When the Security Council authorizes a new mission, it asks the Secretariat to undertake the process both of creating the new administrative structure, and of soliciting from member states both the soldiers to serve in it and the money to pay for it (although tacit commitments of resources by countries are often made in advance of the vote).

For peacekeeping and traditional collective security missions, the personnel for the new institutions are drawn exclusively from forces seconded by national militaries. In other words, personnel for these missions work for their home governments, and are on loan to the Security Council. These forces retain their own command structures, so coordination across the different national components within individual missions can be problematic. Furthermore, maintaining standards of conduct can be difficult, because the UN as an organization does not have the ability to discipline the soldiers wearing its blue helmets. For nation-building missions, personnel can be seconded both from member countries and from other UN IOs with relevant expertise. These sorts of missions sometimes also employ people directly.

The creation of new institutions for each Security Council mission has the advantage of flexibility—organizational structure can be arranged to suit each specific mission. It also has the advantage, from the perspective of member states, of maximizing state control over the use of military force by minimizing the operational discretion of the UN bureaucracy in such matters. The pro-liferation of mission-specific organizations, however, also has disadvantages. One is resource inefficiency, in that each new mission has to create its own bureaucratic structure. Another disadvantage is that each new mission must solicit donations of forces from member countries, which takes time and is not always as successful as it might be. A third disadvantage is that it makes coor-dination both across and within missions more difficult. Coordination across missions is more difficult because of the institutional peculiarities of the indi-vidual organizations and because there is little in the way of central bureau-cratic capabilities to oversee communication among institutions. Coordination within missions is made more difficult because the proliferation of specific institutional structures undermines the orderly development of standardized procedures and expectations.

A final category of institution created by Security Council resolutions is war crimes tribunals. These tribunals tend to employ the bulk of their staff directly. Because they are courts of law, it is important for reasons of judicial credibility that they be staffed by people committed to the court itself, rather than to member countries. At the time of writing, two such tribunals were active, cov-ering war crimes and crimes against humanity committed in the conflicts in Rwanda and the former Yugoslavia. Because of the creation of the International Criminal Court (ICC), which will be discussed in the next chapter, these two tribunals are likely to be the last of their kind to operate under the auspices of the Security Council.

The Security Council and IO Theory

What do these institutional specifics tell us about the role of the Security Council in collective security? This question can be addressed through the lens of the four distinctions discussed in the preceding chapters, beginning with the distinction between efficiency and legitimacy. The efficiency and legitimacy roles of the Security Council are closely integrated. It was clearly designed with efficiency in mind. The UN Charter specifically identifies it as the body with ultimate authority in deciding issues of international peace and security. This is a way of specifying property rights, particularly ways of deciding breaches of sovereign property associated with the use of force. The Council is perma-nently in session, members are required to have representatives available at all times, and emergency meetings can be called in a matter of hours, a rarity in IOs. This both decreases transaction costs and improves information flows by making the debating forum available to members quickly and easily. The small size of the Council has a similar effect, making debate more efficient and decision-making smoother. And the two-tier voting structure is designed to draw a clear link between those who are making decisions about the use of force, and those who will actually have to contribute the bulk of the force. This should increase transparency in the implementation of Council decisions. It should also, in the long run, increase the Council's credibility by decreasing the frequency with which it makes pronouncements that cannot be implemented.

Because most of the veto powers are also the traditional great (imperialist) powers, the Council's two-tier voting structure might also be expected to undermine its legitimacy. The diplomatic crisis leading up to the war in Iraq in 2003, however, indicates that the legitimacy accorded to the Security Council, both by states and by populations at large, is surprisingly high. Before the war, the United States went to some lengths to try to get Security Council approval, and polls suggested that popular opinion in many countries would have been much more favorable to the war had the United States succeeded in getting such approval. U.S. forces in the end occupied Iraq without authorization from the Security Council, although the Council did legitimize a temporary occupation of the country after the fact. There was some discussion that this action could diminish the legitimacy of the Security Council (and of the UN more broadly) in the long term, and that it undermined such basic multilateralist concepts as collective security and respect for international law.

While the crisis leading up to the war was a difficult time for the UN, it also highlighted the extent to which general populations, at least among industrialized countries, accept the Security Council as the arbiter of legitimacy in the use of force internationally. After the war, the United States, although in military control of the country, nonetheless felt the need to seek Security Council approval of its postwar administration there.[11] Furthermore, the U.S. government continued using the Security Council to deal with issues ranging from Iran's nuclear program to crimes against humanity in Darfur, even in the aftermath of its failure to get the Council's approval for the war in Iraq. And the more recent conflicts in Libya and Syria have suggested that if anything the role of the Security Council as legitimator of international intervention is becoming stronger. Despite a decidedly mixed record in maintaining collective security over the years, the legitimacy function of the Security Council appears to be alive and well.

The second distinction is that between IOs as regimes and IOs as institutions. The Security Council is best looked at in this context as a regime; its activities and procedures are dominated almost exclusively by representatives of member states. Since the Council has no independent bureaucracy, it is difficult for it to develop either an independent voice or bureaucratic pathologies, in the way organizations with their own secretariats do. The third distinction is that between power and interdependence. One can certainly make the argument that interdependence is less pronounced in the issue-area of collective security than in many of the issue-areas discussed in the coming chapters. At the same time, however, the importance of interdependence is not negligible. Security crises in weak states can, and often do, destabilize nearby states and draw in members of the international community more broadly. But the role of power in security issues is clear. Most clear, perhaps, is the role of military power, without which a country simply cannot participate meaningfully on the ground in the maintenance of international peace and security. And the costs of military action can overwhelm normative pressure to intervene in support of the responsibility to protect.

But the structure of IOs conveys power to states as well. This is clearly the case in the Security Council. The five states with vetoes are empowered to deal with security issues in a way that other countries are not. They have the ability to block any Security Council action against themselves and their allies, which may help to explain why they tend to use force abroad more often than most other countries. They also have a permanent voice on the Council, whereas other countries have at best only occasional and temporary voices. And they also have veto power over major structural and constitutional change in the UN, and over the appointment of senior UN personnel, including the Secretary-General. The extent to which permanent membership on the Security Council empowers states is suggested by the extent to which several large countries, including Japan, Germany, and India, have at times been willing to expend significant political capital to try to get a permanent seat, despite the obvious hurdles to doing so.

The last of the four distinctions is between sovereignty and globalization. This review of the history of collective security in the context of the Security Council suggests that states' attachment to sovereignty and resistance to globalization are most pronounced with respect to issues of war. This does not mean, however, that in issues of war and national security, IOs are irrelevant. States are least willing to give up sovereignty in these issue-areas, but IOs nonetheless affect outcomes by empowering some states at the expense of others, by legitimating some actions and delegitimating others, and by making international security cooperation more efficient when states choose to cooperate. Furthermore, broad acceptance of norms such as the responsibility to protect, and the writing of such norms into Security Council resolutions, indicates that support in the community of nations of state sovereignty without state responsibility is not infinite.

7

The Institutions of Collective Security

This chapter discusses the institutional features of some of the IOs other than the Security Council that are involved in collective security issues. These include organizations both at the international and regional levels, and with a range of focus from traditional international security to human security. The chapter will look first at the UN Secretariat, with an emphasis on the Department of Peacekeeping Operations (DPKO), then at regional collective security organizations such as the Organization for Security and Co-operation in Europe (OSCE), and finally at the International Atomic Energy Agency (IAEA) and the International Criminal Court (ICC). It concludes, as do all of the chapters in the second part of this book, by looking at these particular IOs through the lens of IO theory.

The Secretariat

There are three ways in which the UN Secretariat directly involves itself in the maintenance of collective security. The first, as noted in the previous chapter, is by providing secretariat services to the Security Council and to specific institutions subsidiary to the Council. In a general sense, this is done through a wide variety of activities that the Secretariat performs as a matter of course, from financial management and the provision of legal services to basic house-keeping functions. There is one department within the Secretariat devoted specifically to servicing international peacekeeping and peace-enforcing missions: the DPKO. The DPKO is responsible, among other things, for general administrative, logistic, and coordinative functions for Security Council missions. It is also responsible more broadly for training forces of member countries in peacekeeping operations, and for setting standards for behavior on these missions.[1]

A relatively new part of the DPKO is the Situation Centre. This office was created in response to some serious operational problems caused by the structure of Security Council missions operating in the early 1990s. As noted above, the forces committed by various countries tend to maintain separate command structures, with coordination to be provided by the UN headquarters in New York. These forces also often operate under fairly restrictive rules and need authorization from headquarters to escalate levels of force in response to provocations from local actors. But until 1993 it was never clear whom an on-site commander should call for coordination and authorization. One could call headquarters in need of urgent consultation and find no one there at that particular hour. The Situation Centre was created to ensure that there was always someone answering the telephone in New York, who could give on-site commanders an answer or at least get the Security Council to discuss an issue quickly.

The second way in which the Secretariat involves itself directly in issues of international peace and security is by the use of the good offices of the Secretary-General. Although not discussed in the UN Charter, this political role was one that Secretaries-General began to play almost immediately upon the creation of the UN. The role involves the Secretary-General, either in person or through an appointed representative, helping to solve disputes by providing neutral third-party intermediation, and by lending the prestige and moral authority of the Secretary-General's office to negotiating processes. The role that these good offices can play, however, is circumscribed by the fact that moral authority is generally the only kind of authority that the Secretary-General can bring to bear.[2] The Secretariat has neither any legal authority nor any recourse to economic or military incentives or threats to back up its involvement.

The Secretary-General currently has roughly 100 Special Representatives, Special Envoys, and Special Advisors, assigned both to mediate particular conflicts and to monitor specific issues.[3] Many of these are associated with specific Security Council missions or subsidiary organizations of the UN, but many are not. In either case, these representatives report specifically to the Secretary-General. The fact that they have been a constant feature of the Secretary-General's office almost since the inception of the UN, and that Secretaries-General are willing to put their limited resources into maintaining so many of them, suggests that they do play some useful role in international politics and in the maintenance of international peace and security, despite the Secretary-General's lack of authority to impose solutions and agreements.

The third way in which the Secretariat is able to affect issues of collective security is by helping to change norms, to change what it is that member countries and their populations expect the international community to do under the heading of the UN's collective security function. The Secretary-General can do this primarily through public pronouncements and reports, and to a lesser extent through private diplomacy. An example of this mechanism can be found with the Responsibility to Protect. The idea was first developed as part of a discussion generated by Secretary-General Kofi Annan in 2001. And a report by Secretary-General Ban Ki-moon in 2009 played a significant role in keeping the concept active on the international agenda, and led directly to the adoption of the concept in a resolution in the General Assembly (it had already appeared in Security Council resolutions).[4]

Regional Security Organizations

Chapter VIII of the UN Charter encourages the creation of "regional arrangements" (i.e., regional collective security organizations) to address security issues that can successfully be dealt with on a regional level. These arrangements allow the Security Council to focus its attention on broader threats to international peace and collective security. There are regional security organizations in many parts of the world that are explicitly designed to fit within Chapter VIII. A good example of such an organization is the Organization of American States (OAS). Some regions have two tiers of collective security organizations, to deal with both continental and subcontinental crises. The African Union (AU),[5] for example, is designed in part to deal with threats to peace and security in Africa in general, while the collective security arms of the Southern African Development Community (SADC)[6] and the Economic Community of West African States (ECOWAS) are designed to deal with threats specifically within southern and western Africa, respectively.

A particularly interesting region in which to look at regional collective security arrangements is Europe, because there are a number of different kinds of regional security arrangements in operation there. The institutions that represent two of these arrangements, the OSCE and the North Atlantic Treaty Organization (NATO), are sufficiently robust to be able to take on significant security obligations. The OSCE fits explicitly within the realm of Chapter VIII. It has the bigger membership of the two organizations, with fifty-six members, including all of the countries of Europe and all fifteen countries of the former Soviet Union (the United States and Canada are members of both organizations). NATO, on the other hand, began as a traditional security alliance; it was designed to protect its members against an external threat (the Soviet Union), rather than internal threats. But when its primary mission became obsolete with the end of the Cold War, it transformed itself into a sort of hybrid traditional alliance/collective security organization. It has twenty-eight full members. In an attempt to bridge the gap between its roles as an exclusive alliance and an inclusive collective security IO, it has also created "partnership agreements" with another twenty-two countries.[7]

The OSCE, as its name suggests, is a forum designed to increase the ability of member countries to enhance security cooperation in Europe. Of the various multilateral collective security organizations, the OSCE has perhaps the broadest definition of security, including human security, environmental security, and the promotion of democracy and good governance. It has a substantial secretariat, with a staff of about 550, and various associated political bodies (made up of state representatives), dealing with various issues related to its broad definition of security, such as minority and language rights, and gender equality. Unlike either the UN Security Council or the GA, it works on a consensus basis. It does not have the authority to call on member countries for enforcement measures, either economic or military, but does work with Security Council missions that have the authority to use force.

The OSCE evolved from the Conference on Security and Co-operation in Europe (CSCE). The earlier body was a forum for discourse among member states, an attempt to improve communication between East and West in Europe during the Cold War. The CSCE met only occasionally and did not have a permanent bureaucracy. As the Cold War wound down, member countries began to add functions, resources, and a permanent bureaucracy to the CSCE in an attempt to increase its capabilities. In 1994, these accretions had enlarged the institution sufficiently that it formally promoted itself from a "conference" to an "organization." The OSCE has retained the forum function of the CSCE, but has added to it a permanent secretariat that is able to monitor potential security threats in Europe, and provide advice and expertise in institution- and democracy-building to countries in need of it.

NATO is a special case, not being, strictly speaking, a multilateral IO as defined in the first chapter of this book. As such it will not be discussed in great detail here. But it does have capabilities not shared by other IOs. In particular, NATO has a military infrastructure and capabilities. The organization requires of its members that they impose certain common technical standards on their armed forces. This gives NATO armies a relatively high degree of interoperability—they can communicate with each other and provide technical and logistical support to each other to a much greater degree than is common among militaries of different countries. NATO also has some committed military assets, including command, transportation, and information-gathering capabilities. These assets are still part of national military forces (more often than not part of the U.S. military) but are committed for use for NATO purposes. These institutional features give NATO the ability to coordinate uses of force by its member countries to a far greater degree than is the case for traditional collective security organizations such as the Security Council.

An interesting comparison of the roles of the Security Council, the OSCE, and NATO can be found in the international community's intervention in Bosnia in 1995 and Kosovo in 1999. In both cases, force was used by other countries (most of the force used in both cases was provided by U.S. air power), leading in effect to an international administration designed to build local governmental institutions to the point of viability. In both cases the OSCE was assigned responsibility for most of the institution-building and civil administration. In the case of Bosnia, the use of force was sponsored by NATO and approved after the fact by the Security Council. In the case of Kosovo, it was authorized from the outset by the Security Council. In Bosnia, NATO's use of force helped to convince the local combatants to sign a peace treaty that explicitly invited NATO forces into Bosnia to oversee implementation of the peace. This invitation suggested a mutual consent to the presence of outside forces, which is how NATO got around the absence of direct Security Council legitimation of its military presence in Bosnia.[8] In Kosovo, such an invitation was not necessary because the Security Council authoritatively legitimized the presence of the foreign military forces. Although the role of the OSCE was similar in the two missions, because of their different histories the OSCE Secretariat coordinated the mission in Bosnia, but in Kosovo it was subsidiary to the UN Secretariat, which is responsible for overall coordination there.

The IAEA

The discussion to this point has primarily been about the role of IOs in dealing with conflict after it breaks out. Another role that some IOs play in collective security is working to limit the potential human security effects of conflict through arms control. Many kinds of weapons are limited or prohibited through formal international cooperation, ranging from weapons of mass destruction (nuclear, biological, and chemical) to landmines and small arms. Some of these agreements generate only limited new organizational structures, or are implemented through existing structures, such as the UN. For example, the Mine Ban Treaty calls on state parties to report to the UN Secretary-General, and calls on the Secretary-General to undertake fact-finding and dispute-resolution functions, but does not create a new IO.[9] Other agreements, particularly those pertaining to weapons of mass destruction, are overseen by their own IOs.

Of these, the relationship between the arms control agreement, the Nuclear Non-Proliferation Treaty (NPT), and the IO, the IAEA, is the most complicated. The chemical and biological weapons regimes are conceptually simple. They ban not only the use but also all production and deployment of weapons within their categories. But the nuclear regime is more complicated. The NPT allows five member countries to deploy nuclear weapons, whereas all other parties to the treaty are not allowed to (three countries that have stayed outside the regime, India, Israel, and Pakistan, and one that has left, North Korea, deploy nuclear weapons). In exchange, the five nuclear powers (which are also the five permanent members of the Security Council, although there is no direct cause-and-effect link between the two) agree to support the development of civilian nuclear technologies in the other member states. They also commit themselves to work toward eventual nuclear disarmament. The NPT calls on the IAEA to verify compliance with the treaty, as well as facilitate the transfer of civilian nuclear technologies.[10]

The IAEA, which was created in 1957, actually preceded the negotiation of the NPT. Furthermore, their memberships are different in important ways. More than thirty signatories of the NPT, mostly smaller and poorer countries without the ability to make effective use of nuclear technological assistance, are not members of the IO. At the same time, India, Israel, and Pakistan are all founding (and continuing) members of the IAEA.[11] The IAEA has the twin responsibility of monitoring and verifying compliance with the NPT, and assisting member states in the development of civilian nuclear technologies. The IAEA, headquartered in Vienna, is a relatively large IO, with a staff of over 2,300 and a budget in the range of $400 million annually.[12] Although the organization is best known for its role in monitoring member countries for the development of nuclear weapons technologies, its resources are roughly evenly split between its two main tasks of monitoring and technological assistance.

This latter category includes assistance with a wide range of civilian nuclear technologies, from ensuring the safety and security of nuclear-powered electricity generators to the application of radioactive isotopes to medical and agricultural uses. This part of the IAEA's work is relatively nonpolitical, consisting of technical experts assisting developing countries with technologies that pose little threat to international security. But it is its role in verifying compliance with the NPT that generates far more publicity for the organization. This is particularly true of it efforts to monitor first North Korea, and more recently Iran, as the two states learned the processes for making weapons-grade nuclear materials. This is a much more political role, in that the Director-General of the IAEA is called upon to negotiate inspection schedules directly with countries to be monitored, and to interpret the result of inspections. However, it is ultimately up to the Security Council to decide if a country is formally in breach of its commitments under the NPT, and if so what is to be done.

The NPT and the IAEA between them constitute a relatively successful regime. While a few states have developed nuclear weapons both inside and outside the NPT, this number is likely far fewer than would otherwise have been the case, and the IAEA does a credible job of making noncompliance transparent. Critics of the regime argue that the five nuclear powers that are party to the NPT are moving too slowly on their commitment to eventual nuclear disarmament, and that the IAEA can be too slow and bureaucratic in dealing with safety issues in civilian nuclear power stations. But overall the compromise that underlies the regime seems to be holding, and to be making civilian nuclear technologies safer, and nuclear weapons rarer, than would otherwise be the case.

The ICC

A very different sort of IO from the IAEA is the International Criminal Court (ICC). Whereas the IAEA is focused on monitoring and technical assistance, and leaves any adjudication to the Security Council, the ICC is a true court—it focuses entirely on adjudication. Furthermore, the IAEA works primarily with states, as do most IOs. The ICC, however, applies international human rights law to individual people rather than states. It is in this respect fundamentally different not just from most IOs but also from most international courts. International law generally applies to states that have international legal personality. This means, in effect, that states are for international law what people are for domestic law—they are the individuals that the court recognizes as having legal standing. Most international courts, from the International Court of Justice and the World Trade Organization's Dispute Settlement Mechanism to ad-hoc tribunals set up to adjudicate specific disputes, deal only with states. When rulings affect the actions of individuals, member states are expected to change individual behavior through the mechanisms of domestic law. Even something like the European Court of Human Rights (discussed in the next chapter), which allows individuals to initiate proceedings based on violations of the European Convention on Human Rights, generally rules on whether states, rather than individuals, are meeting their human rights responsibilities. The ICC, however, tries individuals for gross violations of international human rights law.

The ICC is meant to play, permanently and globally, the role that the International Criminal Tribunal for the Former Yugoslavia (ICTY) and its equivalent for Rwanda (ICTR) play for those specific conflicts.[13] Previous tribunals had been set up under the auspices of, and were answerable to, the Security Council. The Rome Statute, which created the Court in 2002, was meant to institutionalize the idea that nobody should be able to commit crimes against humanity with impunity. The ICC is empowered to try individuals for war crimes, genocide, crimes against humanity, and the crime of aggression (although its jurisdiction over the crime of aggression does not begin until 2017).[14] The ICC can try nationals of and people accused of crimes within countries that have signed on to the Court. It can also try individuals in cases that have been specifically referred to it by the Security Council. The ICC is a court of last resort—it can only try individuals if the national courts with first jurisdiction over the crime are deemed to have failed to prosecute them, or if the national government refers the case to the ICC. It is thus designed to backstop international human rights law, not to replace functioning national courts in prosecuting individuals.

The Court has two primary parts, along with a secretariat (called the Registry). The first is the Judicial Divisions (pluralized because there are pretrial, trial, and appeal divisions). There are eighteen judges, elected by member states for nine-year terms (as a general rule, one-third are replaced every three years). Judges are nominated by their governments, and are required to "possess the qualifications required in their respective States for appointment to the highest judicial offices."[15] No more than one judge is allowed at any given time from a member state. The second part is the Office of the Prosecutor, which is responsible both for prosecuting trials and for conducting investigations. The Prosecutor, who is elected by member countries for a term of nine years, has the authority to generate investigations independently, with the approval of a chamber of the pretrial division. She or he (currently she) is also required to investigate cases referred by member states or by the Security Council. The judges and prosecutor are supported by a staff of some 700 people. The ICC has no ability either to arrest individuals before trial or to incarcerate them. It relies on states to arrest individuals when necessary, and on the Netherlands (where it is headquartered) to incarcerate them when necessary. At the time of writing, one trial has been concluded, with a conviction resulting in a fourteen-year prison term. Several other trials are ongoing, all of them concerning alleged crimes committed in Africa.[16]

A total of 121 counties are currently parties to the ICC. This number does not include three of the five permanent members of the Security Council—the United States, China, and Russia. The United States has a particularly fraught relationship with the Court. President Clinton signed the Court's Statute near the end of his term of office, but showed no intention of getting it ratified by the Senate. The Bush administration that followed was initially so hostile to the ICC that it attempted to unsign the Rome Statute (an action without clear meaning in international law). It attempted to get allies to commit to guaranteeing immunity from the Court's jurisdiction to U.S. personnel. This hostility mellowed over time, however, and by 2005 the United States abstained on, thus allowing the passage of, a Security Council resolution that referred to the ICC the cases of fifty-one people implicated in crimes against humanity in Darfur.[17] The Obama administration is actively supportive of the mission of the ICC, and the United States now has observer status at meetings of the states parties, but shows no inclination to actually become a party to the Rome Statute.[18]

Collective Security and IO Theory

Beginning with the fourth of the theoretical distinctions with which this book began, the institutions discussed in this chapter generally work to achieve both efficiency and legitimacy, but the balance between the two differs in different institutions. Of these IOs, the DKPO is most focused on efficiency, almost exclusively so. It is specifically designed to increase efficiency and transparency of peacekeeping and other Security Council–organized uses of armed force by reducing the transaction costs of cooperating, and by increasing information flows among participant forces. It does play what might be called a background legitimating function through its involvement in training forces to be used for Security Council missions, thereby decreasing the chances that those forces will behave in the field in a way that undermines the legitimacy of Security Council missions more generally. But this stretches the interpretation of the legitimacy function, and the inability of the DPKO to punish misbehavior impedes any legitimating effect. If anything, recent revelations of misconduct by soldiers operating under UN auspices are having the effect of delegitimizing Security Council peacekeeping and peace-building operations.

Also nearer to the efficiency end of the spectrum is NATO, largely because it is not a multilateral collective security organization in the traditional sense. NATO's resources and capabilities allow it to play a much more substantial role in maximizing the efficiency of member countries' military activities. The OCSE plays a somewhat greater legitimating role, and is likely to be more widely accepted in the state-building role, both by the target country and by the international community, than single outside states or NGOs. An interesting indicator of the different levels of legitimacy accorded to NATO and the OSCE by the UN can be seen in Security Council Resolution 1031, the resolution discussed above that legitimated the agreement that ended the Bosnian war. It refers to the OSCE by name as a participant in the mandated state-building process, but it clearly avoids specifying NATO by name, even while legitimating a NATO peacekeeping force.[19]

At the other end of the spectrum are the good offices and legitimation functions of the Secretary-General. These functions do have a minor efficiency-maximizing role, in that the Secretary-General or his appointees can successfully increase meaningful communication and exchange of information among the parties to a crisis, and clarifying norms helps states in general understand what the ground rules of international politics are. But there is no shortage of skilled third-party mediators, and international norms are reinforced by a wide variety of actors. The major difference between the Secretary-General's mediation and norm reinforcement and those of other actors is the prestige and legitimacy of the office and person of the Secretary-General.

Both the IAEA and the ICC fulfill both efficiency and legitimacy roles at the same time. The IAEA plays a crucial transparency role—monitoring the nuclear activities of member states is arguably its key function. At the same time, it plays an important role in anchoring the norm of nuclear nonproliferation, and in negotiating the contradiction between a system designed to protect the nuclear weapons status of some states, and deny that status to other states. The ICC, meanwhile, needs to operate efficiently enough to maintain its credibility as an operating court. But perhaps its most important function is to transmit and reinforce the developing global norm in international politics of an international humanitarian law that applies to people as individuals, not just to states.

The next distinction is that between IOs as regimes and IOs as institutions. The good offices of the Secretary-General provide an interesting contrast in this context with the Security Council as discussed in the last chapter. Whereas the Security Council is best looked at as a regime, the Secretary-General acts to a large degree on his own decision-making authority. The good offices, in other words, operate at the discretion of the bureaucracy, rather than as part of a set of clear rules and procedures that states expect to be followed. Neither institution, of course, is an ideal type of the regime or the institutionalist model, but they are closer to the ideal types than are most IOs.

The other four institutions discussed in this chapter have more even mixes of regime and institutional dynamics. Both NATO and the OSCE embody sets of rules and procedures that help to define actor expectations in the issue-area of European security. At the same time, both organizations have substantial bureaucracies that can and do develop institutional pathologies and that can put bureaucratic interests ahead of the defined interests of the organization. An example of this phenomenon can be found in the efforts of NATO headquarters to define a new mission for the organization after the end of the Cold War, in an attempt to keep itself relevant.[20] The IAEA anchors the nuclear nonproliferation regime, but the Secretariat does have significant discretion in designing specific monitoring arrangements and interpreting the results. The ICC has even more discretion as an actor, given the ability of the prosecutor's office to choose whom to investigate.

The third distinction is that between power and interdependence. Whereas the structure of the Security Council has the effect of empowering the five veto powers at the expense of other Council members, and even more so of nonmember states, membership in other collective security IOs has the effect of empowering smaller states with fewer military resources. For example, because the OSCE operates on a consensus basis, it has the effect of giving small European countries with negligible military capabilities a real voice in those issues that the OSCE is active in. The voice is, for various reasons, not as great as that of countries with significant military capabilities, but it is in all probability greater than it would otherwise be. The IAEA, conversely, to an extent empowers the five permanent members of the Security Council, by recognizing their right, and only their right, to nuclear weapons.

With respect to the distinction between sovereignty and globalization, this review of the institutions of collective security suggests that states' attachment to sovereignty and resistance to globalization are most pronounced with respect to issues of war. The focus on sovereignty becomes on the whole less pronounced the farther the issue gets from national security and the more it gets to be about human security. The Security Council, which can authorize the use of force, is made up almost entirely of representatives of sovereign states, with no one who directly represents the interests of global governance. The OSCE, on the other hand, which has no such authority, has much more leeway to act in the interests of good global governance, because its structure does not allow it to directly threaten the national security interests of member states. The IAEA is closer on this spectrum to the Security Council, and the ICC to the OSCE. This conclusion will probably not surprise anyone. It does not mean, however, that in issues of war and national security, IOs are irrelevant. States may be least willing to give up sovereignty in these issue-areas, but IOs nonetheless affect outcomes, by empowering some states at the expense of others, by legitimating some actions and delegitimating others, and by making international security cooperation more efficient when states choose to cooperate. By promoting norms of human security rather than international security, collective security IOs are in fact promoting a globalization of individual rights at the expense of the sovereign right of rulers to do as they see fit.

8

Human Rights and Humanitarian Aid

While the UN Charter clearly establishes collective security as the central goal of the UN, it accords human rights and humanitarian aid much less prominent roles. Nonetheless, over time both the protection of human rights and provision of humanitarian aid have become major roles of the UN system, and of regional international organizations (IOs) and international NGOs as well. This chapter compares the role of the UN system as protector of human rights with its role as provider of humanitarian aid. Even though the two roles would seem at first to have much in common as two parts of a broader human security agenda, the UN's role in the two issue-areas is very different.

In the field of human rights, the three focal organizational forms discussed in this chapter are the Office of the United Nations High Commissioner for Human Rights (UNHCHR), the United Nations Human Rights Council (UNHRC), and the various human rights committees. These will be contrasted with the role of the Council of Europe (COE) in protecting human rights in Europe. In the issue-area of humanitarian aid, the two IOs discussed here are the Office of the United Nations High Commissioner for Refugees (UNHCR) (not to be confused with UNHCHR) and the World Food Programme (WFP). The human rights organizations at first glance seem weak, often to the point of irrelevance, whereas the two humanitarian aid organizations seem robust and efficient. But in the end, an argument can be made that the human rights organizations can also be effective in helping to change how international politics works in the long term.

Human Rights

Although the phrase "human rights" does not appear in the UN Charter, it quickly became a significant focus of UN activities. An early result of this activity, and one that remains a seminal part of the international human rights discourse, is the Universal Declaration of Human Rights (UDHR) of 1948, which has been accepted by all members of the UN. There had been a few treaties prior to this date that are now classified as human rights treaties, such as the Convention to Suppress the Slave Trade and Slavery (1926) and the Convention Concerning Forced Labour (1930), although these treaties did not actually use the phrase "human rights." But 1948 marked the beginning of a tradition of international human rights discourse that continues to this day. Along with the UDHR, 1948 saw as well the creation of the Convention on the Prevention and Punishment of Genocide and the Convention Concerning Freedom of Association.

The UDHR was followed by a variety of human rights treaties over the years, of which some refer explicitly to human rights while others do not. Some of these are regional treaties that are general statements of human rights, such as the European Convention on Human Rights and the American Convention on Human Rights. Others are agreements dealing with particular sorts of rights, such as civil and political rights, labor rights, and regional and minority language rights. Still others are aimed at eliminating certain kinds of behavior, such as torture, slavery, trafficking in people, racial discrimination, and the mistreatment of prisoners of war or civilians under foreign occupation. And there are many treaties designed to protect particular categories of people, such as women, children, refugees, migrants, and indigenous peoples.[1]

Many of these more specific treaties mandated the creation of oversight committees, made up of human rights experts nominated and elected by signatory states.[2] The role of these committees is to field complaints against signatory countries, and to report both about individual country compliance and about general issues relating to their treaty.[3] They report to the General Assembly (GA), the Economic and Social Council (ECOSOC), and the Secretary-General, although they are officially subsidiary to the GA. While these committees are certainly useful monitoring mechanisms, they are quite limited in their abilities. They tend to have limited personnel (usually around ten people), often not working for them on a full-time basis, with limited institutional and financial support. And their output is limited to reports to other UN bodies. The committees themselves have no direct means of enforcement, and they cannot engage in the sorts of publicity campaigns against specific human rights violations that have often proved successful for human rights NGOs.

A more general body to oversee human rights issues is the Human Rights Council. This was created in the GA in 2006, to replace the earlier Commission on Human Rights. The Commission had been created by ECOSOC in the early days of the UN as one of ECOSOC's functional commissions. The Commission was seen as something of a farce, because it often included as members some of the most egregious human rights violators. An example of such an irony was the election of Libya as president of the Commission for its 2003 session.[4] The situation became bad enough that a Panel created by the then Secretary-General, Kofi Annan, noted that the Commission "has been undermined by eroding credibility and professionalism," and suggests a number of possible reforms, including the creation of the Council.[5]

The Council is directly subsidiary to the GA rather than ECOSOC, and, like the GA, is a political body. Forty-seven states are members of the Council, elected by the membership of the UN for staggered three-year terms (meaning that roughly one-third are elected every year). States cannot be members for more than two consecutive terms. The Council oversees a "Universal Periodic Review," in which each member reports on its human rights actions every four years, and a complaint procedure, a mechanism for non-state actors (organizations and individuals) to inform the Council of human rights violations. It also houses an Advisory Committee, which it describes as an in-house think tank on questions of human rights implementation.[6] Some analysts see the Council as doing some good work by creating transparency and legitimacy in the area of human rights in much the same way the committees do. Others see it as simply replicating the problems of the earlier Commission.

The plethora of specific human rights bodies within the UN system led to the creation of the UNHCHR in 1993. This office was created by a resolution of the GA, but it operates as part of the Secretariat.[7] Its job is to coordinate among and provide administrative infrastructure and support to the various UN human rights commissions and committees. It is also meant to support the activities of the High Commissioner, who is appointed by the Secretary-General, subject to the approval of the GA. The High Commissioner is the public face of the UN on human rights issues, and is tasked with representing the Secretary-General on these issues and promoting the universal recognition of and respect for human rights.

In other words, the UNHCHR is designed to fulfill both efficiency and legitimacy functions, each of which is fairly distinct from the other. The efficiency function mostly involves coordination among existing bodies, to maximize information flows among them and from them to the Secretary-General and the public, and to minimize bureaucratic waste and duplication of effort in their operation. The legitimacy function is in ways similar to the good offices function of the Secretariat. By specifying who the UN's voice will be on human rights issues, the hope is that the moral authority of that voice can get things done even in the absence of formal authority or material resources. This design has clearly benefited from lessons learned from the problems of older UN human rights bodies, which were plagued by multiple voices and poor coordination. The UNHCHR is, however, limited by both the bodies it is supposed to coordinate and its own skill in representing the UN and promoting human rights issues. The UNHCHR does help to improve the efficiency of existing UN human rights bodies, but those bodies are themselves either sufficiently modest in resources or sufficiently political in operation, or both, that even their increased level of efficiency does not necessarily translate into an effective UN human rights infrastructure.

The UN is not the only organization that is active in the field of human rights. A plethora of NGOs are dedicated to this role, the best known of which are Amnesty International and Human Rights Watch. The success of these NGOs, with Amnesty being the best example, has made them de facto fixtures in global governance and the international human rights discourse, and, in individual cases, has given them some real power in changing the behavior of states. Some national governments also report on human rights abuses internationally. Both the NGOs and these national governments tend to take the standards promulgated by IOs, and by international treaties, as their baselines, and embarrass governments by showing ways in which they fail to live up to standards they have committed themselves to.[8]

There are also some regional IOs that are involved in human rights issues, perhaps the most notable of which is the COE. This IO currently has forty-seven members, which includes all of Europe except for Belarus and the Holy See.[9] Roughly half of its current membership has joined since the end of the Cold War. An integral part of the COE is the European Convention on Human Rights (formally the Convention for the Protection of Human Rights and Fundamental Freedoms), and member states are legally bound by the terms of the Convention.[10] Countries are always legally bound by the treaties that they sign; this does not mean that they always comply with them. What makes this Convention, and the COE, different is the European Court of Human Rights. Residents of member states have the right to take their government to this Court if they feel that the government is not living up to its obligations under the Convention, and if they cannot get acceptable legal redress within their national court system. The Court has heard thousands of cases, and has often ruled against states. Perhaps more remarkably, the states have usually done what the Court has told them to, either by changing rules and procedures or by providing restitution to individuals, or both.[11]

In short, then, one could at first glance be highly critical of the extent to which IOs create meaningful behavioral change in human rights issues. The various UN bodies make some efforts at monitoring the human rights behavior of states and at embarrassing recalcitrant states into changing their behavior. But these efforts are limited by the material resources and the legitimacy that the UN brings to bear on the issue. States are willing to sign up to human rights treaties, but are not willing to give these treaties teeth. The result is human rights IOs that are enfeebled in their role as actors in international politics, having little power. The biggest exception to this rule is the COE and its European Court of Human Rights, because of its close association with the European Union (EU) and because its human rights rules are coupled with significant resources in other issue-areas that member countries can draw on.

Having said this, the combined effects over the past six decades of the various international efforts, both intergovernmental and nongovernmental, at promoting human rights norms have been huge. One could argue that they have fundamentally changed the way international politics works.[12] A concept neither widely known nor accorded much importance at the beginning of the process has now become a major constraint on the behavior of states toward their own citizens. An example of the effect that human rights IOs can have in global politics can be found in the Helsinki Final Act. This was a human rights agreement signed by countries on both sides of the Cold War, including the United States and the Soviet Union, under the auspices of the Conference on Security and Co-operation in Europe (CSCE) (forerunner to the Organization for Security and Co-operation in Europe [OSCE]). The Soviet side was willing to sign the agreement because they saw it as a toothless exercise in international propaganda. But when domestic opposition to the communist regimes in Eastern and Central Europe began to grow in the late 1980s, the Act served as a focal point for dissent, and may have played a significant role in the process of peaceful regime change at the end of the Cold War.[13]

States do, of course, still violate human rights. But they do it self-consciously and are, for the most part, embarrassed about it. Because of their higher level of consciousness on human rights issues, and the range of organizations devoted to monitoring these issues, states are much more loath than used to be the case to engage in habitual violations of rights. In other words, states still violate human rights, but on the whole they do it much less often than they used to. This suggests that the mechanisms of global governance have over time been fairly successful at legitimizing human rights norms internationally.

Humanitarian Aid

There is no clear dividing line among such activities as protecting human rights, providing humanitarian assistance, engaging in humanitarian inter-vention, and ensuring collective security broadly defined. Yet there is a clear subset of organizations within the UN system that focus primarily on emer-gency humanitarian assistance, defined as providing basic necessities of life to people who suddenly find themselves without access to food and shelter. Humanitarian aid, by this definition, can be distinguished from humanitar-ian intervention, because it always involves the consent of the local authorities and is not delivered using military capabilities. It can be distinguished from development assistance because it is designed to ameliorate a need in the short term, rather than to develop capabilities in the long term. The two foremost humanitarian aid IOs within the UN system are the UNHCR and the WFP (there are other IOs, such as UNICEF, that provide significant amounts of emergency aid, but this is not their primary activity).[14]

Humanitarian aid IOs tend to be far more robust institutionally than human rights IOs. Both the UNHCR and the WFP are large organizations, with employees numbering in the thousands, budgets in the billions of dollars, extensive networks of NGOs with which they work closely, and active fundrais-ing programs. Their funding patterns are similar as well. Neither organization can count on income from general UN funds or from member dues. The WFP is funded entirely by voluntary donations, while the UNHCR gets roughly 97 percent of its funds from such donations.[15] The resulting need to keep donors convinced that their money is being well spent may well be a significant con-tributing factor to the focus of both organizations on providing services effec-tively and visibly to those in need. The same focus on the short-term provision of services, however, provides part of the logic for the criticism made of both organizations that their focus on short-term aid can exacerbate long-term prob-lems. This criticism is discussed in more detail below.

The office of the UNHCR was created by the GA in 1950 for reasons similar to those that lay behind the later creation of the UNHCHR.[16] The UN was involved in refugee issues in an ad hoc and inefficient way, and the UNHCR was designed to make the UN's refugee program more efficient by coordinating the efforts of various other organizations. The High Commissioner reports to the Secretary-General, and is appointed by the Secretary-General subject to the approval of the GA. The organization is headquartered in Geneva.

The UNHCR deals with its remit not by coordinating the efforts of other IOs, but by centralizing the UN's refugee activities in one office.[17] It still engages in much coordination, because it subcontracts extensively to a wide network of NGOs, both international and local, to provide many services on the ground. But it does so as contractor, not as facilitator—it provides funds and directions, rather than information and advice. It also maintains a presence on the ground in much of the world, with field offices in 120 countries and a staff of more than 7,000.[18] When faced with a new refugee crisis, the UNHCR will publicize the crisis and attempt to raise funds to deal with it, and will either coordinate or manage directly the creation and maintenance of refugee camps in which refugees can find food, shelter, and basic medical care. The UNHCR cares for millions of people in such camps. The organization also provides legal assistance to refugees, and helps with resettlement when refugees attempt to return home.

The provision of basic necessities to refugees that have fled to countries that cannot or will not provide for them is not the UNHCR's only activity. It also monitors compliance with various treaties that deal with refugee issues, and acts as advocate for refugees and refugee issues in international politics, much in the same way that the UNHCHR is supposed to act as advocate internationally for human rights issues. The UNHCR helps to keep refugee issues on the international political agenda and visible to the international public, and works to raise funds for the Commission's activities. Despite efforts to raise funds privately, 97 percent of voluntary contributions come from states and other IOs, to fund a budget of about US$2 billion. Of these, the largest single contributor is the United States, followed by Japan, the EU, and Sweden.[19]

The WFP was created in 1963 by joint resolution of the GA and the Food and Agriculture Organization (FAO) to oversee the food-related humanitarian efforts of both organizations. It was designed from the outset as a functional organization, a primary provider of services, rather than a coordinator of the activities of other IOs. It reports to the secretariats of both the UN and the FAO, and its Executive Director is appointed by both in consultation and subject to the approval of both the GA and the Director-General of the FAO. Because of its relationship with the FAO in Rome, it is headquartered there. Like the UNHCR, it subcontracts much of the logistics of its food distribution to NGOs. It does not play as active a role politically in international relations as the UNHCR, because there is little debate as to who constitutes starving people, and whether or not they should be left to starve. But it does play the same sort of role in trying to keep the issue of famine visible to the international public and to donor countries, and in publicizing specific cases of immediate need.

The WFP raises most of its funds for specific food emergencies rather than for general programmatic needs. Although a large majority of its funds are donated by member governments, it is increasing its efforts to raise funds from NGOs, corporations, and individuals as well (it is now possible to donate online at its website[20]). Despite this range of sources, however, more than a third of its funds consistently come from one source: the U.S. government.[21] The WFP as an organization is about twice the size of the UNHCR, both in terms of size of budget and of number of employees.

Both the UNHCR and the WFP are fairly efficient providers of humanitarian assistance. In 2010, for example, the WFP fed some 109 million people, and the UNHCR helped approximately 34 million people.[22] But both organizations have been criticized for the long-term effects of their short-term aid. The UNHCR has been criticized for creating and becoming the focus of what is essentially a refugee industry, committed to taking care of refugees in place. Many countries, particularly those that are home to the largest refugee flows, prefer that refugees be kept separate from domestic populations and be dealt with primarily by the international community. This often results in huge refugee camps, which are overseen by the UNHCR. The organization tries to promote voluntary repatriation of refugees from these camps to their original homes, but it is often the case that the situation on the ground does not permit this to happen for long stretches of time. The UNHCR's commitment to short-term aid in place and long-term repatriation means that some refugees remain in internationally sponsored camps for generations, without permanent communities or viable economies to sustain them. The international community can ignore them, and the host countries can isolate them, because the High Commission is there to prevent short-term humanitarian disasters. The humanitarian aid, in other words, often contributes to the degree to which refugee problems are allowed by the international community to fester in the long term.[23]

In the case of the WFP, it would seem at first that feeding starving people should be nonproblematic. But emergency food aid often has the effect of undermining the local agricultural infrastructure. When the WFP gives food away for free, people will be less willing to pay local farmers for the food that they grow. So the bad harvests that often lead to famines and thereby to international food aid can also (because of this aid) lead to decreases in local prices for agricultural products. In other words, farmers not only grow less, they also face lower returns on what they do grow. At the same time, the sorts of logistics brought in by industrial-scale international emergency aid can overwhelm local transport and distribution infrastructures. The WFP is trying to deal with this problem, often referred to as the "aid trap," by buying an increasing proportion of the food it donates from developing countries.

There are ways of getting around the aid trap. For example, emergency food aid could be coupled with aid to local farmers in the form of seed and equipment for the next planting season and harvest. But the WFP's resources are limited, and thus medium-term aid to farmers comes at the expense of short-term food aid. For an organization that depends entirely on voluntary donations, emergency food aid can be a more effective fundraising tool than medium-term farm aid. Furthermore, medium-term aid both creates different aid traps and takes the WFP outside of its remit and into conflict with that of one of its parent organizations, the FAO. Having said all of this, however, the emergency aid infrastructure maintained by organizations such as the WFP and the UNHCR clearly save many lives that otherwise could not be saved.

Human Rights, Humanitarian Aid, and IO Theory

In terms of institutional effectiveness narrowly defined, there is no question that, on the whole, the UN's humanitarian aid organizations are far more effective than its human rights organizations. The humanitarian aid organizations are bigger, better funded, and have greater reach and clearer operational goals. They are also, as far as IOs go, quite efficient. They identify and publicize areas of need, they serve as effective focuses for humanitarian aid funding, and they manage to get basic necessities to millions of people in need of them, often in a timely fashion and in logistically difficult situations. They provide useful coordination to NGO humanitarian efforts, and represent an impressive storehouse of practical information and knowledge about the provision of emergency aid. Their legitimacy functions are less pronounced, but are important nonetheless, particularly in the case of the UNHCR, which is the UN's guardian of both the concept of and the rights of refugees.

The various human rights organizations are not particularly effective in this sense. They do fulfill some efficiency and transparency functions, such as monitoring state compliance with treaty commitments and specifying and defining various categories of rights. But they do not fulfill transparency functions particularly effectively; as a result, NGOs and states are often looked to as the more reliable monitors of human rights treaty compliance. They fulfill as well some legitimacy functions, but not nearly as well as one might expect of the human rights arms of an organization such as the UN. Because of their institutional structures and their frequent high levels of politicization, they are often not seen as credible legitimators of international human rights norms.

The relative institutional weakness of human rights IOs can be related to issues of sovereignty and power. Humanitarian aid does not threaten the sovereignty of states. Neither the UNHCR nor the WFP can operate in a state without that state's permission. Nor do the norms underlying humanitarian intervention particularly affect state autonomy, although norms relating to refugees do commit states to certain minimum standards of behavior toward them. Human rights norms, on the other hand, directly affect state sovereignty. Their whole point is to limit the autonomy of states by delegitimizing entire categories of behaviors by states toward their citizens. Therefore, robust IOs designed to deal with humanitarian aid are likely to be more acceptable to states concerned about maintaining norms of sovereignty than robust human rights IOs.

Issues of sovereignty are also implicated in the tension between the short-term missions of humanitarian aid IOs and their inability to deal with the longer-term issues surrounding these missions. Both the refugee trap, in the case of the UNHCR, and the aid trap, in the case of the WFP, involve contradictions inherent in the missions of these two organizations, the contradiction between the need in some cases for immediate humanitarian aid, and the broader and longer-term effects of that aid on the ability of affected communities to develop. When the WFP is responding to short-term need created by natural disasters, such as the tsunami that devastated much of South and Southeast Asia in December 2004, this contradiction is not really an issue. In such cases, the resources of humanitarian IOs can prove invaluable. But when humanitarian IOs respond to famines and refugee flows created by political negligence, incompetence, or malice, the contradiction can end up keeping bad governments in place longer than would otherwise be the case.

From the perspective of the countries in which the aid is needed as a result of political rather than natural factors, emergency aid helps to isolate the effects of problems such as famine and refugee flows from their causes. If countries know that IOs will take care of refugees and of the victims of famine, governments need worry less about their roles in causing these problems in the first place. Similarly, emergency aid is less likely to come with conditions than other forms of aid. From the perspective of donor countries, emergency aid creates the belief that something is being done, that people are being saved, without the need to look in any great detail at the workings of the international system that would be created by attempts to deal with the more fundamental long-term problems leading to famines and to refugee flows.

In terms of power, there are two ways to look at the relative weakness of human rights organizations. The first is to note that humanitarian aid issues are more likely to have cross-border effects than human rights issues. For example, wealthier states know that if they do not help to take care of refugees in areas where they first flee, they are more likely to have the refugees show up at their borders. And they know that they need the participation of the poorer states that the refugees usually get to first in order to prevent a greater influx into the wealthier states. To a certain extent the same argument can be made for human rights—countries that respect human rights are less likely to generate refugees and other cross-border effects that the West wants to avoid. But by and large, those countries committed to human rights domestically can ensure these rights at home regardless of what is happening in other states. So governments do not need to cooperate on human rights for reasons of interdependence. Since powerful states, often the states that care most about human rights, do not need the help of others to protect these rights at home, they can cooperate on their own terms with other states less respectful of human rights.

The second way to look at the relative weakness of human rights IOs in terms of power is through the lens of neocolonialism. One of the critiques heard most often from the global South about the international human rights regime is that these rights are expressions of Northern, particularly American and European, culture. Whereas humanitarian aid does not particularly threaten local cultural forms and local power structures, critics of the human rights regime argue that the imposition of human rights norms can threaten local cultural forms and undermine local governance structures.[24] To these critics, international human rights norms are being imposed on the rest of the world by the Northern governments and by Northern NGOs.

Either way, the countries most interested in promoting human rights norms internationally are generally the most economically developed. For them, the international politics of human rights can be undertaken most effectively by creating relatively weak IOs to allow for the direct bilateral application of power when appropriate. International organizations tend to empower weaker and poorer countries at the expense of stronger and richer ones, because of the legal equality, and often the equal voting power, of states. Since it is the economically and militarily most powerful states that are most interested in the status of human rights norms globally, they have an interest in minimizing the effects of IOs where other states are relatively empowered, and resorting to more bilateral or less formal kinds of relationships, where more traditional forms of power in international relations are less constrained.[25]

9

Economic Institutions and Trade

One of the issue-areas in which IOs are both most active and most contentious is the international political economy. The three most prominent organizations in this issue-area, and three of the most prominent IOs overall, are the World Trade Organization (WTO), the International Monetary Fund (IMF), and the World Bank. These IOs operate in the issue-areas of international trade, balance-of-payments and currency stabilization, and economic development, respectively. The WTO has dominated the international trading system to an extent that few IOs can claim in their issue-areas. The IMF and the World Bank are the world's two predominant multilateral lenders, so much so that they are often referred to in development parlance simply as "the multilaterals." This chapter looks at the first of these issues, with a particular focus on the WTO. The next looks at questions of international finance and balances of payments, with a particular focus on the IMF. Chapter 11 then deals with questions of development, in which the World Bank is one of a number of active IOs.

The WTO on one hand, and the IMF and the World Bank on the other, provide an interesting comparison. Beyond their centrality to the international political economy's system of multilateral governance and to debates on globalization, they are different in almost every way. They have very different outputs: primarily rules in the case of the WTO, and primarily loans in the case of the IMF and World Bank. As a result, they play different roles with respect to such issues as sovereignty and globalization. They also have different internal structures, different job descriptions, and different degrees of institutional power and agency. The WTO is a relatively small organization that operates primarily as a forum for its members, while the multilaterals are the best funded and among the largest IOs, and are important actors in global politics in their own right.

This chapter looks at the WTO as an institution, and begins a comparison of its place in global governance with the multilaterals that continues in the next chapter. It concludes with a discussion of the roles of two less-visible but nonetheless important IOs in the governance of the international political economy, the World Intellectual Property Organization (WIPO) and the

Organization for Economic Co-operation and Development (OECD). But before getting to the issue of international trade specifically, it is useful to look at how the big three international economic institutions are perceived in international politics.

The International Economic Institutions and Their Critics

While conclusions may vary about how effective each of the big three international economic institutions is individually, collectively they play a key role in legitimating the structure of the post-War and contemporary international political economy. The IMF and the World Bank in the 1990s legitimated a certain model of development that to an important degree became the standard against which developing country policies were compared. This model is often referred to as the "Washington Consensus" because of the proximity of the two organizations to each other in Washington, DC (and because of the enthusiasm of the U.S. government for the model as well). The model has changed over time, but at any given point in time, it legitimizes a particular orthodoxy of development. The model has, however, weakened since the mid-1990s; the IMF and World Bank do not agree on what it should contain to the extent that they did two decades ago, and the set of financial crises beginning in the late 1990s and culminating in the global recession beginning in 2008 have dented its credibility.

Similarly, the WTO has legitimized a model of international trade based on the idea that trade should be rule-based and nondiscriminatory. This model of trade may seem obvious to the early-twenty-first-century reader—this is a sign of the effectiveness of the WTO, and its predecessor organization the General Agreement on Tariffs and Trade (GATT), at legitimizing these norms, which were quite exceptional when first proposed in the mid-twentieth century. Much of the benefit of all three organizations can be seen in their legitimating roles rather than their market-perfecting effects. But much of the criticism of the WTO, IMF, and World Bank as regimes focuses on these roles as well. While critics of specific economic IOs may argue that they fail to increase the efficiency of cooperation (as is discussed with respect to individual organizations below), critics of the broader legitimating function of the international economic institutions often argue that they are too effective, because the content of the cooperation is flawed.

The WTO, the IMF, and the World Bank have been, and continue to be, criticized not necessarily for failing to do well what they do, but for being too successful at doing the wrong thing. In particular, all three organizations have been criticized for globalizing a model of economic policy, the Washington Consensus, both too hard and too far. This criticism has recently become much more visible, in a pattern first seen when some 50,000 protestors showed up at the WTO's biennial meeting in Seattle in November 1999, and seen frequently since then at all of the major meetings of the big three international economic institutions.[1] The thrust of this criticism has been twofold: that the policies that the international economic institutions have been promoting are flawed, and that the processes through which they are promoting them are undemocratic.

The first of these criticisms can take a range of forms, from criticism of specific sets of IMF loan conditions or World Bank project decisions from people who are broadly sympathetic to market capitalism, to more fundamental criticisms of the role of these IOs in promoting market capitalism in general. The latter group often point to the training of the personnel in these organizations—that they hire only a particular kind of professional who believes in their goals from the outset, and is therefore unable to examine those goals critically. In the IMF, this means professional economists, generally orthodox neoclassical economists. In the WTO, this means trade experts, trained both in the discipline of economics and that of trade law. Critics of both organizations often suggest a link between this personnel specialization and a narrow view of what the international economy should look like.[2]

Criticism of the policies of the WTO, IMF, and World Bank also often points to their focus on economic issues to the exclusion of other goals, such as maintaining labor or environmental standards, or empowering women.[3] The Seattle protestors represented a range of these criticisms, from labor activists who supported the status quo in general and wanted the status quo protected from further globalization, to environmental activists who objected to market capitalism and international trade in principle. All three organizations have taken these criticisms seriously, and have made attempts to address them (although the IMF, in part because of its focus on macroeconomic rather than microeconomic issues, has done the least in this regard). But to the extent that the international economic institutions act in support of a global capitalist economy that critics see as inherently hostile to environmental and gender issues, the efforts of these institutions at reform will inevitably be seen as wanting.

The second criticism, that international economic institutions such as the WTO, IMF, and World Bank are undemocratic, is actually more germane to the subject of this book. The argument from this perspective is that in the IMF and World Bank a bunch of unelected economists are dictating policy to elected governments, and in the WTO a bunch of unelected trade lawyers are dictating policy to the world as a whole. In essence, this is a critique of contemporary globalization, and an argument in favor of reinforcing national economic sovereignty. The standard response to this charge from the perspective of IOs is that they are in fact very democratic.

The IMF and World Bank are unusual among IOs in not having a voting structure based on the international law norm of one country, one vote. How this voting structure interacts with concepts of democratic governance will be discussed in the next chapter. The WTO does hew closer to the norm in this respect, and in fact works on a consensus basis. It claims that its consensus decision-making makes it even more democratic than majority-rule governance systems, as does the fact (as is generally the case with international law) that new rules do not apply to countries until they explicitly accept them.[4] This answer refers, of course, to democracy among countries rather than among the global population at large. But those people are represented through their governments, and a majority of those governments in turn are democratically elected.

The WTO

The WTO is a relatively recent IO, having come into existence in 1995. It does, however, incorporate the GATT, which dates from 1947. The GATT in turn was originally meant to be a part of an International Trade Organization (ITO). The ITO was the result of multilateral negotiations on the creation of a rule-based international trading system following World War II, and included, among other things, a set of rules for trade in manufactured goods (the GATT), and an authoritative arbitration body to settle trade disputes. The ITO never came into being. It was undermined, among other things, by the opposition of the U.S. Congress, which objected to two features of the proposed organization. The first was the arbitration body, which was seen as a threat to national sovereignty. The second was the provisions for the liberalization of trade in agricultural products, which threatened the system of agricultural supports created in the United States during the Great Depression and Dust Bowl era in the 1930s. The GATT proved less objectionable than the broader ITO, and was adopted as the basic set of rules for international trade among countries outside of the Soviet sphere of influence.[5]

The WTO, which resulted from the Uruguay round of international trade talks held between 1986 and 1993, recreates much of what had been part of the ITO, including a formal dispute settlement mechanism. It incorporates the GATT, the Dispute Settlement Mechanism (DSM), and the General Agreement on Trade in Services (GATS), as well as a host of subsidiary agreements that spell out more detailed rules in specific issue-areas.[6] These agreements are the core of the WTO system—they are the rules that are the raison d'être of the organization. The WTO currently has 155 members, including all of the world's major trading powers. A majority of the non-member countries are in the process of negotiating membership (which can be a time-consuming process – negotiating Russian entry, for example, took 18 years).

The basic rule of the WTO is nondiscrimination, the idea that states that are members should treat all other members equally. There are a number of exceptions to this rule for developing countries, countries with industries in distress, and regional trading organizations. But the basic principle is equal treatment. The principal function of the WTO is to encourage and oversee negotiations that reduce general tariff levels, bring new kinds of goods and services into the rules-governed trade system, and generate agreement on how individual countries will put the rules into effect. The WTO is therefore best seen as a forum for negotiations leading to more open and more specific international trade rules. The WTO, as an institution, is heavily weighted toward its legislative function, its rules and rule-making apparatus. Its judicial function, considerably strengthened in the transition from GATT to WTO in 1995, plays a less important, but still central, role. The executive function for an organization of its size is minimal; the system is designed to be rule-based and self-policing, so there should be little need for an active executive.

Organizationally, there are two central components to the WTO: the decision-making structure and the Secretariat. Decisions about WTO rules are taken by member countries through a multilayered decision-making structure. At the top of this structure is the Ministerial Conference, a meeting of ministerial-level representatives of all member countries that must convene at least every alternate year. Until 2005 the pattern had been for meetings to circulate among member countries – the 2005 meeting was in Hong Kong, and the two previous meetings had been in Cancun, Mexico, and Doha, Qatar. The Hong Kong meeting went sufficiently badly (more on this below) that no Ministerial Conference was held in 2007. The 2009 and 2011 Conferences were held (at an intentionally smaller scale) at WTO headquarters in Geneva.

Subsidiary to the Conference is the General Council, a body that meets frequently at the WTO's headquarters in Geneva. All member countries are represented in the Council, usually by their permanent representatives to the WTO. Subsidiary to the General Council are three specific Councils, on Trade in Goods, Trade in Services, and Trade-Related Aspects of Intellectual Property Rights. These Councils collectively oversee some two dozen committees and working groups that deal with specific trade-related issues and negotiate changes in the WTO's rules. All member countries are represented in most of these councils and committees.[7] The DSM is also technically subsidiary to the General Council,[8] although the actual panelists on specific dispute settlement panels are experts in trade law and are supposed to be politically impartial. They are chosen by the Director-General of the WTO in consultation with the parties to the particular dispute. However, most contentious DSM decisions are appealed. Appeals to panel rulings are heard by a standing tribunal called the Appellate Body, which consists of seven independent jurists appointed for four-year terms.

The Secretariat consists of a Director-General, chosen by consensus by the membership,[9] and a Secretariat staff of approximately 600 people. They serve to provide technical and logistical support to the decision-making structure, mostly in the form of expertise on specific trade issues under negotiation in the various councils and committees. They also provide technical assistance and training in trade policy enforcement to countries that need it. The Secretariat performs little in the way of executive functions, simply because there are few executive functions to be performed within the structure of the WTO. The rules for trade that are the core of the regime are supposed to be monitored and enforced by member states, not by the WTO itself. This limits the role of the Director-General to administration of the bureaucracy and to political entrepreneurship, using the moral authority of the position to promote world trade and to cajole countries into negotiating in good faith.

A key feature of the WTO, and of the GATT process before 1995, is its voting structure. The basic voting rule is unanimity; the regime is strongly biased toward consensus rather than majoritarian control. Technically speaking, each new negotiating result leads to a formal change in the rules of the WTO and is thus not binding on any state that does not accept the change. Because a rule-based trading system requires that everyone be using the same rules, changes are only made when all participants accept them. But in practice, the unanimity rule is not quite so clear-cut. One or two small countries could probably not obstruct acceptance of a new set of rules, because other countries could credibly threaten to simply leave them out of the trading system. The United States, the European Union (EU), or China, on the other hand, could obstruct such acceptance, because a threat to run a global trading system without them is not credible.[10] Smaller, poorer countries often deal with this practical power imbalance by negotiating in blocs big enough to make credible threats of nonparticipation.

The result of the consensus structure of WTO negotiations is that they take a very long time. The Uruguay round of negotiations that led to the creation of the WTO took seven years; the Tokyo round of GATT negotiations before it took six. And this means full-time negotiations concurrently in a variety of committees, not just occasional plenary meetings. It also leads to very high levels of detail in the resultant documents: the list of national commitments under the Uruguay round filled some 22,500 pages, which mostly contained details about commitments to lower tariffs on a specific good with respect to a specific trading partner, or to change a particular regulatory policy to allow greater transparency or competition.[11] The danger of the consensus structure, in combination with the practice of comprehensive rounds rather than negotiation of individual issues separately, is that it can be prone to failure.

A new round of negotiations was launched at the Ministerial Conference in Doha in 2001. This round was supposed to be concluded by 2005, but at that date many major disagreements among member states had yet to be resolved. In fact, the Ministerial Conference in Hong Kong in that year that was supposed to wrap up the round was such a failure that the 2007 Ministerial failed to happen at all. A key difference between the Doha Round and earlier negotiations is that developing countries as a group have become much more willing to pursue their interests, and veto agreements that do not meet their perceived needs. One of the major areas of current disagreement, ironically, is the extent to which WTO rules should apply to agricultural products—the same issue that contributed to the demise of the ITO more than half a century ago. Doha Round negotiations are ongoing, but without much momentum or political will, and at this point there is no conclusion to them in sight.

The WTO, Efficiency, and Legitimacy

Does the WTO work as an international regime? From a rationalist perspective, the answer is a qualified yes. A core function of the institution is transparency, and as such a good starting point in discussing its effectiveness as a regime is with a rationalist analysis of the extent to which it increases the efficiency of international cooperation. The WTO's primary function, from an efficiency perspective, is to improve property rights in the issue-area of international trade. The rules of the international trading system, the core of the WTO, are in effect specifications of property rights, and the DSM is a mechanism for clarifying and adjudicating these rights. The specification of these property rights is not perfect, but it is clearly better than what had gone before.[12] In this sense, the WTO, as a regime, has been remarkably successful. It has also had some success at decreasing transaction costs and at improving information flows, but this success has been more muted. Trade negotiations carried out under the WTO's auspices retain high transaction costs, in that they can last more than half a decade and employ thousands of people, although this process is probably more efficient than holding a large number of bilateral trade negotiations. The WTO also collects and publishes trade statistics, but this often duplicates information available elsewhere. This more modest role in dealing with transaction costs and information flows, however, should not be taken as a serious criticism of the WTO, because its primary design function is the specification of property rights with respect to international trade.

From a reflectivist perspective the answer is also a qualified yes. As suggested earlier in the chapter, the WTO and its predecessor the GATT have been enormously successful at institutionalizing the idea of rule-governed trade as a fundamental and widely accepted norm of the international political economy. And the DSM has come to be accepted as the core adjudicative body in the realm of international trade. But there are two contemporary categories of threat to the WTO's role as the legitimate core of the international trading system. The first is the issue of democracy and representativeness discussed earlier in the chapter. The charge that the institution in general is not democratic was addressed above. But the charge has been applied specifically to the DSM as well. Only countries party to a dispute have a right to be heard there, whereas individuals, and NGOs representing the interests of social, labor, environmental, or indigenous groups, are generally excluded.

This seems, on the face of it, an odd criticism, because the DSM is intended as a court, a legal body, and not as a political body. In liberal democratic societies, including the United States, the role of courts is generally assumed to be the impartial adjudication of the law, and as such, courts are generally thought most effective when they are most insulated from political pressures. The critique that the DSM is unrepresentative, therefore, is based on the idea that international arbitration should not work in the way that domestic arbitration works, but should instead be a political activity. The implication is that the rule of law at the international level undermines, rather than reinforces, democracy. This critique is not really directed at the DSM in particular, but is a much broader indictment of the idea of globalization, and an argument in favor of stronger national sovereignty.

The second category of threat to the legitimacy of the system of global trade centered on the WTO stems from the repeated failures of the Doha Round. The lack of progress in global trade talks has led many of the world's major trading powers to focus on regional and bilateral trade agreements instead. Some regional agreements, such as the EU and the North American Free Trade Agreement (NAFTA) have been around for decades, and have their own established institutional structures. But the pace of negotiation both of regional agreements in regions not previously prone to them, such as the Asia-Pacific, and of bilateral agreements that are not region-based, such as that between the United States and South Korea, is increasing. At a certain point, the increasing diplomatic focus on regional and bilateral agreements will inevitably threaten to undermine the concept of global cooperation and of nondiscrimination that the WTO was designed to legitimate.[13]

Other International Economic Institutions

There are many IOs other than the big three international economic institutions that deal with economic issues as well. These include organizations based on trade agreements such as NAFTA, and those that focus primarily on issues of international finance, which will be discussed in the next chapter. The line separating an international economic institution from an organization focusing on, say, development or technical co-operation is unclear, and some of the organizations that straddle this line are discussed in other chapters throughout this book. The rest of this chapter briefly discusses two particular organizations that focus primarily on issues of economic cooperation that tangent with, but are not focused primarily upon, trade. These two IOs are the World Intellectual Property Organization (WIPO) and the Organization for Economic Co-operation and Development (OECD).

WIPO is an IO that oversees a system of twenty-three treaties dealing with issues relating to intellectual property, including patents and copyrights, and has a current membership of 185 countries. It is a specialized agency of the UN, affiliated with rather than subsidiary to the General Assembly (GA) and ECOSOC. While WIPO has existed with its current name and structure only since 1970, it is a direct linear descendent of one of the oldest IOs, the United International Bureaux for the Protection of Intellectual Property (or BIRPI, the acronym of its French name), created in 1893; BIRPI itself traces its roots back to 1883. WIPO's major challenges in the near future involve coping with the growth of the Internet and related technologies, and expanding international intellectual property rules to cover the new electronic economy.

WIPO's structure is fairly typical of IOs, with a legislative body made up of member states, and a Secretariat led by a Director-General. The Secretariat has a staff of some 1,200 people and administers a budget of over a quarter of a billion dollars a year. Unusually for an IO, over 90 percent of this budget comes from service charges levied by WIPO on companies and individuals, mostly for use of its international patent registration system, rather than from membership dues or voluntary donations.[14] The role of the Secretariat is to oversee the implementation of treaties, and as such it plays mostly a technical and informational role. But the Secretariat nonetheless does have some independent impact on international relations through the technical advice it gives, and through its efforts to promote intellectual property issues and foster international cooperation on these issues. In this sense, the WIPO Secretariat, as an actor, is comparable to the WTO Secretariat. Basic policy decisions are taken through the modification of existing treaties and the creation of new ones, meaning that states need not accept new rules that they do not agree with. As with the WTO, this promotes a tendency toward consensus decision-making. WIPO sees its task primarily as one of maximizing efficiency, by getting member countries to agree to a common definition of intellectual property rights. But it does play a role in legitimating internationally the idea that intellectual property rights should be strongly protected and enforced.[15]

The OECD is less typical of IOs in that while it is a multilateral organization, it is not part of the UN system, and has a limited membership of thirty-four countries, all of which are relatively wealthy (it has recently allowed some middle-income countries, such as Mexico and Turkey, to join). It is, in essence, the club of rich market democracies. The forerunner of the OECD, the Organization for European Economic Co-operation (OEEC), was created to oversee the distribution of Marshall Fund aid in the late 1940s. This aid was specifically tied to the creation and maintenance of democratic political and market-based economic systems in the recipient countries.[16] The membership of the OECD (which was created from the OEEC in 1961) has always been limited to market-oriented democracies. Unlike most multilateral organizations and UN-related organizations, it does not have a membership that is open to all countries; membership is by invitation only.

The OECD is best known for its research on international economic issues, particularly issues of concern to developed countries, and for its reports and statistics. This research is compiled by a staff of 2,500 at its headquarters in Paris. The organization also creates standards (nonbinding rules) in a variety of different realms of economic activity, such as guidelines for multinational corporations, and standards for competition policy and insurance industry oversight. There has also been the occasional formal treaty negotiated under its auspices, such as the Convention on Combating Bribery of Foreign Public Officials in International Business Transactions (1997). It has also had one notable and public failure, in its attempt to generate a Multilateral Agreement on Investment (MAI) in the late 1990s.[17] The MAI dissolved under a barrage of criticism from the antiglobalization movement within OECD member countries.

Organizations such as the WTO, WIPO, and the OECD overlap in terms of membership and often in terms of function. On some intellectual property rights issues, for example, negotiation could reasonably happen under the auspices of any one of the three organizations. If it took place under WIPO, then the issue would likely be discussed on its own and by most of the world's countries. If under the OECD, then it would still be discussed on its own, but only by industrialized countries. And if under the WTO, then it would be discussed by most of the world's countries and in the context of a much broader negotiation. This range of possibilities allows countries trying to pursue a particular goal multilaterally to engage in what is called forum-shopping—to raise an issue in whatever forum is most likely to yield the result that the country in question is looking for.[18] This helps to explain why the MAI, for example, was pursued under the auspices of the OECD—the countries party to the negotiations were looking for a venue where rich countries could maintain control of the agenda.

10

International Finance

The onset of the global recession in 2008 pushed trade issues to the background of discussions on the management of the international political economy, and brought financial issues to the foreground. To a certain extent this change is a sign of the resilience of the global trading system. While the recession created a set of crises in global finance, the trading system has weathered the downturn quite well. The set of norms underlying the trading system, of rules-based governance and nondiscrimination, has held up, and has prevented the sort of tariff increases and other trade-based beggar-thy-neighbor policies that caused the international economy to spiral down into the Great Depression in the early 1930s.

The recession has, however, been more problematic for global finance, both private finance in the form of banking collapse and public finance in the form of fiscal crisis. These various crises have highlighted weaknesses in systems for, and assumptions about, collective management of international financial and monetary issues. IOs have been called upon to respond through widely varying means, ranging from lending money to governments to overseeing the creation of more effective financial regulatory standards. A wide variety of IOs are involved in managing the international financial and monetary systems as either their primary task or as one of several. Five particular organizations will be discussed in this chapter: the IMF, the G-7, G-8, G-20, and the Bank for International Settlements (BIS). The latter four will be discussed briefly, to give an overview of the range of IO activity on this issue. The chapter begins with the IMF, one of the big three international economic institutions and probably the best-known IO focusing primarily on global financial and monetary issues.

The IMF

The IMF was one of two institutions created at the conference held at Bretton Woods, New Hampshire, in 1944, designed to recreate an international monetary system after the end of World War II. The other institution, the World

Bank, was designed to fund specific projects to assist countries in postwar reconstruction and in development. The IMF was designed to assist in the maintenance of macroeconomic stability and of the fixed exchange rate system (known as the Bretton Woods system) by lending money to assist countries having balance-of-payments difficulties. The system of fixed exchange rates fell apart in the early 1970s, but the IMF continues to operate, and continues its focus on macroeconomic stability and on balance-of-payments difficulties.

The Fund and the Bank are often referred to together as the International Financial Institutions (IFIs). They are similar in many structural respects, and are collectively quite different from most other intergovernmental institutions. Much of what is said here about the structure of the IMF, therefore, also holds true for the World Bank. Many of the differences between the IFIs and other IOs can be explained by the fact that the IFIs are, in important ways, hybrids of the standard model of IOs and regular banks. They are like the standard model of IOs in that their members are states, and in that they are designed to address specific problems of international cooperation: in this case, the provision of infrastructural needs to the international monetary and financial systems. They are more like for-profit financial institutions, however, in their operation and governance. The most straightforward aspect of this observation is that they operate at a profit. They charge interest on their loans to member governments, and this interest is more than sufficient to cover both their operating costs and losses from loan defaults.[1] As a result, member governments do not need to contribute operating funds on an annual basis, as they must with most IOs. Rather, they are asked on a more occasional basis to contribute funds to the IFI's working capital.

The idea of working capital informs the IFI's voting structure, which is more like that of corporate shareholding than like that of most IOs. There is no one-member, one-vote rule. Rather, the proportion of the total vote that each member country has is determined by the proportion of the organization's total working capital contributed by the country. In other words, the more shares you buy, the more control you get. In essence, this means that the big industrialized countries have not only de facto but also de jure control over the activities of the IFIs. In the IMF, this means that the United States alone has 16.75 percent of the vote, and that voting together, the United States, the EU, and Japan have a majority. Many decisions can be made by this simple majority of the vote, but other more fundamental decisions require 70 percent of the vote, and major changes to the structure of the IMF require 85 percent. The 70 percent threshold can be met by the twenty-three countries with the biggest votes (although many of these are developing countries). At the 85 percent threshold the United States can individually vote a measure down, but all of the countries of Africa and Central and South America voting collectively cannot.[2]

This voting structure affects major decisions of the IFIs, but in both the IMF and the World Bank a considerable degree of authority over operations, including authority over most lending decisions, has been delegated to the Managing Director and the executive staff. The highest levels of management of the IFIs are their respective Boards of Governors, which are made up of the finance ministers or central bank directors of all of the member countries. These boards meet once a year at the IMF and World Bank's joint annual meeting, usually held in Washington. Day-to-day management rests in the hands of the twenty-four Executive Directors. The United States, Japan, Germany, France, the United Kingdom, China, Russia, and Saudi Arabia, as eight of the largest shareholders, each have their own Executive Director.[3] The other sixteen are elected by groupings of states, although the Director chosen is often from the country with the most votes in each group.[4] Reporting to the Executive Board is the Managing Director, whose position is equivalent to that of Secretary-General or Director-General. Although in principle the Managing Director is chosen by the membership of the IFIs as a whole, in practice it is an unofficial but generally accepted rule that the Managing Director of the World Bank will be an American, and that of the IMF will be a European.

The Managing Director of the IMF has a staff of approximately 2,400 people and an annual operating budget (which does not include the value of loans made) of just over $1 billion.[5] The staff is organized both regionally and functionally.[6] The total value of loans and credits by the IMF currently outstanding is $110 billion.[7] The IMF describes its three main activities as surveillance, financial assistance, and technical assistance. Surveillance means that the Fund "highlights possible risks to stability and advises on needed policy adjustments."[8] Financial assistance means the lending of money and the extension of credit lines. Technical assistance means in practice the lending of IMF economists to help countries improve the management of their fiscal and financial systems.

In practice, these three activities come together in what the IMF calls conditionality. This entails making loans to countries contingent on their governments' fulfillment of (or promise to fulfill) a set of macroeconomic policy conditions, usually involving neoliberal reforms to national fiscal and regulatory policy. The reforms required by IMF conditionality usually include some combination of reducing budget deficits, increasing fiscal transparency, fighting corruption, opening markets, reforming domestic financial and banking structures, and privatizing government-held businesses.[9] These conditions are designed to make governments and economies more efficient, and to stabilize countries' currencies. The conditions are often unpopular within recipient countries, however, because they often result in lower government spending, higher taxes, a less valuable currency (meaning that imports become more expensive), and weaker labor regulation. Economic theory suggests that these changes should be good for the economy in the medium term, but they inevitably create hardships for many individuals within the country in the short term.

Conditionality brings together all three of the IMF's central activities in that the surveillance identifies what the conditions should be, the technical assistance helps governments to implement the conditions when they cannot do so themselves, and the financial assistance provides the tool with which the IMF enforces conditions. The logic underlying conditionality is based on the fact that IMF loans are designed to help countries overcome macroeconomic instability. The assumption is that such instability is usually caused (at least in part) by macroeconomic policies, such as monetary and fiscal policies, that interfere with the operation of a market economy. Overcoming instability therefore requires a change in macroeconomic policy to get at the underlying cause of the instability, as well as funds to deal with the effects of the instability in the short term.[10]

Criticisms of the IMF

And yet the practice of conditionality provides one of the two key sources, along with its governance structure, of criticisms of the IMF. Critiques of conditionality come from both a principled and a practical perspective. The principled critique is that conditionality does not adequately respect national sovereignty. The practice, in effect, means that the economists at the IMF, unelected employees of an intergovernmental organization, are telling national governments how to run their countries, often in ways that undermine the democratic legitimacy of those countries. For almost four decades after the early 1970s the IMF lent only to developing countries, and it was commonly assumed that loans to developed economies were a thing of the past, adding a neocolonialist element to the critique. But the global recession and crisis of the Euro beginning in 2008 brought IMF lending back to Europe. This does nothing to address the antidemocratic element of IMF lending, but does reduce the neocolonialist element.

The practical critique of conditionality is that it quite often involves inappropriate conditions. Critics of the IMF charge that despite the Fund's claims that it takes local circumstances into account, the reality is that it imposes conditions based on economic theory to countries in a cookie-cutter fashion, conditions that are often grossly inappropriate to local circumstances. They also charge that the IMF is prone to subscribing to economic fashion: for example, they allege that it recommends currency boards to countries when the idea of currency boards is popular among development theorists, then changes its mind once countries have already committed themselves to putting the idea into effect.[11] The IMF has mellowed somewhat since the beginning of the recession in 2008, and is now more Keynesian than many member governments and central banks. While this change from a tradition of strict macroeconomic orthodoxy is welcomed by many, a cynic might note that it happened when the Fund, always headed by a European, was called upon to lend to European governments for the first time in four decades.

The second key source of criticisms of the IMF stems from its governance structure. The WTO, as discussed in the previous chapter, responds to criticisms that it undermines democratic governance by arguing that its structure is in fact democratic. The IMF, however, cannot claim to be a participatory democracy in the way that the WTO can. Its weighted voting structure is more suggestive of corporate governance than of political governance, and it has considerable executive powers in dealing with individual countries. The IMF has argued that it should not in fact be expected to be a democratic institution, for two reasons.

The first is that a corporate governance structure is appropriate to its primary activity, lending money at interest. In other words, it is designed to make lending decisions based on economic rather than political criteria, and therefore requires an economic rather than political decision-making structure.[12]

The second argument against democratizing the IMF is that many of its functions are the international equivalents of what central banks do for domestic economies. It is the current international fashion to depoliticize central banks as much as possible and to insulate them from electoral politics to allow them to focus on their primarily technical goals, such as stabilizing currency values and moderating business cycles. The same logic that argues that central banks should be insulated from political pressures should in principle hold true for the IMF as well.[13] And yet, the basic critique of the IMF remains: it is an undemocratic institution dictating economic policy to sovereign governments, which are themselves often democratically legitimate. Were it the case that the IMF was seen as always dictating unambiguously good policy, this criticism might be more tenuous. But this has not always been the case. In particular, its policy prescriptions in a set of crises in the late 1990s and early 2000s, particularly in the East Asian financial crisis of 1997 and the currency crisis in Argentina in 2000 were seen by many in the affected countries as problematic.

Partially as a result of these crises, by the middle of the 2000s the IMF was running out of countries to lend money to. The middle-income economies that had for decades been responsible for the bulk of the Fund's profits were mostly able to either build up strong foreign currency reserves or borrow directly from international financial markets. While in principle the decline in demand for IMF loans is a good thing if it indicates international financial and balance-of-payments stability, in practice the IMF needs income from loans to pay its expenses. By 2007 the Fund was losing money, threatening its ability to provide information and other services to member countries.[14] It even devised a plan to sell some of its gold reserves to create an endowment from which to pay its staff.[15] The crisis beginning in 2008, which brought a new set of large-scale borrowers to the IMF, has made the organization comfortably profitable again.

The Fund has in the past decade or so begun to look for ways to increase the participatory, if not democratic, legitimacy of its lending conditions. It has increased its institutional transparency and has begun to try to work with various NGOs and civil society groups, to attempt to make its lending conditions reflect points of view other than just those of the economists on the IMF's staff. At the same time, it has begun to use the term "program ownership" in tandem with conditionality. This implies an effort to work with governments to create lending programs and conditions that they approve of and support, rather than simply dictating conditions to governments.[16] Whether this change in language will lead to a significant change in the practice of conditionality remains to be seen. Even if it does, however, it will undoubtedly not affect the more fundamental critiques of the role of the IMF.

The IMF is also adjusting its voting structure to more accurately reflect the financial positions of its members in the contemporary international political economy. Because voting power reflects total capital invested, rather than annual contributions, it tends to reflect the historical rather than current distribution of national financial power. This has been an issue for some time, but the global recession, and in particular the increased potential demand for IMF funds from relatively large Euro-zone economies, has brought it to the fore. In 2008 the IMF's members agreed to expand its capital by 20 percent, with most of the increase coming from, and therefore most of the new votes going to, large developing economies such as China, India, and Brazil. In 2010 the members agreed to double its capital base, again with a disproportionate amount coming from middle-income developing countries; however, at the time of writing this plan has not yet been implemented.[17]

The IMF and IO Theory

From the perspective of IO theory, the IMF is in ways almost the opposite of the WTO. Whereas the latter's efforts at making the international political economy more efficient focus on creating rules that specify property rights more clearly, the emphasis of the IMF's market-perfecting activities is on increasing information flows and reducing transaction costs. The IMF increases information flows by researching the economic situation of various countries and publishing the information. It also develops standards for the reporting of national accounts (such as GDP) and balance-of-payments figures, increasing the comparability of these figures across countries, and thereby increasing the amount of comparative economic information available in the system as a whole.

At the same time, the IMF reduces the transaction costs of international cooperation in macroeconomic management and lending by acting as a central authority for both. This decreases the degree to which countries have to coordinate anew with each other each time questions of macroeconomic management arise, or when the need for lending to countries in macroeconomic crisis makes itself apparent. Its relatively strong and independent executive gives the IMF the ability to reduce transaction costs by acting on its own initiative in many such cases. The absence of such executive powers probably hinders the WTO's capabilities in this regard. But in a world of sovereign states that are only legally bound by new rules when they choose to accept them, the consensus-building structure of the WTO allows it to authoritatively create new property rights more effectively than the IMF.

Both the executive independence and the transparency-building function of the IMF run into limits with respect to one of its particular roles: an international lender of last resort. The IMF lends money to bail out countries that are facing financial crises.[18] Last-resort lending is one of the few economic functions where perfectly specified property rights can be problematic because of what is called moral hazard, the risk that if investors (or governments) know that they will be bailed out in crises, they will undertake riskier behavior, which in turn makes a crisis more likely. Furthermore, the large lines of credit often needed by countries in crisis mean that these loans can become political issues, decided upon by the Executive Directors rather than by the application of purely economic criteria by the IMF's professional staff.[19] As a result, the criteria for small and nonemergency loans by the Fund are far better specified than the criteria for large and emergency loans.

Looked at as institutions, the IMF and WTO are very different. Among other things, the IMF is simply a much larger organization, with a staff and an operating budget (i.e., excluding loans) more than five times larger than the WTO. This means that the amount of research and analysis that the IMF can do, and the amount of technical assistance that it can provide, is far greater, as is the breadth of expertise that it can bring to bear. The IMF also has an existing source of funds, and does not need to be funded by its member countries every year. Its primary output is money, in the form of loans, while that of the WTO is rules. These differences combine to make the IMF more of an independent agent in international politics than the WTO, both because it is more independent from the states funding it and because it can threaten to withhold its loans from the states that need them. Rules and reports, once they are agreed on by most countries, exist for any country to make use of. But loans can be withheld from specific countries. This latter difference not only makes the IMF a more independent actor in international politics than most other IOs, but also a more powerful one. In other words, the IMF is more of an actor in international politics, the WTO more of a forum.

Other International Finance IOs

While the IMF is the most visible IO in multilateral financial and monetary politics, it is not the only one. There are several other organizations that fulfill functions distinct from those performed by the IMF, some of which have been deeply and visibly involved in the international response to the financial and Euro crises. Interestingly, many of these organizations, like the IMF, are not organized in the same way as most traditional IOs. The BIS has as its members central banks rather than states, and the G-7, G-8, and G-20 have no institutional structure of their own. Another organization that is central to the recent set of global financial crises, the European Central Bank (ECB), is an integral part of the EU rather than answerable directly and only to member states.[20] This pattern suggests that with respect to international finance and monetary politics the tension between sovereignty and globalization works itself out differently than the patterns of multilateralism found in most other issue-areas.

Of these other organizations, the BIS is structurally most similar to the IMF. It describes itself as "a bank for central banks."[21] It is structured as a bank in much the same way as the IMF, as a profit-making institution with shareholders, except that in the case of the BIS these are other central banks, of whom sixty are shareholders. These are heavily weighted toward the first world, with more than half the member banks from Europe, and only one representative from sub-Saharan Africa (South Africa). Unlike the IMF, the BIS pays annual dividends to its shareholders. Although it is a relatively small organization, with some 550 employees, it has financial assets of over $300 billion.[22]

The BIS performs three main categories of functions. The first two fit neatly in its self-description as the institution that meets central banks' investment banking needs. It acts as a counterparty for transactions among central banks, making these transactions cheaper and more efficient. And it offers financial services to central banks, helping them both to safely hold and to earn some returns on their currency reserves. Both shareholder and non-shareholder central banks make use of these services. The third function is a much more traditional role for an IO; it hosts meetings of central bankers and finance ministry officials on issues relating to central banking, international financial stability, and banking supervision. The best-known result of this function is a set of standards on reserve requirements and risk management for banks, called the Basel standards after the city in which the BIS is housed. The most recent set of standards, Basel III, was published in 2010 and is currently being implemented by participant countries.

The BIS was created in 1930 to help manage the payment of German reparations from World War I. Because it was created as a commercial entity rather than an IO, and was housed in neutral Switzerland, it continued to operate with both German and Allied participation throughout World War II. This in turn led to suspicions that it had helped Germany to launder looted funds, and as a result it was almost closed down at the end of the war. But inertia prevailed, and it continued its role as counterparty for central bank transactions. It became the focus for the creation of international standards for bank capital requirements both because it is central banks that generally have the expertise and authority to regulate banks, and because it had a limited membership that nonetheless included all the countries that housed major international banks.

Despite its centrality to the negotiation of many of the world's financial and banking rules and its huge asset base, however, the BIS plays a far smaller role as an independent agent on the international stage than the IMF. With respect to the rules, the BIS is mostly a forum rather than a participant. The organization's small staff, particularly in comparison with the resources that member central banks are willing to invest in negotiations, means that the organization plays primarily a hosting and coordinating role. In regime terms, it reduces transaction costs and increases transparency, but does little to add to the legitimacy that member central banks bring to the table. And while the BIS has almost as large a capital base as the IMF, it has little leeway in how to deploy that money, and in any case does so for financial rather than political reasons. It cannot therefore use it as a source of power with respect to other actors in international politics.

The G-7, G-8, and G-20 (the relationship among these groups is discussed below) are basically exercises in great power economic and political summitry. They are not IOs, in that they are not legal entities. They are examples of multilateralism, in that they are attempts by countries to act in concert rather than unilaterally. But it is less clear that they are examples of globalization because they involve leaders of countries negotiating directly with each other, with no institutional mediation. None of these groups has any independent staff, budgets, offices, or formal rules. Leadership, which entails the responsibility for hosting meetings and the right to set the formal agenda, rotates among participants on an annual basis. Nor do the groups have clear or official areas of responsibility. They are designed as forums in which the leaders of the great powers can meet collectively to discuss common approaches to key economic and political issues.

The first of these groups to be formed traces its roots to a summit of the heads of state of the United States, Japan, Germany, the United Kingdom, France, and Italy, at the invitation of the President of France, in 1975. The leaders decided to make the meeting an annual event, and to invite Canada as well, thus creating the G-7 in 1976. While a range of issues was generally discussed in any individual meeting, macroeconomic coordination consistently remained a key focus. The finance ministers and heads of central banks of the G-7 countries also meet as a group, often in conjunction with the annual meeting of the IMF and World Bank in Washington.

In 1998 Russia was invited to join the group, creating the G-8. Because Russia's economy is structurally quite different from those of the original G-7 members, the change had the effect of undermining the group's utility for discussions of macroeconomic stabilization, and the G-8 has tended to focus on political and development issues. The G-7 still exists to discuss macroeconomic issues, but has been demoted from a meeting of heads of state to a meeting of finance ministers. The G-20, meanwhile, was an attempt to create a summit group of all of the world's leading economies, not just the traditional developed market economies. It includes the members of the G-8, as well as the biggest of the emerging economies, and the EU, and has met annually since 2008.

There are two ways to look at the role of the G-groups in international politics. The first is as a powerful cabal of great powers. This view is shared by some of the countries not included in the groups, and by the protesters at many of its summits. The second is as a sideshow to international politics, highly visible but not prone to generating meaningful results. To this view, the summits are useful for getting great power leaders to know each other on a personal basis, but the absence of institutional structure or mandate undermines the ability of the forum to produce meaningful outputs. History largely bears out this second view. The G-7 is too elitist to be the source of effective multilateral cooperation, and the G-20 is too big to act effectively as a small coordinating group.

Having noted the ways in which organizations dealing with international financial and monetary issues differ from the standard structure of IOs found in other issue-areas, it merits noting that there are in fact some IOs in this issue-area that hew much more closely to the standard structure. An example is the Financial Action Task Force (FATF), which was created at a G-7 summit in 1989, and generates standards for combating money laundering and terrorist financing. The FATF's secretariat functions are provided by the OECD (their memberships overlap strongly), but does have its own budget generated by member dues. As well as recommending standards, it monitors countries' performance (both member and nonmember) with respect to money laundering. It fits, in other words, well within the standard model for IOs.

11

Development

The role of international organizations (IOs) in development can be divided into three rough categories: development lending, development assistance, and development discourse. This chapter examines the leading institutions in each of these three categories: the World Bank, the United Nations Development Programme (UNDP), and the United Nations Conference on Trade and Development (UNCTAD), respectively.

The World Bank and Development Lending

The World Bank is the world's premier development lending institution. Its job is to lend money to development projects in poorer countries. The Bank is, in many ways, a sister institution to the IMF. The two institutions are often referred to as the International Financial Institutions, or IFIs. Their genesis was at the same conference in Bretton Woods in 1944, and they have similar organizational structures. In particular, the World Bank shares with the IMF a corporate shareholding and management structure and a similar pattern of voting power. It is also a profit-making institution—most of its loans are at market rates, and it is one of the last creditors that countries would consider defaulting on. As such, many of the criticisms of the IMF that were discussed in the previous chapter hold true for the World Bank as well, including the pattern of development that it promotes and legitimizes, and concerns about democratic governance.

There are also, however, a number of important differences between the Bank and the Fund. A key difference, of course, is that they perform different tasks. They both lend money to developing countries, but for different purposes. Whereas the Fund makes credit available to governments for general budgetary purposes, the Bank lends money to finance specific development projects. These are usually infrastructural projects, either in the form of the physical infrastructure needed for economic development, such as roads or electrical systems, or the human infrastructure that promotes economic development, such as better education. A government will come to the Bank with a project proposal, although Bank personnel often participate in preparing the proposal. The projects that the Bank funds are supposed to generate economic returns sufficient to pay off the loan; they are supposed to be financially viable. For example, if a country wants to borrow money from the Bank to help fund a new school, the proposal needs to show that the increased productivity generated by the increase in educational achievement will generate enough new revenue over the long term to pay for the cost of building and running the school.

Because of the difference in focus between the two institutions, the Fund tends to think in terms of macroeconomic stability, and the Bank in terms of microeconomic growth. This has led to the growth of different expertise within the two IOs, and a reputation on the part of the Bank for being less "orthodox," less focused on economic theory, and more willing to take social considerations in borrowing countries into account. Because the focus on microeconomic development means that the Bank needs to know about individual national economies in greater detail, it has also led to the evolution of a much bigger research bureaucracy: the permanent staff of the Bank, at more than 9,000 people, is more than three times the size of the Fund's staff.

A second difference between the IMF and the World Bank is that there is only one Fund, and no regional monetary funds.[1] There are, however, regional development banks, organizations that are structured like the World Bank and operate in the same basic manner, but focus their lending within a specific region. This does not mean, however, that all of the member countries are from the region. The United States, for example, is not only a member but also has the largest share of the vote in all of the major regional development banks. The major Western European countries, Japan, and Canada are also members of all of the major regional development banks. These banks include the Asian Development Bank (ADB), the African Development Bank (AfDB), the Inter-American Development Bank (IADB), and the European Bank for Reconstruction and Development (EBRD).[2] While the capital that each of the regional development banks can call on, and the amount that each lends, is far smaller than the equivalent figure for the World Bank, the regional banks collectively lend amounts similar to those lent by the World Bank. Nonetheless, they remain far less central to international development issues than the World Bank because of the more central role that the latter institution plays in the discourse on and legitimization of models of development.

A third difference between the IMF and the World Bank is that the latter is actually made up of a number of different components, each with separate tasks. The original component, and still the core of the institution, is the International Bank for Reconstruction and Development (IBRD), which is what people are in fact often referring to when they speak of the World Bank. This is the component that lends money to member governments for development projects, at a profit. The IBRD in 2011 lent roughly $27 billion. The International Development Association (IDA) provides loans to the poorest of countries at concessional rates (often charging no interest, but still requiring repayment of the capital, over a long term). The International Finance Corporation (IFC) makes loans to corporations in developing countries rather than governments. The IDA lent about $16 billion in 2011, and the IFC about $12 billion.[3] The other two components of the Bank are the Multilateral Investment Guarantee Agency (MIGA), which provides investment insurance to investors in developing countries in order to reduce risk premiums, and the International Centre for the Settlement of Investment Disputes (ICSID), an arbitration body.[4]

The World Bank, as a regime, has been criticized from both efficiency and legitimacy perspectives. From the efficiency perspective, there have been some recent questions as to whether development banks are still necessary in a globalizing world in which there is free movement of capital and an increasing number of financial mechanisms that developing countries can use to raise capital on world markets. From this perspective, there may still be a need for the IDA (with its concessionary lending) and the ICSID (with its arbitration function), as well as for the World Bank's efforts at collecting and disseminating development information and coordinating development efforts in particular countries.[5] But from the perspective of neoclassical economics, the imperfections in the international market for development finance that were behind the creation of the Bank in the first place have largely disappeared, and creditworthy development projects should have no problem obtaining finance from private sources. The Bank's response to this observation is to stress that it is a development agency, not a bank. It lends money for projects that would have trouble finding private financing, and lends to countries at lower rates of interest, and for longer periods of time, than private lenders would. The Bank also notes that it provides a wide array of development services in addition to lending.

From a legitimacy perspective, the World Bank regime has been subjected to many of the same criticisms as the IMF. The details of the criticisms are marginally different because the Bank supports specific projects rather than macroeconomic adjustment, but the basic gist of the criticism is the same: the Bank promotes a particular idea of development, one that many people find problematic. It does so through the mechanism of moral suasion, by using its position as the lead multilateral development lender and voice of the international community on development issues as a source of legitimate authority and as a bully pulpit. But it also does so institutionally, by causing the creation of bureaucracies in developing countries that are designed primarily to interact with the Bank (and the IMF). By creating government bureaucracies in developing countries that are by design concerned primarily with responding to the World Bank and IMF, the IFIs have the effect of legitimizing their models of development within the governments of the countries they lend to.[6]

One can certainly argue that the Bank's vision of development has beneficial aspects. For example, the shift in emphasis in the internationally accepted idea of what development means—from industrialization to poverty alleviation—in the 1960s and 1970s has been traced to the Bank.[7] But critics argue that the Bank remains too focused on physical infrastructure at the expense of social infrastructure, and that it is insufficiently sensitive to the social and environmental effects of the projects to which it lends.[8] At the extreme, this sort of criticism argues against development lending in general, inasmuch as it by definition promotes the development of a monetary economy at the expense of alternative economic forms, be they traditional or radical. Nonetheless, there are many critics who accept the principle of development lending, but argue that the Bank lends inappropriately.

The World Bank has, particularly in the past two decades, taken these criticisms to heart. It has changed its lending policies to reflect social and environmental concerns. It has modified the definition of development that it legitimizes to focus more on the development of human capital and infrastructure at the expense of physical infrastructure. And it has put a variety of institutional mechanisms in place that are designed to ensure that social and environmental concerns are incorporated into specific lending projects.[9] For example, before the Bank lends money to fund a dam, it will conduct studies into how much environmental damage the dam will do, how many people the dam's reservoir will displace, and what the effect of the dam on any indigenous populations will be, among other things. The Bank is also becoming less sympathetic to projects that focus on physical infrastructure, such as dams and highways, and more sympathetic to projects that fund human infrastructure, such as primary education and health care.[10]

Critics contend, however, that these changes are (at least to some extent) only cosmetic, that the basic institutional structure of the Bank does not allow it to reform itself effectively. The argument is that the basic task of the Bank is to lend money, and that employees are rewarded on the basis of how much money they lend and how much of that gets paid back. As attention to environmental and social side effects is a distraction from this goal, the lenders will attempt as much as possible to marginalize those in charge of social and environmental reviews. And loans to social infrastructure do not generate a clear cash flow that can be used for repayment.[11] The Bank is doing a better job of dealing with these issues than it used to, but the question remains, however, whether or not it is in fact doing a *good* job of dealing with these issues.

From the perspective of the study of IOs, the pattern of change in lending focus within the Bank is interesting not only because of its impact on development, but also as a case study of leadership and agency in IOs. In particular, a number of studies have asked how much difference changes of leadership at the Bank make to institutional norms and policy. These studies have tended to suggest that leaders can in fact make quite a difference, that the priorities of particular presidents of the Bank have had a real impact on Bank policies.[12] Since Bank policies in turn affect accepted models of development, this means that the President has real institutional power in international politics. By tradition the United States has always chosen Presidents of the World Bank. In 2012 there was a push from within the international development community to break this pattern by appointing a Nigerian, Ngozi Okonjo-Iweala, to replace Robert Zoellick, whose term was ending. But a voting majority supported the American nominee, Jim Yong Kim.

The UNDP and Development Assistance

Development assistance is used here to mean programs that transfer resources to developing countries (in other words, provide aid), as opposed to development lending, where resources are lent but repayment is expected.[13] The volume of money lent by the development lending institutions is an order of magnitude greater than what the multilateral development assistance institutions can spend. But this comparison understates the importance of the development assistance institutions, for three reasons. The first is that assistance does not increase the indebtedness of the recipient countries, and therefore does not feed into the cycle of debt that the lending institutions both contribute to and are called upon to alleviate. The second reason is that the development assistance institutions can fund programs that do not have a direct economic logic, or that do not yield a cash flow for repayment. In other words, they can fund many kinds of programs that the development lenders would not, such as the development of democratic institutions. And finally, the development assistance institutions are important actors in the development field because they are more like normal IOs than the development lenders. In particular, their policy-making bodies work on a one-country, one-vote basis, unlike the corporate voting structures of the IFIs. This gives them greater legitimacy in the eyes of developing countries than the IFIs, which are seen by some to be Northern-dominated and neocolonial.

There is a variety of IOs that fit under the heading of development assistance institutions, and the distinction between these institutions and organizations that offer humanitarian aid is not always clear. Various UN-related organizations, such as the UNDP, the United Nations Children's Fund (UNICEF), the Food and Agriculture Organization (FAO), the World Food Programme (WFP), and the World Health Organization (WHO), as well as the World Bank and IMF, focus on their own specific issue-areas, but also try to coordinate their activities where they overlap, in a process that will be discussed at the end of this chapter. The organization that is most directly focused on development assistance per se is the UNDP. Its particular remit is to provide technical assistance to developing countries, primarily by providing and promoting technical expertise.

The UNDP is a subsidiary body to the UN General Assembly (GA) and the Economic and Social Council (ECOSOC). It was created in 1966 from the merger of already-existing technical assistance funds within the UN.[14] Its executive board consists of representatives of thirty-six countries elected for three-year terms from within ECOSOC. It has a relatively weak central secretariat; most of its bureaucratic structure is to be found in its regional offices and its 129 country offices. In other words, unlike many of the IOs examined to this point, it emphasizes on-site implementation rather than centralized rule-setting or oversight. The central office, through the executive board, sets general funding priorities, which currently include poverty reduction with a particular focus on achieving the Millennium Development Goals (MDGs), as well as democratic governance and sustainable development.[15] But regional and country offices have a significant degree of latitude in implementing these priorities, in deciding which particular programs to fund in specific countries. UNDP country offices also often cooperate with the local offices of other IOs, such as the World Bank or UNICEF, and with an array of development NGOs, to provide funding.

The institutional history of the UNDP, as an amalgam of voluntary development funds rather than an IO created *de novo,* is reflected in its current funding structure. The organization does not have access to any of the UN's membership dues and does not charge any dues of its own. It is funded entirely by voluntary contributions from its members. These contributions yielded some $970 million in core resources, and $4.05 billion in contributions earmarked for specific projects (by donor countries, multilateral organizations, and matching funds by recipient countries) in 2010.[16] The voluntary nature of the contributions means that they tend to come disproportionately from those countries that are favorably disposed toward the idea of multilateral development assistance. In 2010, for example, while the largest overall donor to the UNDP was Japan, and the second-largest the United States, the third-largest was Norway, a country of only 5 million people. Looked at another way, the U.S. contribution amounted to $1.30 per person, the Japanese contribution to $3.30, and the Norwegian contribution to $55. The Scandinavian countries as a group account for over a quarter of total UNDP core funds.[17]

Viewed as a regime, the UNDP has both efficiency-maximizing functions and legitimating functions. Its primary efficiency-maximizing function is to reduce the transaction costs of development aid. In maintaining offices in most developing countries for the purpose of technical assistance for development, it eliminates a need for donor countries to do so individually. It also creates a network of development professionals able to pool their knowledge, and make that knowledge available to countries in a way that is sensitive to particular needs at the local scale. By some accounts this network function is the most important and effective role of the UNDP.[18]

The UNDP as a regime also has legitimizing functions. At the most basic level, the organization legitimizes the idea of multilateral development assistance, such that all of the large industrialized countries, even those with extensive bilateral aid programs, donate some funds. The UNDP's role in determining what constitutes legitimate development programmatically is less clear. The organization's priorities are a good indicator of internationally accepted development priorities. Its inclusion of, for example, democratization and HIV/AIDS, neither of which would have been priorities two decades ago, indicates that these two issues have become a generally accepted part of the development agenda. But the UNDP's role in setting this agenda is unclear—is the organization driving the agenda, or simply responding to it? In the case of the MDGs, it is at least in part responding.

As an institution, the UNDP is somewhat diffuse, with considerable decision-making autonomy devolved to the country offices. These offices can at times be quite important within their countries, particularly when governments are not functioning effectively or lack access to the expertise needed to govern. At the same time, the offices tend to be more focused on the governance needs of the particular country, and less on the development priorities of the central IO bureaucracy, than is true of World Bank local offices. This suggests that, institutionally, it may be more accurate to think of the country offices as relevant independent actors within specific developing countries than to think of the UNDP, as a whole, as a key actor in the international discourse and practice of development.

UNCTAD and Development Discourse

The third category of international institutions active in the issue-area of development comprises those that promote development discourse, institutions that serve primarily as forums for discussion. There are a variety of such institutions, including the regional and functional commissions that report to ECOSOC. The premier development discourse IO, however, is UNCTAD. Like the UNDP, UNCTAD was created by the GA in the mid-1960s (UNCTAD was in fact the earlier institution, created in 1964), has the same membership as the GA, and reports to ECOSOC. Beyond this common lineage, the two organizations are fundamentally different.

Unlike the UNDP's dispersed decision-making structure, most of UNCTAD's activities take place at its headquarters in Geneva. And unlike the UNDP's funding base of voluntary contributions, UNCTAD is financed primarily from the GA's regular budget. Both the organizations have programs to promote technical cooperation, but the programs themselves are fundamentally different. Whereas the UNDP's technical cooperation programs are focused on North–South cooperation and involve the creation of on-site expertise, UNCTAD's programs focus on South–South technical cooperation and involve the creation of guidelines and formats for cooperation through negotiation in Geneva, rather than the implementation of technical cooperation on the ground.[19]

UNCTAD grew out of the rapid increase in developing country membership in the UN in the early 1960s (thirty-two new members joined the UN between 1960 and 1964). Suddenly, the third world had a voting majority in the GA, and UNCTAD was one of the first institutional results of this development. It was created to assist developing countries with issues of trade and development, and was designed from the outset as an institutional counterweight to the Northern-dominated system of international trade and development. While all members of the UN are also members of UNCTAD, the organization was designed primarily as a forum for developing countries to discuss development issues. It has generally reflected the positions of developing countries, and has always been closely associated with the G-77.[20]

UNCTAD is perhaps best known as the forum of the New International Economic Order (NIEO), an attempt by developing countries to alter the international terms of trade in favor of exporters of primary products.[21] The idea of an NIEO has more or less died, and UNCTAD has accepted the basic premise that free markets are the main engines of international trade. But UNCTAD remains more focused on the prerogatives of the developing world in the international system (as opposed to development projects within countries) than other development organizations. It can do so in part because of its funding structure. Whereas the UNDP has to raise funds anew from volunteer donors every year, UNCTAD gets most of its funding from the regular UN budget. This has the effect of keeping its operations small—it has an annual budget of less than $70 million, and a total staff of some 400 people. This size constraint means that UNCTAD operates mainly as a forum, as a place where developing countries can set the agenda for discussions on issues of trade and development. Although UNCTAD does attempt to offer some technical assistance programs to countries dealing with the technical requirements of international trade, such as help with the bureaucratic processes of conforming to internationally accepted technical standards, these efforts are quite modest. But the resulting freedom from the need to raise funds from developed countries gives UNCTAD the political leeway to be more critical of market economics than other UN agencies.

As a regime, UNCTAD functions more in the realm of legitimacy than in the realm of efficiency-maximizing. In other words, it is primarily about political rather than technical cooperation. It does generate some efficiency gains, in the way that international forums do, by decreasing transaction costs of consensus-building and increasing information flows on relevant political positions among participants, as well as doing some of its own research on trade and development. But its main function is to act as a political counterweight to the formally Northern-dominated IFIs, and to other more democratic but still informally Northern-dominated economic IOs, such as the GATT, the WTO, and, to a lesser extent, the UNDP. It is not clear that UNCTAD does so particularly effectively.

Development, Efficiency, and Legitimacy

As a whole, does the community of international institutions working in the field of development make a difference? This question can be addressed from two perspectives: efficiency and legitimacy. From an efficiency perspective, one can ask whether or not the resources committed to development IOs are used more efficiently than they would be if they were used for bilateral development aid, and whether or not the current institutional structure could be redesigned to use those resources yet more efficiently.

The efficiency gains of multilateral development assistance are, as was discussed above, greatest for wealthy but smaller donor countries, as these countries make greater proportional use of development IOs. Even for larger donors that maintain their own local development offices, however, multilateral coordination can lead to more efficient allocation of development resources by improving information flows about various projects and thus eliminating some program duplication. This gain is mitigated somewhat by the proliferation of multilateral development organizations. The UN is dealing with the efficiency costs of various IOs with overlapping remits by creating new, country-specific coordinating bodies.[22] These in turn improve information flows among specific national offices of development IOs, but at the expense of creating yet another layer of bureaucracy. In short, the international development organization community is aware of the problems in balancing regime efficiency (having a central location for information and decision-making) with institutional efficiency (keeping the size of specific bureaucracies under control). But it is a difficult balancing act.

Critics of the IFIs argue that many of their functions, with the possible exception of crisis lending, could be performed equally effectively by the private sector. To the extent that they are right, the IFIs function more as vehicles for rich country power than as efficiency maximizers in the process of aiding development. In any case, the major donors to the IFIs are also those that, by virtue of being the biggest economies, would suffer the fewest efficiency losses in managing development lending bilaterally rather than multilaterally. Perhaps the greatest efficiency gains that the IFIs provide in this context are in the realm of property rights. They maintain a pool of capital that is committed to development lending, in a way that would make it very difficult even for the biggest donor countries to change. Thus, the developing world can expect that this pool will remain (conditionally) accessible to a greater degree than would be the case if the funds were controlled by separate national governments.

From the perspective of legitimacy, the success of the community of international development organizations is mixed. In their favor, it can be argued that they have had two beneficial effects. They have increased levels of development funding by legitimating minimum development funding levels of 0.7 percent of GDP for developed economies, a target that has been broadly accepted for almost half a century. They have also affected definitions of what constitutes a legitimate development project, and therefore, what projects should be funded. More generally, the simple existence of the various development IOs and their constant calls for funding probably do increase overall levels of development funding, by embarrassing countries that fail to contribute. However, it is probably impossible to determine how much difference the development IO community has made to overall development funding levels. There is also some evidence that development IOs can expand existing definitions of legitimate development to include issues such as poverty alleviation, as discussed earlier, whether through IO-specific programs such as those of the UNDP and World Bank, or broader targets such as the MDGs.[23]

On the other hand, the success of the development IO community both at increasing funding levels for development and at legitimating particular understandings of development has been partial at best. The international community has agreed in principle to the 0.7 percent funding level. But only five countries, all of them small, regularly meet the target, and many developed countries remain well below half of it. Furthermore, overall aid levels do not seem to be converging on the target (although we do not know if funding levels would be falling faster absent the IOs).[24] Similarly, while UNCTAD was active throughout the 1970s promoting the NIEO, this activity ultimately had very little effect on the structure of international trade and commerce. In fact, the structure of the international trading system became more liberal at a time when the NIEO was arguing for greater checks on liberal international trade. Leaving UNCTAD aside as an outlier for the moment, the picture remains unclear. International organizations clearly have some independent effect on understandings of what constitutes legitimate development, even after allowing for the interests of their donor countries. But the question of what effects they have is confused by the fact that the development IO community itself is not in agreement as to what should be considered legitimate.

On a final note, some of the most successful attempts at legitimating particular development goals have come not from a development IO, but from the GA. The 0.7 percent target comes originally from a GA resolution in 1970 entitled "International Development Strategy for the Second United Nations Development Decade."[25] The UN MDGs originated in a GA Resolution entitled the "United Nations Millennium Declaration" in 2000.[26] The Declaration included a number of specific development goals, such as reducing the number of people living on less than one dollar a day by half by 2015. Because all UN member countries have signed on to the MDGs, they represent an international consensus. And because the goals originated in a report by the Secretary-General, the UN bureaucracy is enthusiastic about them as well. As a result, many development IOs, including the World Bank, UNDP, and UNCTAD, have incorporated the MDG into their own development programs, as have many national development agencies.

12

The Environment

The environment presents a unique set of challenges for global governance, and has generated a set of institutions and regime complexes that is distinct from those found in other issue-areas. Whereas security and trade issues are about direct relationships among states, and development and humanitarian institutions are focused on providing assistance to specific populations, environmental issues are for the most part about the global commons, understood as those things held in common by different countries and peoples. Global commons can be geographical, areas such as the high seas, the atmosphere, Antarctica, and outer space that are not under the jurisdiction of individual states. They can also be things like species of life, which are part of the Earth's common heritage even if they are physically located within countries. Global environmental governance is about restraining pollution and resource use in such a way that actions by specific countries or their nationals do not prevent access to elements of the global commons by others.[1]

Three particular features make global environmental governance distinct from the governance of other issue-areas. The first is the difficulty of enforcing cooperation. The issue structure of commons cooperation means that non-cooperating countries can actively undermine cooperation. This issue structure is distinct from something like international trade, where a state can choose not to participate without undermining the ability of other states to do so. Since increased pollution or resource use by a state can undo the positive effects of cooperation by others, environmental cooperation requires either consensus among relevant countries (those in a position to contribute meaningfully to pollution or resource use), or effective means of coercing states to participate. This issue structure makes international environmental cooperation particularly difficult to do effectively.[2]

The second feature is the importance of science. Effective environmental governance requires detailed scientific understanding in a way that is not true of most other issue-areas. Actors must agree on what poses threats to specific elements of the natural environment before they can agree on how to manage them, and these threats are often complex or nonintuitive (or both). While considerable technical knowledge underlies much of the technical cooperation discussed in the next chapter, this knowledge is about understanding how our own technology works, rather than the much more complex question of how natural systems work. The third feature is the range of distinct issues it covers, from reducing carbon emissions globally, to regulating the mining of deep-sea minerals, to protecting specific habitats of migratory birds.

The system of environmental IOs that has developed, mostly over the past four decades, reflects these three features. It is marked by a few central IOs that address the range of environmental issues, but at a fairly general level, and a much larger number of small IOs and regimes that address specific environmental problems. These IOs are much more likely to have in-house mechanisms for generating science that are designed to be seen as politically unbiased than IOs in other issue-areas. This chapter addresses these features of the system, beginning with a discussion of the most central of the IOs, the United Nations Environment Programme (UNEP), and continuing with a survey of smaller and more specific environmental IOs and regimes. It then looks at the role of science in the system.

UNEP

UNEP grew out of the United Nations Conference on the Human Environment in Stockholm (UNCHE, sometimes called the Stockholm Conference) in 1972. This conference was convened by the UN General Assembly (GA), at the initiative of the government of Sweden. It was attended by representatives of 113 states, and is often credited with putting the environment on the international political agenda. UNCHE began a process of decennial global environmental conferences. In response to fears in the developing world that concerns about the environment would crowd development out of the agenda, the meeting in Rio de Janeiro in 1992 was called the United Nations Conference on Environment and Development (UNCED, also often referred to as the Rio Conference). UNCED began a process of changing the focus on global environmental governance from environmental issues specifically to the concept of sustainable development more generally.[3] Also, some important multilateral environmental agreements (MEAs) were signed there, such as the United Nations Framework Convention on Climate Change (UNFCCC) and the Convention on Biological Diversity (CBD).

The World Summit on Sustainable Development met in Johannesburg in 2002, followed in Rio again in 2012 by the United Nations Conference on Sustainable Development, also known as Rio+20. Increasingly, these conferences have been attended by not only representatives of states but also NGOs and global civil society actors, yielding almost 20,000 attendees at Rio in 1992, and as many as 50,000 in 2012. These conferences have had some real impacts on global environmental governance. They have served to legitimate first the natural environment and then sustainable development as central focuses of multilateralism. The two more recent conferences, however, have been criticized as being more show than content. The consensus texts to come out of them have been aspirational, and have not contained specific constraints on state behavior.[4] Nor have they generated new formal IOs. They have been useful at reinforcing networks of actors, particularly nongovernmental actors, in global environmental politics, but from a rationalist regime perspective they have produced little. Political forums yield little in the way of cooperative efficiency gains in the absence of political common ground.

Prior to UNCHE there were a few small environmental IOs dealing with specific issues, for example, the International Whaling Commission (IWC). Several larger IOs were beginning to incorporate environmental concerns into their activities, such as the Food and Agriculture Organization of the United Nations (FAO), but there was no central coordination among these efforts. There was, in other words, no voice for the natural environment in general in the UN system. UNEP was designed to be this voice, to both advocate for the environment within the UN system and coordinate environment-related activities across the system. It was also designed to help generate concern about environmental issues in developing countries, and to this end became the first major UN body to be headquartered in the developing world, in Nairobi, Kenya.[5]

UNEP is directly subsidiary to the GA, and has neither its own membership nor its own compulsory member dues. It gets a small amount of money from the GA, but this covers only 3 to 4 percent of expenses. The rest is raised from voluntary contributions, which yield a budget of about $200 million annually, a relatively small budget for a major UN body. Just over half this budget consists of contributions to one of 84 trust funds that support individual programs and the secretariat functions of specific environmental treaties and conventions. The other half finances general UNEP activities, and is called the Environment Fund. The largest recent contributors to this fund have been the Netherlands and Germany, at just over $10 million per year each, with the United Kingdom in third place. The United States, in fourth place, contributes about $6 million, roughly two cents per citizen per year.[6]

The provision of secretariat functions is one of the key roles of UNEP. Many MEAs require some secretariat functions, such as running meetings and collecting and disseminating information on environmental conditions and state compliance. But some of these functions overlap, and it is often the case that significant efficiency gains can be found by centralizing MEA secretariats. As such, UNEP provides secretariat services for several MEAs, including the ozone regime (the Vienna Convention, the Montreal Protocol on Substances that Deplete the Ozone Layer, and the Multilateral Fund), the CBD, and the Convention on International Trade in Endangered Species (CITES), in a variety of different locations.[7] The availability of UNEP to provide MEA secretariats makes it easier to create agreements on specific environmental issues without having to create new IOs from scratch.

Beyond providing MEA secretariats, UNEP engages in several activities in its role as the voice for the environment in the UN system. It facilitates the development and negotiation of international environmental law and of new MEAs, and helps to coordinate regional as well as global environmental cooperation. It helps to implement environmental policy, particularly in those countries that lack the capacity to do so themselves, and facilitates collaboration in finding technological and economic solutions to environmental problems. An example of the latter category is the Green Economy Initiative, an attempt to reorient economies toward more environmentally conscious sectors that is beginning to make its way into the international environmental discourse. It is an implementing body for the Global Environment Facility (GEF), a funding agency for environment-related projects (dealing with issues such as climate change, biodiversity, and industrial pollution). It provides and coordinates scientific advice on the environment, providing assessments, early warning of impending issues and crises, and hosting a set of scientific advisory groups. And finally, it coordinates environmental activities and management across the UN system.[8]

UNEP is thus trying to do a wide variety of things with a relatively modest set of resources. Not surprisingly, while it has had some real successes in its advocacy and coordinating functions, it has been criticized for not being up to all of the demands put on it. Various critics identify four factors that limit UNEP's role. One is its size and budget—it simply does not have the resources to do everything that it has been called upon to do. The second is its structure, as a program subsidiary to the GA rather than as a UN specialized agency. Voices from both the academic and policy worlds have suggested that UNEP be replaced by a specialized agency, proposed names for which include the World Environment Organization, modeled on the WTO. This idea has gained considerable political support recently within the EU, although it is less popular elsewhere.[9]

Proponents argue that the transition to a specialized agency would create an environmental IO with greater resources, greater legitimacy, and greater autonomy than UNEP currently has.[10] Others counter, however, that an agency would not necessarily have greater resources, and that the way to increase UNEPs funding is simply to give it more money. Furthermore, the autonomy may come at the cost of access within the UN—the Executive Director of UNEP (currently Achim Steiner) is also an Undersecretary-General of the UN, a role that helps with the task of coordinating environmental policy across the UN, and one that would likely be lost in the transition to a specialized agency. Finally, there is no reason to believe that such a transition would necessarily increase the legitimacy of the organization.[11]

The third factor that critics identify as limiting UNEP's role is its lack of power to coerce and enforce multilateral cooperation. But this criticism betrays a misunderstanding of how the multilateral system works. IOs have only such power as sovereign states give them, and states do not choose to give UNEP, nor would they choose to give a specialized agency, such power. Complaining about the IO in this context misses the point, which is that the requisite political will for action on many environmental issues, most notably climate change, does not exist among the major powers.

Finally, the fourth factor is UNEP's location in Nairobi. While a headquarters in Africa does help to legitimize environmental multilateralism in the developing world, it also creates logistical difficulties for the organization. Part of UNEP's role is to coordinate environmental activity across the UN, but most UN decision-making happens in New York and Geneva, leaving UNEP potentially out of the decision-making loop. Furthermore, it can be more difficult to attract talented employees to Nairobi than to other cities where UN bodies are headquartered.[12]

Despite discussions about the architecture of global environmental governance, little is likely to change in the near future. Rio+20 resulted in commitments for increased funding of UNEP and some of the trust funds that it oversees, but it is likely to remain one of the smaller of the main UN bodies. It may be the case that development funding becomes increasingly sensitive to the demands of the green economy, although whether this changes the institutional pathways through which development is funded remains to be seen. The conference also called for minor adjustments in UNEP's governance, increasing representation on its Governing Council from fifty-eight states to all UN member states, in lieu of more fundamental changes to its structure.[13] The chances of UNEP's headquarters moving from Nairobi, meanwhile, are negligible, for political reasons; the G-77 is unlikely to allow the one major UN body headquartered in the developing world to move.

Other Environmental IOs

Beyond UNEP, most of the actual governance of specific international environmental issues happens through a plethora of MEAs. Some of these, as already noted, have their secretariat functions hosted by UNEP. Some have their secretariat functions provided by other UN bodies. Those of the Convention on Long-range Transboundary Air Pollution (LRTAP), for example, are provided by the UN Economic Commission for Europe. Many others have their own secretariats, usually quite small. The Northwest Atlantic Fisheries Organization (NAFO), for example, operates on a budget of under $2 million per year.[14] Membership in MEAs can vary widely in size, depending on whether the issue in question is regional or global. NAFO has 12 members, LRTAP has 51, and the UNFCCC has 195.

MEAs for the most part operate as standard IOs. They have an executive body made up of representatives of member states, often called a conference of the parties, that meets annually or at other regular intervals, to set overall direction for the regime. Their secretariat functions tend to be relatively small because their core role in international governance is to serve as locations where rules are made and norms of behavior are set with respect to specific environmental issues, rather than to act as agents or implementing bodies. There are two general patterns through which these rules are made in MEAs: treaties that are structured to allow for regular review of rules without the necessity of new legislation, and what is called the convention/protocol process.[15]

In the first of these patterns, the MEAs are structured so that specific rules can be reviewed frequently, often annually. Commissions within the MEA meet to set and review specific rules for behavior. For example, NAFO generates new fishing quotas every year, in response to new data on the health of the fish stocks that it regulates. These quotas set a total overall catch for each stock, which is then divided up among member states. Most fisheries treaties that set rules (of which there are about twenty) work in this way. Similarly,

CITES maintains a list of endangered species of animals and plants, and if a particular species is on this list it cannot be traded internationally. Changes to the list are made at its annual meeting every year, without needing to change the treaty framework.

Not all MEAs work this way. Many begin with framework conventions, which are agreements that indicate a commitment to cooperate on a particular environmental issue and provide a framework for that cooperation, but do not contain specific rules of behavior. States that are parties to the convention then set rules in protocols to the original agreement, of which there can be just one, or many. For example, the UNFCCC in 1992 led to the Kyoto Protocol five years later, which committed some signatory states to reduce their greenhouse gas emissions by a fixed percentage relative to a 1990 baseline. The Kyoto Protocol has expired, and at the time of writing there is no sign of a replacement. The Vienna Convention on substances that deplete the ozone layer, negotiated in 1985, led to the Montreal Protocol in 1987, which required states to cut emissions of CFCs, the key ozone-depleting chemical, in half. Several follow-up meetings made the rules more stringent, with the cumulative effect that total emissions of ozone-depleting chemicals have been cut back more than 97 percent from their peak. Each new iteration of the rules was in effect a treaty modification.

By either pattern, MEAs are generally structured so that states will not have to accept new rules that they disagree with. When new rules are part of a new protocol, states can avoid new behavioral obligations simply by not joining the protocol. They can do this without leaving the original treaty. The United States, for example, remains a party to the UNFCCC, and is active in its governance, despite never having ratified the Kyoto Protocol to that Convention. When new rules are set without new protocols, they are usually agreed to by consensus, or there is a mechanism for states to object to the rules and thereby opt out of them.[16]

MEAs have in common that they deal with specific environmental issues, and that their institutional structure, whether run through a separate secretariat or through a bigger IO, is designed to implement a treaty that focuses on the multilateral management of that issue. Some MEAs are embedded in broader agreements or sets of agreements that yield IOs that deal in significant part with particular environmental issues. The Secretariat of the Antarctic Treaty, for example, is the implementing body for the Environment Protocol to the Antarctic Treaty (the Convention for the Conservation of Antarctic Marine Living Resources, or CCAMLR, has its own Commission, which is structured much like most fisheries-related MEAs). The United Nations Convention on the Law of the Sea created the International Seabed Authority (ISA), which deals in part with the environmental regulation of deep-sea mining.

There is a wide variety of other IOs, however, that deal with environmental issues in different ways as a part of their remit, rather than supporting specific environment-focused treaties. Some of these have already been discussed. The World Bank, for example, lends money to many projects designed around environmental or sustainability goals, and the UNDP (often in collaboration with UNEP) frequently develops or helps to manage similar projects. The GEF is a fund specifically designed to help finance projects at the nexus of environment and development, and has granted more than $10 billion to such projects since its inception in 1991. It is the official mechanism for the financial support called for in a variety of MEAs, including the CBD, UNFCCC, and the UN Convention to Combat Desertification. It also funds specific projects proposed by a variety of other IOs, including UNEP, UNDP, and the major development banks.[17]

Some IOs act as implementing bodies for MEAs while also dealing with the non-environmental aspect of their remit. As was noted above, the UN Economic Commission for Europe acts as the secretariat for LRTAP. The International Maritime Organization, which is tasked to oversee regulation of international shipping, acts as the implementing body for a variety of treaties designed to limit maritime pollution, as well those dealing with the safety both of ships and of sailors at sea. The FAO focuses on food security, of which sustainability is a key component. So while several fisheries MEAs, including NAFO and CCAMLR, generate quotas and other rules for fishing particular stocks, the FAO proposes general codes of conduct for fisheries and aquaculture, and collects global statistics on fisheries catches.[18]

Environmental IOs and Science

While collecting information is a common task of IOs, environmental IOs tend to focus more than other IOs on questions of science. Environmental governance builds on natural sciences that identify ways in which natural and social systems interact. At the same time, however, environmental regulation often generates economic winners and losers. As such, it is prone to being used, or to being seen as being used, for political purposes. Successful international environmental governance, therefore, requires that IOs not only fulfill the transparency function of improving flows of information, but also the legitimizing function of ensuring that the information is believed. The prevalence of scientific bodies in environmental IOs follows from this twin requirement.[19]

MEAs tend to have specific arrangements designed to generate science in support of their governance mandates that is seen as legitimate. Few employ their own scientists because it is expensive, and is therefore limited by the relatively small budgets of most MEAs. Furthermore, MEAs do not have the physical infrastructure to support scientific research, and therefore in-house research would likely fall behind work being undertaken by universities and governments. Most MEAs make use of scientists who either are seconded by their national governments or are volunteers. Furthermore, most of the work that scientists do for MEAs, and for environmental IOs in general, is aggregation and review of existing research, rather than the original research itself.

NAFO, for example, takes the first route. Each state that is a contracting party to the IO is a member of its Scientific Council, which in turn has four standing committees, on fisheries science, the fisheries environment, research coordination, and publications. States are expected to provide a scientist to each standing committee.[20] This model of institutional science works by trying to average out rather than eliminate political interference in scientific inputs. Scientists formally represent their countries, but all member countries have input. LRTAP goes further, encouraging member states to develop (and finance) national program centers, which are research centers that focus on specific aspects of long-range transboundary air pollution. This gives LRTAP the ability to request specific avenues of research, rather than just responding to them, an ability most MEAs do not possess.[21]

UNEP generally favors the second route, having eminent scientists volunteer for committee work. It has several scientific advisory groups, the leaders of which are officially appointed by UNEP, sometimes in consultation with other IOs, often unofficially in consultation with member governments. Scientists serve on these committees in their professional capacity as scholars rather than as representatives of states, so that their input can be seen as nonpolitical.[22] They are in effect equivalent to employees of IO secretariats rather than of member states, except that they are generally volunteers, meaning that they continue to hold full-time employment elsewhere, usually in universities or research institutes, and their work for the committees is additional to this. As a general rule, the legitimacy of the science produced by these committees correlates with the extent to which the committees' membership mirrors the range of scientific work done on the subject, and the extent to which it includes the leaders of the relevant scientific community.

The best known of these committees is the Intergovernmental Panel on Climate Change (IPCC). The IPCC was created by UNEP and the World Meteorological Organization (WMO), with the support of the UN GA, in 1988.[23] Its task is to review the state of the science of human-induced climate change. It is not tasked with conducting or sponsoring original research. Rather, its task is to produce a comprehensive literature review of the state of climate science, a task that to date it has performed four times. The first assessment report, released in 1990, suggested that observed warming was consistent with models of human-induced climate change, but also within the range of natural variability. The second, in 1995, concluded that the balance of evidence indicated a human effect. The third, in 2001, concluded that recent warming is likely due to increases in greenhouse gas concentrations, and the fourth, in 2007, that this is very likely.[24] The fifth assessment report is expected in 2013 or 2014. These reports involve several thousand contributing authors. They are widely cited, and generally accepted as representing the state of the art in climate science.

Because it was created jointly by UNEP and the WMO, and because its work requires coordinating the activities of so many people, the IPCC has its own administrative structure and operating procedures. It has its own secretariat, with twelve employees, hosted at WMO headquarters in Geneva. The secretariat is responsible for coordinating meetings and communications; it is not responsible for any of the scientific review. Because the IPCC was set up as a separate body, it has its own membership of 195 states. Representatives of member states do not participate in the writing of the assessments, but do review them, adding a political component particularly to the executive summaries. Member states also have the right to nominate, but not to appoint, scientists to the panel. Scientists can also be nominated by other participating organizations, and by scientists already involved in individual working groups.[25] The process as a whole is complicated and messy, but this complexity allows it to err on the side of inclusiveness.

One final note on the prevalence of this model of generating and compiling scientific information is that it is, from the perspective of MEAs and other environmental NGOs, remarkably cost effective. These organizations often seem small and under-budgeted. But they are availing themselves of the labor of many thousands, possibly tens of thousands, of researchers. While this labor is part-time, it is also supported by the research infrastructures of the universities and governments that are the researchers' primary employers. Environmental IOs, in other words, are getting hundreds of millions of dollars worth of free scientific advice. And because this advice often comes from the leading scientists in the relevant fields, it probably ends up being seen as more legitimate than what would result if the IOs received bigger budgets and hired their own researchers.

Environmental IOs and IO Theory

As regimes, environmental IOs as a whole have a mixed record. In rationalist terms, most work to improve information flows and reduce transaction costs, and some work to specify property rights to global environmental goods by creating rules limiting the consumption of those goods. UNEP itself does little rule-making, and focuses more on implementing rules made through specific MEAs. Some of those rules are very successful. The Montreal Protocol, for example, has mostly solved the problem of a shrinking ozone layer, and CITES has overseen the successful recovery of some endangered species, such as elephants. It must be kept in mind, however, that regimes can only make international cooperation more efficient when participant states have the political will, and sufficiently overlapping interests, to create effective rules in the first place. Where environmental IOs have failed, they have often done so because the political will among states for effective cooperation has been weak.

In reflectivist terms, the record has also been mixed. The decennial conferences have generated considerable enthusiasm for global environmental governance, but this enthusiasm has often not translated into meaningful action. Environmental IOs as a whole have done a good job of generating legitimate science, although this science reliably fails to convince people who are ideologically opposed to environmentalism, or to the behavioral changes it would require. Environmental IOs in general, along with other parts of the UN system, have effectively ensconced the idea of sustainable development on the international political agenda, although it remains unclear how that idea will be put into effect in practical terms. Individual MEAs tend to have relatively little effect on the legitimization of specific environmental issues. States tend to participate because they exogenously believe management is necessary, or because they have political motives to do so, and rarely because MEA IOs themselves have legitimated the issue. There are exceptions, however. For example, LRTAP generated a scientific process that convinced states that they were being damaged by acid rain. These states then became willing to reduce sulfur emissions when previously they had not been.

Some environmental IOs do have real agency in international politics. These IOs fall into two main categories, those that put environmental issues on the international agenda and those that pay for environmental action. The main actor in the first category is UNEP, which was designed from the outset in part to be a voice for the environment both within the UN system and in global politics more generally. UNEP can be quite effective in helping to put particular issues on the international agenda, such as ozone depletion, climate change, and the pollution of regional seas. But it can only be effective at promoting cooperation when sufficient political will exists among relevant states.

International environmental cooperation is driven by interdependence—governing the global commons necessarily requires cooperation. Environmental IOs are designed to reflect this, and generally operate either on a consensus basis or in a way that allows individual states to opt out of specific rules they object to. The power-based mechanisms of enforcement that are found in international security, trade, and finance IOs are generally not to be found in MEAs. Carrots are used more often than sticks—MEAs often contain mechanisms for financial aid for developing countries. But power is nonetheless to be found in international environmental politics, most often when environmental rules are backed up by threats of trade sanctions. The United States, for example, has done this with fisheries and species-protection issues, and the EU has threatened to do it with climate change. But as the global balance of power shifts southward, such uses of economic power to support mechanisms of global environmental governance are likely to become rarer until countries like China come to favor stricter regulation.

Finally, there is the tension between globalization and sovereignty. Globalization is part of the impetus for environmental cooperation—international environmental threats require a globalized response. But states remain effective at using the prerogatives of sovereignty to block effective cooperation. So much so, in fact, that many environmental activists are beginning to argue that the traditional mechanisms of multilateralism and international law are not only failing now, but are inherently incapable of dealing effectively with the scale of global environmental degradation. Partly in response, the mechanisms of global civil society are increasingly becoming the focus of global environmental governance. To a certain extent, in other words, environmental issues are supporting the universalist tradition at the expense of the internationalist. This new pattern involves environmental IOs working with NGOs, sub-national and local governments, and business to create a greener international economy. In this sense, therefore, the constraints of the sovereign state system are driving a globalization of governance outside of that system. It remains to be seen, however, whether voluntary governance through global civil society can generate effective environmental governance in the absence of authoritative regulation by states.

13

The Technical Details

Chapters 6–12 looked at specific international organizations (IOs) as agents of international cooperation in issue-areas that have strong political components. The IOs themselves were designed in part to answer political questions, to decide in favor of one set of state preferences over others as a prior condition to cooperation. But there is a wide range of IOs, relatively small and narrowly focused, that are designed to deal with technical and functional, rather than political, cooperation. They are designed to take goals that all countries agree on—such as efficient international postal delivery, the safety of international civil aviation, and combating dread diseases—and allow them to cooperate on achieving those goals more effectively. All countries agree on goals such as international peace and development, but disagree about what exactly those goals mean and about the conditions under which they should be achieved. With a goal such as safe international civil aviation, there is likely to be less disagreement about both goal definition and the conditions of cooperation.

The organizations that deal with this type of technical and functional cooperation tend to get much less press than the more political IOs. And yet, they can be quite important in the everyday lives of a wide range of people. We assume that mail will get delivered internationally, and that airplanes will be able to communicate effectively with ground control overseas. International commerce, among other things, would be severely impacted were these services to stop functioning. Therefore, we should apply theories of international organization to better understand technical and functional IOs, and to make them work as effectively as possible. These IOs can also yield useful observations about some of the broader questions in IO theory that are different from those suggested by the more political IOs.

In particular, the trajectory of cooperation managed by technical IOs speaks to the first of the theoretical distinctions discussed in the first half of this book: the distinction between sovereignty and globalization, between an internationalist model of global governance and a universalist one. One way of looking at this distinction is through the theoretical lens of functionalism, as discussed in

Chapter 3. Functionalist theory argues that as increasing economic complexity drives demands for more international regulatory coordination, technical cooperation among countries will drive political integration. This theoretical approach fell out of vogue in the late 1960s as scholars recognized the limits of technological cooperation in the absence of political cooperation. But a major part of the antiglobalization critique of many IOs is that they are too technical, and not political enough; that rules that affect individuals the world over are made by narrowly focused technical experts and bureaucrats without sufficient popular input.

Three such technical organizations are the Universal Postal Union (UPU), the International Civil Aviation Organization (ICAO), and the World Health Organization (WHO). These three IOs represent a wide range both in terms of scale (size of bureaucracies and budgets) and in terms of issue-area of focus. The extent to which they represent examples of technical expertise driving international cooperation and, in particular, international political integration, should tell us something about the extent to which functionalist theory accurately describes contemporary international organization.

The UPU

The UPU is in many ways a prototypical functional IO. It claims to be the second-oldest multilateral IO, having been founded in 1874 (it was brought within the UN system in 1948).[1] It is specifically designed to increase transparency and reduce transaction costs in international postal delivery, goals shared by all of its members, and generally does not address politically contentious issues. Although its members are national governments, in practice, these governments are represented by national postal bureaucracies, which tend to be bureaucratically distinct from broader national executives and legislatures.

The UPU was created to replace a complicated system of bilateral postal agreements with a single, simpler, multilateral one. The original system was in fact quite simple: the member countries agreed that for all letters sent internationally, the postal service of the sending country would receive all of the stamp revenue, and that of the country to which the letter was sent would receive none. The logic underlying this system was that the number of letters sent by any given country should be roughly equal to the number received, so that the revenues across postal services should even out over time. By the 1960s, it had become clear that this was not the case; more letters were sent from rich to poor countries than from poor to rich. This meant, in essence, that the postal services of poorer countries were subsidizing those of richer countries. In 1969, in response to this situation, the UPU created, and continues to oversee, a system of "terminal dues."[2] This system in essence compensates postal services for international letters they deliver in excess of those that they send.

Whereas the core function of the UPU is managing a set of rules to create transparency in the delivery of mail internationally, in the past several decades the organization has branched out into other areas. It now focuses much of its energy on technical assistance to postal services in developing countries, and helps postal services to deliver mail, and serve other needs of their customers, more quickly and efficiently. Among these other needs is what it calls "financial inclusion,"[3] the provision of financial services to the poor, such as savings and electronic payments (post offices in many countries also operate as savings institutions, primarily for customers of moderate means). It also coordinates efforts to create international standards for new technologies that relate to postal services, primarily the increased use of information technology, such as offering online services to customers and using bar-code technologies in mail sorting. On a more ideological note, the focus of the UPU's activities on these fronts is on helping postal services to transform themselves from traditional government bureaucracies to consumer-oriented service companies. This focus seems to reflect a general movement among member countries toward a neoliberal consensus on postal reform, and the desire of the postal services themselves not to get left behind in a rapidly globalizing industry.

The UPU is one of the most broad-based of IOs, with a membership of 192 countries (membership is open to all UN members, and to other countries by vote of two-thirds of existing members). Its governing body is the Universal Postal Congress, which meets every five years and at which all members are represented. The Congress elects two councils of forty members each, the Council of Administration and the Postal Operations Council, each representing the geographic diversity of the UPU. The UPU's secretariat, the International Bureau, coordinates its day-to-day activities and provides technical assistance. As well as working with the postal services of member countries, the International Bureau also coordinates its activities with those of other IOs when appropriate. For example, the UPU will coordinate with the United Nations Office on Drugs and Crime (UNODC) on issues relating to the shipment of drugs by mail, and with the ICAO on issues relating to international airmail coordination.

The UPU is one of the smaller of the UN-affiliated IOs. Its secretariat has a full-time staff of about 250 people and a budget of 37 million Swiss francs per year (about $39 million). The budget comes predominantly from membership dues, which are calculated in an interesting way. Members can essentially choose how much to pay when they join. Five countries—France, Germany, Great Britain, Japan, and the United States—have chosen to pay the maximum (just over $2 million a year), while some forty countries have chosen to pay the minimum allowable, just over $20,000.

As suggested above, the UPU can be understood quite well from a rationalist, efficiency-maximizing perspective. The organization's goal is quite straightforward—to make international postal service work more efficiently—and its activities mostly fit uncontentiously within this goal. It works primarily by reducing transaction costs, clarifying and standardizing rules, and bringing standards of postal services internationally up to the point where they can participate effectively in the system. The UPU has little effect in creating or legitimating new ideas. The exception to this rule is the recent bias noted above toward making postal services less like government bureaucracies and more

like private companies. This bias probably reflects the interests of those countries that pay the largest share of the UPU's budget, rather than any internal
bureaucratic interest. The organization also has little effect on national interests; states generally begin with an interest in efficient international postal
services, and look to the UPU to facilitate them.

In many ways, then, the UPU fits the bill for functionalist theory. It is a
forum for technical cooperation, with participation largely by experts in the
field rather than by political appointees. It tends to be an efficiency maximizer
rather than a forum for political competition. And, by and large, it works.
International mail delivery may not be perfect, but the mail generally gets
through with little difficulty. If it sometimes takes a while to do so, it is more
the fault of the national postal services than of the UPU. As the need for effective postal cooperation has expanded, so has the UPU; first, in response to
the postal needs of new countries in the system and second (more recently), in
response to advances in communications technologies. But in another sense,
the UPU does not fulfill the promise of functionalist integration theory. This
approach sees international cooperation not only as a solution to specific technical problems, but also as a driver of broader patterns of integration. Despite
the increasing complexity of its issue-area and the increasing breadth of its
technical abilities, it is difficult to see the UPU as a driver of integration,
managerial or political, outside of its immediate issue-area.

The ICAO

The ICAO, which was created in 1944 to provide the same sort of transparency to the business of international civil aviation that the UPU provides to
international mail delivery, would seem at first to be a similarly functionalist
organization. In many ways it is. Its membership is almost the same size as the
UPU's, with 191 members at last count. Administratively, it is a larger organization than the UPU, with a budget a little more than twice the size, reflecting
the technical complexities of the aviation business. Some of the organizational
details of the ICAO are discussed in Chapter 3, and need not be repeated
here. The gist of that discussion is that the ICAO secretariat has within it
several functional bureaus specializing in specific technical issues relating to
both the safety and the commercial viability of international civil aviation.
The primary output of these bureaus, and of the ICAO in general, is a set of
agreed-upon rules and technical standards for civil airliners flying internationally. Secondarily, the ICAO also provides technical advisors to help poorer and
smaller countries to implement these rules and standards.

As with all functional IOs, these parts of the secretariat make recommendations that are then submitted to the governing political element of the IO for
approval. The ultimate governing element of the ICAO is the Assembly, which
meets every three years and at which all member countries are represented.
The Assembly elects a Council of thirty-six countries from among its members
to represent both geographic diversity and "states of chief importance in air
transport."[4] While the Assembly is responsible for setting the general direction

and goals of the organization, the Council is the practical governing body, responsible for approving or rejecting the rules and standards recommended by the various parts of the Secretariat.

So far, the ICAO appears to be functionally similar to the UPU. They both exist to standardize procedures to make international cooperation in their issue-areas more efficient, and they both supplement their rule and standard-setting functions with technical assistance to less-developed countries to help them meet and participate in international standards. But there are two differences in their operation that make the former a less purely technical organization than the latter. One difference is to be found within the bureaus of the Secretariat, and the other is to be found in the degree of political contentiousness of some of the issues facing both the Council and the Assembly.

The technical rule-making and standard-setting functions within the secretariats of both the UPU and the ICAO are similar, in that they involve technical experts in the field of postal management and civil aviation, respectively, making suggestions based both on their own expertise and on extensive consultation with and inputs from the industry that they regulate. But the two industries are very differently structured. The postal industry is mostly made up of government monopolies that are required to provide a universal service. It is in fact these monopolies that generally provide the representatives to the organization, removing most of the potential tension between the goals of the technical experts and the goals of the political representatives. The civil aviation industry, on the other hand, is made up of companies, some government-owned but many not, in a highly competitive industry. The ICAO works closely with the International Air Transport Association (IATA), the industry group of the airlines that operate internationally, as well as with representatives of both airport operators and pilots' unions. The technical recommendations of the ICAO's secretariat, therefore, are more likely than those of the UPU to represent industry interests that may not match the broader political interests of the organization's governing body.

The second difference between the ICAO and the UPU as functionalist IOs is to be found in the sorts of issues that confront the political governing bodies. Postal cooperation is simply less political than cooperation in civil aviation. Few issues in postal cooperation generate much in the way of value trade-offs or ideological disagreement. Even the recent trend in the UPU to focus on the professionalization of postal services is relatively uncontentious. Civil aviation, however, does involve more contentious issues. One of these is the question of who can fly where. There are complex laws about what airlines from one country can do in another country, and these laws are often governed by bilateral agreements between countries. A simple set of multilateral rules, or at least norms, would be more efficient. But such a major change in the rules would inevitably favor the airlines of some countries over those of others. This puts the Secretariat in the difficult position of on the one hand, trying to make the industry more efficient by rationalizing international civil aviation rules, but on the other hand, running the risk of alienating various elements of its membership.[5] In other words, the ICAO can improve efficiency when all countries benefit similarly, but is constrained when some countries will benefit more than others.

Another trade-off that the ICAO is beginning to face is that between providing affordable international air travel and dealing with environmental damage, particularly climate change. Civil aviation contributes roughly 4 percent of the human-generated climate change effect, but international aviation is not currently covered by negotiations to limit climate change. For example, it is exempt from emissions quotas under the Kyoto Protocol to the United Nations Framework Convention on Climate Change (UNFCCC). The Kyoto Protocol calls specifically on the ICAO to regulate these emissions. Given the lack of progress in negotiating a successor agreement to the Kyoto Protocol, it seems likely that the ICAO faces some serious political hurdles in trying to regulate carbon emissions from international civil aviation among member countries that have very different positions on climate change. The current compromise is a set of aspirational goals and a call for members to create "action plans," but no binding commitments.[6]

The WHO

The WHO was created in 1948 as the UN specialized agency for health. Unlike the UPU and ICAO, which were created as autonomous organizations and later brought into the UN system, the WHO was created explicitly as a UN agency from the outset. Its official mandate is to work toward the "attainment by all peoples of the highest possible level of health."[7] Within this broad remit, the organization has considerable latitude in defining its specific health goals and operational priorities at any given point in time. The WHO undertakes a wide range of activities, ranging from long-term health planning and coordination, to functional assistance in the provision of health services in developing countries, to the coordination of international responses to specific international health crisis, such as the global spread of bird flu since 2003.[8]

Given the breadth of its mandate, one can question whether the WHO is a functional organization of a kind that can reasonably be compared with the two IOs discussed above. The WHO, as an organization, is an order of magnitude bigger than the UPU and ICAO, with a staff of more than 8,000 people in the organization's headquarters in Geneva, 6 regional offices, and 147 country offices. It has a budget of just under $500 million per year from mandatory assessments of its 194 member states, and raises three times that figure through voluntary contributions from governments.[9] As such, it is organizationally more like development agencies such as the United Nations Development Programme (UNDP) or the United Nations Children's Fund (UNICEF) than the smaller functional IOs.

On the other hand, the WHO does resemble the smaller functional IOs in terms of its focus on professional expertise. Its structure is designed to maximize the input of health care professionals into organizational policy, in order to encourage decision-making based on medical rather than political criteria. This emphasis can be seen almost up to the highest governing body of the organization, the World Health Assembly, which is composed of representatives of all of the member countries. It meets annually to set overall policy and to choose the organization's executive management. More immediate political governance, however, is provided by the Executive Board. As is the case with many IOs, the thirty-two members of the Executive Board are appointed by countries chosen by the Assembly. But countries cannot appoint whom they choose to the Board; they can only appoint people who are "technically qualified in the field of health,"[10] meaning that governance is provided by people with at least some background in and knowledge of this field.

Both the size of the WHO and the breadth of its mandate provide it with opportunities not available to the smaller functional IOs, but they also present it with difficulties that the smaller organizations do not share. Size gives the WHO the ability to be active in a wide range of activities, to have a strong global presence, and to have spare capacity on hand in case of new developments and global health crises. The scope of its remit gives it the flexibility to set its own agenda. In other words, the WHO is much more of an independent actor in world politics, with some real power within its issue-area, and is capable of considerable activity on its own initiative. It has the ability to affect the global health agenda in much the same way that the UNDP is able to affect the global development agenda. But the size of the WHO also gives it a bureaucracy that is larger and more unwieldy than that of the smaller functional IOs. The opportunities provided by the broad scope of its various activities also threaten it with loss of direction and focus in the absence of strong leadership within the organization.

Perhaps the WHO's greatest success has been the eradication of smallpox. The smallpox campaign was launched in 1967, and victory over the disease was declared in 1979. This campaign shows what the organization can accomplish when it combines a focus of its institutional capabilities with political will among its backers.[11] The WHO played four essential roles in the campaign. The first was as agenda-setter and publicist. It was central in getting various countries to agree to commit the resources necessary to eradicate smallpox, and in keeping them focused on that goal. The second role was as information coordinator. The WHO was responsible for keeping track of the science of combating smallpox, the spread of the disease, and who was doing what operationally, thus helping to prevent individual countries from wasting resources by duplicating the efforts of others or by using obsolete science. The third role was as provider of funding for smallpox eradiation programs in developing countries. And the final role that the WHO played in the smallpox campaign was to provide its own medical specialists to assist with the campaign in those countries where such outside help was needed most. These four roles are indicative of what the WHO does more broadly.

But the smallpox campaign, and the role of the WHO in bird flu outbreak, are also symptomatic of some of the criticisms of the WHO: that it focuses too much on infectious diseases at the expense of other threats to health, that it focuses too much on the diseases of the wealthy and on publicity-friendly campaigns, at the expense of less-glamorous health capacity-building.[12] The organization has also been criticized for institutional inertia and lack of direction following the success of the smallpox campaign. Recent reforms have attempted to address all of these criticisms. In the past several years, the WHO's bureaucracy has become more transparent, and there has been a greater institutional emphasis on health capacity–building and on addressing the health concerns of developing countries.[13] But whether the reforms have gone far enough remains open to dispute.[14]

Another general criticism of the WHO is that it has not lived up to its broader institutional potential and to the goals invested in it by its founders.[15] Along with the executive functions that the organization performs, such as coordinating activities to combat specific diseases and building health-services capacity in developing countries, its constitution gives it substantial legislative prerogatives. For example, the World Health Assembly has the authority to adopt binding regulations with the approval of two-thirds of the membership (subject to individual country opt-outs), and to propose international conventions (treaties) on health issues. The Assembly has adopted only two regulations (the more recent one in 1951), and only one convention, the Framework Convention on Tobacco Control, in 2003,[16] although it has adopted many nonbinding codes and classifications.

In short, then, the WHO's record as a functional organization is mixed. It clearly does some good work, and it would be difficult to argue that the world is not at least a somewhat better place because of it. But it does not seem to have lived up to the expectations of its founders to the extent that some other functional IOs have. In part, this is because of the nature of the issue-area: all the mail can in principle get through, but everyone cannot in principle always be healthy. But in part it is also because of its greater level of ambition, reflected in the greater size and scope of the organization. Since the WHO has much more leeway in determining what its specific program focuses will be, it is easier for the organization to lose focus. And since it has greater agency in determining its activities, it runs a greater risk of meeting political opposition in its choice of activities. As a functional organization, this leaves it in a dilemma. Either it can make contentious choices, in which case it becomes as much a political as a functional organization, or it can shy away from these choices, in which case it fails to live up to its functionalist potential.

Functionalism and Technical IOs

What does this comparison tell us about functional IOs, organizations that are designed to enhance cooperation within specific technical issue-areas? From a rationalist regime perspective, it tells us that they can work quite well. When the issue-area is well defined, functional IOs can increase transparency efficiently and relatively cheaply. When the issue-area is less well defined, technical cooperation can be hindered both by bureaucratic inertia and by political disagreement. In the language of game theory, the greater the element of prisoners' dilemma mixed in with a coordination game, the less smoothly will cooperation work.[17] This suggests that, from the perspective of efficiency-maximizing, functional IOs are best kept small, issue-specific, and as technical as possible. From an institutional perspective, however, the result is more mixed, as was demonstrated by the discussion of UNEP and as shown by the multilateral environmental architecture. Larger and more diffuse organizations such as the WHO are more vulnerable to bureaucratic pathologies and inertia, but they are also more able to act meaningfully as international political players, to use their institutional position to push particular items onto the international agenda. In other words, there can be a trade-off between technical efficiency and political effectiveness

From the perspective of functionalist theory, the role played by these technical IOs in driving international political integration is surprisingly small. The technical cooperation sponsored by the three organizations discussed in this chapter has grown both deeper and more complex in response to scientific, technological, and managerial developments. But the cooperation sponsored by them has tended to remain squarely within the bounds of the issue-areas that the IOs were designed to oversee. There have been exceptions to this pattern (the ICAO, e.g., is the repository for a convention on the production of plastic explosives, and the WHO has been critical of Israeli policy with respect to the Palestinian Authority),[18] but these have been few and isolated. In fact, far from driving patterns of political integration, the functional IOs have tended to shy away from political issues in the absence of broad agreement among member states. In other words, they have tended to coordinate activity within their issue-areas at the level of the lowest common denominator of political consensus among their members.

This observation in turn suggests that technical cooperation is not driving any broader patterns of political integration. In other words, a technical or functionalist version of the universalist model of global governance is not threatening to supplant internationalist cooperation. Even when looking at the internationalist model, functionalism seems to have little impact in driving changes in patterns of global governance. With respect to the sorts of technical IOs discussed in this chapter, the political authorities of the traditional nation-states appear to retain a firm grasp on the evolution of the formal system of global governance through IOs.

14

The Fuzzy Borders of Intergovernmentalism

This is a book about multilateral intergovernmental institutions. The definition of this category of institutions, as discussed in the introduction, is relatively straightforward. It comprises institutions whose constituent members are states—either all states, or all states meeting certain criteria. Identifying institutions that meet this definition should not be particularly problematic, and in most cases it is not. But there are several institutions that, for a variety of reasons, do not fit neatly into the definition. In other words, there are some institutions that are clearly part of the international organization (IO) system, and are clearly involved in global governance, but are not traditional IOs. This chapter focuses on such organizations.

Sources of global governance can be divided into two broad categories: intergovernmental sources and nongovernmental sources. The latter category includes both networks of not-for-profit NGOs, sometimes referred to as global civil society, and industry and business groups. This book is primarily about intergovernmental sources. But the two categories of sources cannot always be neatly separated. This is true operationally, as has been discussed in earlier chapters. For example, IOs such as the United Nations High Commission for Refugees (UNHCR) subcontract many of their operational duties to NGOs, working with as many as 500 specific ones. Many IOs sponsor forums for NGOs, or have institutionalized mechanisms through which NGOs, as representatives of global civil society, can be heard directly rather than through state representatives. Other IOs, such as the International Civil Aviation Organization (ICAO) or the International Maritime Organization (IMO), work closely with industry groups to gather information about their issue-areas and to set standards.

But beyond these operational relationships, there are some hybrid IOs that involve both states and nongovernmental actors as primary participants. One of the classic works of functionalist theory, Ernst Haas' *Beyond the Nation-State*, looks at one such organization, the International Labour

Organization (ILO).[1] This chapter will look at a number of other hybrid IOs. In some of these organizations, both states and non-state actors can be members. In some, the organization began as an NGO and over time transmuted into an IO. Other organizations remain NGOs, but have been directly co-opted into playing a formal role in international politics and in the IO system. This chapter examines examples of all of these patterns. It looks briefly at six organizations: the International Criminal Police Organization (ICPO, also known as Interpol), the International Organization for Standardization (ISO), the International Telecommunications Satellite Organization (ITSO, formerly INTELSAT), the International Union for Conservation of Nature and Natural Resources (IUCN), the International Committee of the Red Cross (ICRC), and the International Olympic Committee (IOC).

The ICPO, or Interpol

Interpol is at present a relatively standard functional IO. It serves to coordinate efforts among national police forces to combat crime when either the crimes or the criminals cross international borders. It has the standard IO structure, with a General Assembly in which all member states (currently 190) are represented, an Executive Committee of thirteen members elected from among the member states, and a Secretariat, managed by a Secretary-General, with a budget of about $80 million a year. The organization is funded primarily by member dues, which are based on the national GDPs of member countries, and is headquartered in Lyon, France.[2]

While Interpol is currently an IO, it did not start off that way. It started life as an NGO called the International Criminal Police Commission. It was created in 1923 on the initiative of the police chief of Vienna, who invited police officials from twenty countries to an International Police Conference. These police officials undertook to create the Commission under their own authority. They drafted the organization's constitution, which was accepted by a number of police organizations in various countries, but was never submitted to governments for ratification. Interpol's founding membership thus consisted of police departments, not governments. It gradually changed into an intergovernmental organization. It was granted UN consultative status in 1948, was upgraded from a commission to an organization in 1956, and was granted full IO status by Special Arrangement with the Economic and Social Council (ECOSOC) in 1971.[3] Technically speaking, it is still police organizations that are members, but only one such organization per country, "appointed by the competent governmental authority of that country."[4] In practice, this is no different from representation in traditional functional IOs, in which country representatives are generally functional experts chosen from the relevant national bureaucracy.

The main task of Interpol, as the functional IO in the issue-area of criminal policing, is increasing the efficiency of cooperation among police forces. Its General Assembly acts as a forum for international discussion of policing issues, and passes resolutions on these issues. Its Secretariat, both on its own and in cooperation with police forces in member countries, studies and collects data on various key and emerging forms of international criminal activity and coordinates activities among these forces, as well as assisting with capacity-building in those states in need of assistance with policing. One of the best known of Interpol functions is the issuing of "red notices," a type of international arrest warrant. These allow police forces in any member country to request the arrest and extradition of particular criminal suspects in all member countries. They make the process of finding criminals internationally much easier by creating a central clearing-house of suspects rather than requiring police forces to communicate with hundreds of individual police forces abroad. Red notices are currently being issued at a rate of over 6,000 per year.[5]

Interpol does not maintain any independent policing ability; it works entirely through member police forces. Perhaps the most important institutional innovation of the organization is the requirement that member countries identify National Central Bureaus, which are particular offices in member countries that are responsible for coordinating all interactions between domestic police forces on the one hand and the international policing community on the other. National Central Bureaus are sometimes part of national police forces (in Canada, e.g. the Bureau is a part of the Royal Canadian Mounted Police), but are sometimes administratively separate bodies (in the United States, the Interpol–U.S. National Central Bureau is part of the Justice Department, but is separate from the FBI and other specific police organizations). This means that any time a police department needs to deal with a counterpart in another country, or with police forces abroad in general, it knows where to turn to bureaucratically.

The ISO

The ISO acts as an international coordinative body for various kinds of commercial standards. It oversees more than 19,000 international standards, which together fill three quarters of a million pages.[6] These standards cover a vast array of topics, from the definition of units of measurement in the metric system, to definitions of screw, paper, and battery sizes, to postal codes, to the thickness of ATM cards. In other words, the ISO makes sure that an AA battery in one country is the same thing as an AA battery in other countries. Besides these sorts of specific standards, the ISO is also known for two sets of generic business principles: the ISO 9000 and ISO 14000 series. These are quality management and environmental management principles, respectively. When a company claims to be ISO 9000 or ISO 14000 compliant (these claims may occasionally be seen on company advertisements), it is claiming to subscribe to these general management principles. All of the ISO's standards are voluntary.[7]

In many ways the ISO seems like an IO, but technically it is an NGO. Its members are national standards organizations, and it was created by agreement among those organizations rather than among governments per se. It was not created by treaty, and does not have the standing in international law that IOs have. The ISO has three categories of members. Along with full members, there are also correspondent members, representing countries that have not yet developed fully functional national standards organizations, and subscriber members, representing countries that are too small to have their own fully functional national standards organizations. Membership numbers for these three categories are 111, 48, and 5, respectively, for a total of 164 countries represented.[8]

Only one national standards organization per country can be a member of the ISO. Some of the national organizations are either part of their national governments' bureaucracies or are semiautonomous governmental corporations. For example, the Standards Council of Canada (SCC) is a Crown Corporation, a semiautonomous but wholly owned corporate subsidiary of the Canadian government. Other national organizations, however, are private. The Association Française de Normalisation (AFNOR), the French body, is a private not-for-profit organization, loosely supervised by the Ministry of Industry. The American National Standards Institute (ANSI), AFNOR's equivalent in the United States, is also a private not-for-profit organization, which has as members various government agencies, industry and trade groups, and specific businesses. It is this variation in the governmental status of the member organizations that makes the ISO a true hybrid IO–NGO.

The ISO is also notable for the way in which it organizes its work. It is headquartered in Geneva, with a staff of about 150 that acts in a primarily coordinative capacity. The specific standards are arrived at by a network of more than 3,000 committees, subcommittees, and working groups. Each of these committees and groups deals with a specific type of standard, and includes representatives from government, industry, research institutes, consumer groups, and, where relevant, IOs. Standards are arrived at by consensus. The headquarters secretariat in Geneva, however, does not directly oversee and administer the work of these committees and groups. Rather, this work is farmed out to member organizations, of which thirty-eight volunteer to do the secretariat work for particular committees and groups. In other words, ANSI will oversee some international standards, and AFNOR others. The ISO estimates that this system is the equivalent of the thirty-six organizations donating 500 people to the ISO, and saves the latter some $80 million a year. This sort of voluntary group-secretariat approach to institutional organization is unique to the ISO.

The ITSO, or INTELSAT

The ITSO is not an example merely of an interesting hybrid organizational structure, but an example of three different structures: the first lasting from 1964 to 1972, the second lasting from 1972 to 2001, and the third beginning in 2001 and currently ongoing. The ITSO, which until the second of these institutional changes was more generally known as INTELSAT, was created to overcome public goods problems in the provision of commercial telecommunications satellites. In the early 1960s, the United States, by far the world leader in telecommunications and satellite technologies at the time, wanted to ensure both common international standards and a global network of terrestrial base stations for its new technology. Other countries, primarily European allies of the United States, wanted to ensure both access to new satellites and the right to participate in the development of new technologies and telecommunications systems. The resulting compromise was INTELSAT.[9]

The ITSO started off as an intergovernmental commercial venture. It was intergovernmental in that the members were states. The organization was created in 1964 with nineteen member states, but this number grew rapidly, reaching seventy-five by the end of the decade. INTELSAT was commercial in that it was structured on a shareholder basis, like the Bretton Woods organizations, rather than on a one-country, one-vote basis, and was designed to be a commercially profitable entity that charged for use of its product. National contributions to INTELSAT's capital were based on the share of the satellites' capacity that each country expected to use. On the basis of this formula, the United States started off with more than half of the votes in the organization; the next closest country was the United Kingdom, with just over 7 percent. U.S. dominance, in terms of ownership, use, and technology, was so pronounced that INTELSAT was more or less run by the American domestic communications satellite company, COMSAT.[10]

These arrangements had always been intended as temporary, and the original multilateral agreement had called for a renegotiation in five years. This process of renegotiation began in 1969 and yielded a new organizational structure in 1972. By this point, INTELSAT had launched four commercially successful communications satellites, and had some eighty-three members. Also by this point, the technologies involved had diffused to a much greater degree, and some countries other than the United States had developed the ability to build commercially viable communications satellites. The renegotiation of the governance of the ITSO was based on recognition that the organization was fulfilling two functions, one commercial and the other political/governmental. In other words, the organization was both acting as a regulator, ensuring access to satellite telecommunications to all countries, and as a satellite operator.[11]

The results of the renegotiation were twofold. First, it capped U.S. dominance of the organization. Second, it separated the commercial and governance functions to a greater degree than had been the case earlier. A new organizational structure was mandated for the management of commercial operations, to separate INTELSAT from COMSAT. This new structure was to be overseen by national satellite communication or telecommunication bodies. It retained shareholder voting, but the U.S. vote was limited to 40 percent. At the same time, a new level of governance was created that was similar in structure to traditional IOs. This new aspect of the ITSO was to oversee the regulatory functions of the organization, and to make decisions that were of a political rather than commercial nature.[12]

This second organizational scheme remained in place for almost thirty years. By the beginning of the new millennium, INTELSAT operated more than twenty satellites, at a substantial profit, which were used by more than 140 member countries. But the difficulties and inefficiencies of trying to operate a commercial venture with an IO governing structure were undermining

INTELSAT's long-term competitiveness. In response, the members of the organization decided to privatize the commercial part of INTELSAT, and to retain the ITSO as a regulatory IO in charge of ensuring that the new private company fulfilled its public service commitments of providing access in a nondiscriminatory way to all of its member countries. As such, in 2001, INTELSAT became a private company registered in Bermuda, and was sold to a consortium of some 200 companies,[13] the largest single share being owned by Lockheed Martin, an American multinational corporation and a major player in the satellite telecommunication business. At the same time, the ITSO became a standard functional IO, with an organizational structure and voting rules resembling those of most typical functional IOs.[14]

The IUCN

The IUCN is, in terms of its structure, perhaps the most hybrid of the organizations discussed in this chapter. It was created in 1948 to "influence, encourage and assist societies throughout the world to conserve the integrity and diversity of nature."[15] It was designed to be open to all organizations interested in its mission, both governmental and nongovernmental, and remains open to both states and NGOs. The IUCN itself is formally an NGO, incorporated as such under Swiss law and headquartered near Geneva.

The IUCN has two primary membership categories: governmental and nongovernmental. In the governmental category, both states in general and specific governmental bureaucracies can join, as well as IOs and regional integration organizations such as the European Union (EU). In the nongovernmental category, NGOs, both national and international, can join. Membership dues differ both between and within the two categories, on the basis of the size of the country or NGO. For states, dues range from 7,548 to 480,127 Swiss francs (about $8,700 to about $550,000), while for NGOs they range from 433 to 20,828 Swiss francs (about $500 to about $24,000).[16] All members, irrespective of category, can send a designated representative to be a full participant at the World Conservation Congress, the Union's highest decision-making and planning body, which meets once every three years. These triennial Congresses set general policy for the IUCN, pass resolutions, and elect the Council, the Union's primary governing body in between Congresses. The voting structure of the Congresses is essentially bicameral; in order to pass a resolution or elect the Council, a motion requires a majority both of the governmental and the nongovernmental members.[17] In other words, major decisions must be approved by both the governmental and nongovernmental parts of the membership.

The Council, which consists of thirty-eight members, is unlike the equivalent body in IOs in that its members do not represent their home states or particular NGOs, but are supposed to serve the IUCN in a personal capacity (although, unlike the members of the IUCN's Secretariat, they are not employees of the Union, because they cannot be paid for service to the Council). Of the members, twenty-four represent regions of the world, six are the chairs of the Commissions (see below), two are elected as President and Treasurer, one represents the host government (Switzerland), and five are selected by the Council "on the basis of diverse qualifications, interests and skills."[18] The Council, in turn, appoints the Secretariat, which fulfills standard secretariat functions.

The bulk of the work of the IUCN is done by its six commissions. These focus on education and communication; environmental, economic, and social policy; environmental law; ecosystem management; species survival; and protected areas. The commissions are networks of experts in the relevant fields, some 10,000 in all, who work for the IUCN on a volunteer basis. They are responsible for doing research and writing reports on issues within the purview of the respective commissions, and providing expert advice to governments, IOs, and NGOs. This research tends to result in databases, assessments, and guidelines. An example of an IUCN activity that involves all three outputs is its Red List, a comprehensive list of species threatened by extinction. The Red List creates guidelines for what counts as an endangered species, guidelines that are often incorporated into national endangered species lists as well as being used by the IUCN. The Union carries out assessments of specific species and regions to determine which species should be on the list. It also publishes a comprehensive list of endangered species globally that can be used as a database by anyone interested in the subject.[19]

The major function of the Union is thus advisory and research-oriented, rather than regulatory. This function has both transparency effects, by creating and disseminating information, and legitimacy effects, by setting single international standards. The IUCN does, however, also fulfill some official functions within the international system, as mandated by some international treaties. For example, the IUCN is given an official advisory role in the text of the Convention Concerning the Protection of the World Cultural and Natural Heritage.[20]

The ICRC and the IOC

Both the ICRC and the IOC, unlike the organizations discussed above, are true NGOs. They are governed not by representatives of states or of national organizations, but by an autonomous and self-replicating membership. In other words, new members of both committees are chosen by the existing members. This method of governance does not necessarily make the ICRC and the IOC exceptional among NGOs. What does make the two committees exceptional is the formal role that they play in international and, more specifically, intergovernmental politics.

The ICRC's role in intergovernmental politics is the more formal of the two. The Committee is written into the Geneva Conventions on the rules of warfare as an official neutral party and as a guarantor of the rights and conditions of prisoners of war. States that have ratified the Geneva Conventions commit themselves to allowing the ICRC access to prisoners of war whom they hold, noncombatants in war zones, and protected persons in occupied territories. The ICRC in these situations, along with national Red Cross/Red Crescent societies in some cases, is supposed to act both to increase transparency by determining the conditions of treatment of prisoners of war and noncombatants, and to provide medical and humanitarian services. This is the only example of an NGO, over which states or other IOs have no administrative control, being identified exclusively and by name in an international treaty as the guarantor of that treaty.

There are also other ways in which the ICRC is different from other NGOs. Like IOs, but unlike most other NGOs, the ICRC has concluded headquarters agreements with the governments of most of the countries in which it operates. These agreements give the organization international legal standing and the same level of extraterritoriality enjoyed by IOs in those countries. The ICRC also draws more than 80 percent of its funding from national governments. In 2001, eighty-one governments (plus the EU) donated funds, ranging from a contribution of 262 million Swiss francs by the United States to one of 1,328 Swiss francs by Guyana.[21]

The governance structure of the ICRC is based on the premise of Swiss neutrality. It is headquartered in Switzerland, where it was founded in 1863. It maintains operations in more than eighty countries with some 12,000 staff, 800 of whom work at the headquarters in Geneva. It is administratively separate from the national Red Cross and Red Crescent societies, and from the International Federation of Red Cross and Red Crescent Societies. Unlike almost all of the other organizations discussed in this book, individuals, rather than states or NGOs, are members of the ICRC, and all of these members play an active role in the governance of the organization. All of the members (there can be between fifteen and twenty-five at any given time) must be Swiss citizens, on the assumption that Switzerland will be neutral in all interstate conflicts. New members are elected by the existing members. Members tend to be either academics, generally with a specialization in international law, or active members of the humanitarian aid community, or (frequently) both. Many members historically have worked for the ICRC extensively before being invited to join.[22]

The IOC is not a formal part of the multilateral international system in the way that the ICRC is. It is part of the system to the extent that the Olympic Games are an international event. The IOC owns all rights to the Games and has sole authority to decide where the Olympics will be held. And many governments clearly feel that the Games convey legitimacy within the state system. For example, the Chinese government in 2008 clearly felt that the Beijing games that summer were important for China geopolitically. Similarly, when governments decide to boycott the Games, as happened in 1976, 1980, and 1984,[23] they are in effect saying that the Olympics are an important international event, one worthy of grand gestures by states. The IOC has the right to decide which countries the Olympics will legitimate.

The IOC is a much bigger committee than the ICRC. The IOC's rules call for a Committee of 115 members: 15 represent National Olympic Committees; 15 represent International Federations, the international governing bodies of specific sports; 15 are active Olympic athletes elected by their peers; and the remaining 70 need not be any of the above. Most members have had at least some experience in national Olympic committees. As is the case with the ICRC, new members are nominated and elected by existing members.[24] Although its committee is bigger than that of the ICRC, the IOC as an organization is much smaller, having only a very small professional secretariat (located in Lausanne, Switzerland). It provides some coordination for national Olympic committees and international federations of Olympic sports, but does not engage in any activities on the ground in the way that the ICRC does. The IOC raises its funds through the commercial marketing of the Olympics, and thus has no need to raise funds from governments. In fact, it raises sufficient funds from marketing to be able to help support both the national committees and the federations.[25]

Over the past decade the IOC has changed many of its rules, originally in response to allegations of corruption in the awarding of the 2002 Olympics to Salt Lake City. Among other things, it has committed itself to publishing some financial information for the first time. On the whole, however, the IOC does not have a reputation either for transparency or for financial probity. The ICRC, on the other hand, prides itself on its reputation for both. For example, it claims to have been the first humanitarian organization to meet the rigorous criteria of the International Accounting Standards (see below).[26] The difference between degrees of transparency in the two organizations may well be related to funding sources. The IOC, owning as it does the rights to the Olympic Games, has a secure source of funds. The ICRC needs to make the case to governments every year to renew its funding. This means that the ICRC needs to convince donors that their money is being well spent, while the IOC does not.

Is There a Pattern to Hybrid Organizations?

The set of organizations discussed in this chapter is by no means exhaustive. There are several other hybrids, and new ones continue to be created. One of the oldest IOs, the ILO, is a hybrid: both states and national labor unions can be members. Two examples of recently created NGOs that have an authoritative role in international governance are the International Accounting Standards Board (IASB) and the Internet Corporation for Assigned Names and Numbers (ICANN). The IASB was created in 2001, replacing the earlier International Accounting Standards Committee, created in 1973. It is charged with creating a uniform set of international accounting standards, which governments may (and often do) write into their national law as national standards. It is an NGO registered in the United States but operates in the United Kingdom, with a self-perpetuating membership.

ICANN is also an NGO registered in the United States, and is responsible for overseeing the system of names and addresses that allows the Internet and the World Wide Web to function. It was founded in 1998 to take over functions that had previously been performed by the U.S. government. Unlike many of the other NGOs discussed here, the Directors of ICANN are not self-perpetuating; they are selected by a number of relevant user groups, representing both geographical regions and functional constituencies. Many governments, particularly from developing countries, increasingly feel that ICANN's functions should be transferred to a proper IO, where governments rather than users would have a primary say in Internet governance.

Can any general conclusions be gleaned from this review of various kinds of hybrid IO–NGOs? Not really. There are few institutional and organizational commonalities across them. They fulfill both transparency and legitimacy functions in the international system. They tend to reflect either the demands of particular issue-areas or specific historical contexts. They have always been, and remain, a fairly small part of the system of multilateral global governance. And, although new hybrids continue to be created occasionally, the overall importance of their role does not seem to be increasing. Furthermore, as new hybrids are created, existing hybrids are sometimes dehybridized, and made into traditional IOs. Of the organizations discussed here, this happened with both Interpol and INTELSAT, and may well happen in the near future with ICANN. Most of the other hybrids can retain their status because they create voluntary standards, and thus do not pose a threat to the authority of sovereign states or the multilateral system. They function, in other words, because states allow them to. The remaining NGOs, such as the ICRC and the IOC, are unusual enough that they can be looked at as exceptions to broader patterns of global governance.

15

Conclusions

Are international organizations (IOs), and other forces of globalization, replacing sovereign states as the central actors in global governance? No. Are IOs fundamentally changing the way in which international relations work? Yes. In figuring out how these two observations fit together, we find some of the most interesting aspects of the study of IOs.

The introduction to this book began by asking whether or not IOs matter. The answer in general is clearly yes: they matter in a variety of ways. They enable technical cooperation among states in a range of areas that are vital to modern societies and economies. They encourage dialogue and communication among states as a first response to disagreements, and they foster rules-based, rather than power-based, dispute settlement in a variety of functional realms. They act as agents for the international community in dealing with issues of human security that might otherwise go unaddressed. At a more general level, they are changing the basic expectations of states and foreign policy makers about how international relations work, by substituting a bilateral model with a multilateral one.

Nevertheless, the role of IOs should not be overstated. They have their limits, and expecting them to perform beyond those limits is bound to lead to disappointment. They can affect international relations by facilitating cooperation and by legitimating rules. But they do not have the traditional power resources of states; they cannot tax, and they do not have either independent means of force or the right to regulate actors authoritatively. In the end, they are beholden to the states that formed them and are constrained by the interests and preferences of those states. Such power as they do have can be co-opted by some states to promote their interests at the expense of others. In concluding a book that reviews the study of IOs, it is as important to point out their limits as it is to point out their successes. The rest of this chapter, therefore, addresses a more nuanced question than the one that the book started off with: Under what circumstances do IOs matter, and in what way? It also addresses a more practical and policy-oriented follow-up question: How can we make IOs work better?

Efficiency and Ideas

Theories of international organization suggest two primary ways in which IOs can improve cooperation among states: by improving the efficiency of cooperation among states that recognize cooperative interests and by making the perceived interests of states more cooperative. The earlier issue-specific chapters suggest that both of these pathways to cooperation do in fact occur in international relations, and with some frequency. These chapters also suggest some of the limitations of IOs.

Focusing on efficiency, on international regimes as maximizers of transparency in the international marketplace for cooperation, has some definite advantages. From the perspective of the theoretician and policy-maker in the field of international organization, it has the advantage of clarity and specificity. Focusing on transaction costs, information flows, and property rights gives designers of IOs specific, and often quantifiable, measures of institutional performance and success; from the perspective of the student of international relations, it identifies a wide array of issue-areas in which IOs are, and can be, successful.

The focus on efficiency has also yielded several useful lessons about how to design new institutions and how to fix existing ones, lessons that by now have been widely recognized within the IO community. The need to minimize transaction costs, for example, means that IOs should create mechanisms for monitoring and enforcing agreements that require as little extra effort as possible on the part of states. The more the effort required, the more costly it is to ensure compliance with agreements, and therefore the less credible the agreements are. This observation means that, for example, incorporating a more thorough monitoring and enforcement mechanism into an agreement will not necessarily make the agreement work better if the mechanism is likely to be employed only sporadically because of cost or complexity.

Similarly, the need to maximize information flows means that IOs need to be designed both to gather as much credible information as possible and to disseminate that information as effectively as possible. Small investments in increasing information flows, such as the creation of the Situation Centre in the UN Secretariat's Department of Peacekeeping Operations (DPKO), can yield large improvements in cooperative efficiency. And the need to specify property rights means that the rules of cooperation overseen by IOs should be as clear as possible, as should be the process of mediating disagreements among states over the interpretation of those rules.

At the same time, a focus on efficiency in the study of international regimes has three clear limitations. The first is that it applies only to a circumscribed set of situations in international politics. The second is that it fails to fully describe what IOs actually do. And the third is that a focus on efficiency, which is value-neutral in the sense that it says nothing about what is being made more efficient, can be used to mask more traditional power relationships in international politics. This third limitation is discussed below, in the section on power and interdependence.

The first of the limitations is straightforward; rational regime theory only claims to be applicable in situations where states perceive themselves to have overlapping interests *ex ante*. It also applies best in iterated situations, where states care more about long-term patterns of behavior than they do about the outcomes of individual interactions. This limitation makes the efficiency approach highly applicable in areas such as postal cooperation, where cooperative and long-term interests predominate, but makes it more problematic in areas such as security cooperation, where goals are more likely to diverge and where states are more likely to focus on outcomes of particular interactions than on long-term cooperative patterns. It also makes the approach problematic in issue-areas ranging from trade to the environment, where states are sometimes more concerned about the distribution of gains from cooperation than they are about the aggregate size of those gains.

The second of the limitations of the rationalist efficiency approach to studying international regimes is that it fails to capture much of what IOs do and much of what states want them to do. This is where the second approach to studying international regimes comes in: the reflectivist approach, focused on ideas and ideals. The reflectivist approach can explain a range of phenomena that the rationalist approach cannot, but at the expense of specificity. The causal links between how an IO is designed and, say, its ability to legitimate a particular idea are much less clear than the causal links between institutional design and efficiency. This creates difficulties both for the student of IOs, who cannot necessarily tell how much of a state's behavior can be attributed to the ideas generated by an IO, and for the policy-maker, who has fewer clear guidelines in designing effective legitimating institutions than in designing effective efficiency-maximizing institutions.

Despite these difficulties, theories of international regimes that focus on ideas, such as the reflectivist approach, can illuminate some of the broader and more fundamental effects of IOs that the rationalist approach misses. In particular, they can illuminate both processes of change in international relations and the role of IOs in the basic rules of interaction of the state system. In other words, without applying the reflectivist approach we can determine much of the effect that an IO is having on international relations at any given point in time, but we cannot discover much about whether, or how, that organization is changing international relations. We can discover how states with compatible interests can cooperate better with rationalist theory, but we need reflectivist theory to discover how those states came to have compatible interests in the first place.

Regimes and Institutions

Both the rationalist and the reflectivist approaches to regime theory begin with the premise that IOs at best do good, and at worst do no harm. But neoinstitutionalist IO theory warns us that IOs are bureaucracies and can suffer from the same bureaucratic pathologies as other large organizations. In particular, they can evolve to work in the interests of the members of the bureaucracy rather than in the interests of those who created, and fund, the organization. International organizations are also, for the most part, specialist organizations. This specialization gives them the ability to focus on specific goals, but can also lead them to lose track of the bigger picture within which those goals are embedded.

The problem of bureaucratic pathologies can manifest itself in a number of ways, from nepotism and poor financial management to an operational focus on organizational growth at the expense of a focus on specific institutional goals. The best (although not perfect) solution to this problem is external oversight and a focus on institutional transparency and accountability. External oversight can come either from member states, which have the ability to withhold funding from IOs, or from NGOs, which have the ability to embarrass them. Institutional transparency refers to the ability of people from outside the organization to see inside it, to figure out what is being done and where the organization's resources are going. Accountability refers to any system in which the organization needs to account for its activities to an outside body, and report on the extent to which it is achieving its intended goals.

The UN Secretariat, for example, has for some two decades now been under pressure from some of its members (and in particular some of its biggest donor countries) to make itself more transparent and accountable. As a result, the Secretariat now sees transparency and accountability as important even without constant prompting by members. The withdrawal of the United States and the United Kingdom from the United Nations Educational, Scientific, and Cultural Organization (UNESCO) (as discussed in Chapter 2) is one extreme example of the sort of pressure member states can exert on IOs (both have since rejoined, their primary complaints having been addressed). In both the Secretariat and UNESCO, by all accounts, increased external scrutiny, leading to a greater focus on institutional transparency and accountability, has meant that the organizations actually work more effectively at achieving their institutional goals than they used to.

It should be noted, however, that the bureaucratic impulse to self-perpetuation and organizational growth is not necessarily a bad thing. It depends on the situation and on whether the impulse detracts from or contributes to the goals that member states have for the IO. For example, in the early 1970s, the IMF reoriented itself from overseeing the system of fixed exchange rates (the Bretton Woods system) that had just collapsed to acting (among other things) as a sort of credit-approval agency for developing countries. This change was, for the most part, generated from within the organization. But the change was accepted by the major donor countries because it served their interests at the time. The United Nations Environment Programme (UNEP) is another example of an IO whose responsibilities continue to grow and change. This organization regularly identifies new environmental issues that require international cooperation, thereby increasing its responsibilities and, over time, its capabilities. In an issue-area marked by high degrees of uncertainty, this ability to identify new needs for its services is a necessary part of UNEP's function.

The negative effect of institutional specialization—losing sight of the big picture—is a more difficult problem to address. It requires that someone be thinking in terms of the big picture, and be thinking of unintended consequences. Good examples of this problem can be found in such issue-areas as development assistance and aid to refugees. In both cases, well-meaning aid can lead to the creation of long-term dependence on the IO, when the intended goal is precisely to reduce the dependence of the recipients in the long term. This problem is not one of accountability, because in the short term recipients benefit from the aid. It is rather a problem of disjuncture between short- and long-term goals. There are in fact no simple or straightforward solutions to this problem; it requires a careful balancing of the short- and long-term goals. Both development and refugee-assistance IOs are more conscious of this problem than used to be the case, which is a necessary prerequisite to drawing the balance between short- and long-term goals in a thoughtful way. But it is a problem that needs to be kept continuously in mind.

Power and Interdependence

These various observations about regimes and institutional theory are based on an assumption of interdependence. International organizations, in these theories, are designed to enhance international cooperation, and this cooperation is itself made necessary by the fact of interdependence among states and peoples. The logic is that since we are driven to cooperate because of the fact of increasing interdependence in a world of globalization and technological advancement, we may as well cooperate as effectively and efficiently as possible.

But, some critics say, this focus on interdependence masks much of what is really going on in IOs, because it does not address the way in which power is being used through and by IOs and the patterns of cooperation that they represent. The critics would note as well that this focus glosses over the relative powerlessness of more peripheral countries that are full participants in the system, but are unable to affect it in any major way. As the multilateralist system matures, and as both IOs and countries proliferate in the international system, it is worth looking at the way in which power relationships in the system are changing.

Daniel Drezner, for example, argues that standards-setting in global governance will follow patterns of great power interests. A harmony of interests among both the great powers and other countries will generate harmonized standards. When great powers have similar interests to each other, but these differ from the interests of other states in the system, they will generate what he calls club standards, sets of rules from which non-great powers can be excluded. Differing interests among the great powers will likely generate competing standards, and differing interests both among great powers and between them and other states will lead to what he calls sham standards, or to no standards at all.[1] By this logic, IO effectiveness depends more on the underlying balance of state interests and power than on IO design. Therefore, we should look more to changes in great power interests, or to changes in power balances across states, to explain changes in IO effectiveness.

There are also ways in which power in the multilateral system is becoming more diffuse. At an obvious institutional level, new IOs are no longer created with voting structures that are as biased toward the traditional great powers as those of the IMF, the World Bank, or the Security Council. Even when new IOs are created that are not based on the one-country, one-vote principle, voting tends to be distributed in ways that ensure that both sides of the issue in question are represented. For example, the Multilateral Fund of the Montreal Protocol on Substances that Deplete the Ozone Layer requires majorities of both donor and recipient countries to carry a motion, and the International Tropical Timber Agreement requires majorities of both producer and consumer countries. In this sense, the creation of structural power favoring wealthier or more militarily powerful states over others in particular IOs is no longer accepted to the degree that it was half a century ago.

The same phenomenon can be seen in many international negotiations. In the Doha Round of international trade negotiations, for example, developing countries threatened in a way that had never happened before to veto a new agreement if their needs were not met. In a range of environmental negotiations, including those dealing with ozone-depleting substances and climate change, developing countries have wielded the threat of nonparticipation in a way that has allowed them significant input into the form and content of the final agreement, and a more lenient set of obligations. In short, in a significant subset of issues about which states negotiate to create agreements and form IOs, developing countries have accreted considerably more negotiating power than was evident in the earlier days of the multilateral system. But this new negotiating power is inconsistent across issue-areas and is far from evenly distributed across developing countries. It is concentrated in a small group of big and influential developing countries, led by China and India. Smaller countries, and most of Africa, remain essentially powerless. This new negotiating power, in other words, makes big versus small a more important distinction than developed versus developing.

And it remains the case that the big, rich states are by far the most powerful in most international negotiations. In other words, for the most part, the states that are most powerful in IOs are those that would be most powerful without them. This is true not only of observable bargaining power, but perhaps even more so in the background conditions of international negotiations. In fact, in terms of background conditions it can be argued that the multilateral system is actually more unilateral than it has ever been. The system always operated in the tacit recognition of U.S. financial hegemony, which is less pronounced now than in the early days of the system but, arguably, still a meaningful condition. But it is the case now, to a far greater extent than it has ever been before, that the system operates in the tacit recognition of overwhelming U.S. military hegemony. This recognition in all likelihood does not have a great impact on many negotiations, those far removed from military issues. But in any issues related to international security, the UN's official core function, U.S. military hegemony is a fact that helps to set the agenda for discussion.

Critics of the IO system argue that even more than the "hard" power of military and financial capabilities, the West, and particularly the United States, sets the ideological agenda of the multilateral system. Even if the larger developing countries seem to be holding their own in negotiations, they can do so only within the context of discussions that fit into a neoliberal and neocolonial setting. This critique of the system can be made at the level of rational decision-making; third world leaders recognize the rules of the system, and try to do as well as they can within those rules. But the critique can also be made via the cooptation of elites, in which the West convinces elites in developing countries that neoliberalism is a good thing, even though it may in fact not be the best policy for their countries. This latter critique is inherently normative; it cannot be addressed on a purely empirical basis, because it depends on the analysts' determination of what the goals of developing countries should be.

Whatever one makes of the ideological critique of the multilateral system, the grip of neoliberalism over the system appears to be weaker in the early years of the twenty-first century than in the mid-1990s. The Washington Consensus is no longer a clear consensus: the credibility of the neoliberal focus on markets at the expense of regulation has been undermined in a set of crises from those in East Asia in 1997 to the global crisis of 2008. At the same time, eight years of relative neglect of the multilateralist system by the United States at the beginning of the twenty-first century weakened both the system and U.S. power within it. Finally, the growth of Chinese power, combined with a weaker Chinese ideological commitment to the system than that of the traditional Northern powers, is a potential threat to the ideological consensus underlying multilateralism. It remains to be seen what long-term effects these factors will have on the international system.

A final note on power, interdependence, and international organization has to do with the power of IOs themselves. This power is constrained, but nonetheless real. Some IOs have the power to allocate financial and other material resources, but only within reasonably narrow parameters. Most IOs have access to only modest material resources, and when they have access to substantial resources, as in the case of the IFIs, the distribution of those resources is watched by donor states, which in turn have been known to interfere in the IFIs' lending decisions for political reasons. Most of the power that IOs have access to is not material; it is the power of moral authority. In some cases, this moral authority is accepted by third parties as authoritative; thus, the effect of IMF loans in securing the credit-worthiness of developing states, and the World Health Organization's ability to declare regions dangerous to travel for health reasons.

But it is important not to confuse the power of IOs with the power of member states. The Security Council, for example, has the moral authority to legitimize uses of force. However, it has no military power of its own, and depends entirely on the material capabilities of its members to put its moral authority into material effect. The WTO as an IO has remarkably little power, serving predominantly as a forum for member states. Even its Dispute Settlement Mechanism (DSM), which can authorize states to punish other states for breaking trade rules, cannot enforce its rulings on its own. The power of other IOs, particularly those with lower political profiles or with stronger secretariats (or both), lies in their ability to set agendas and to cajole states and other actors, but this power is always severely limited in the face of active opposition by the larger, and richer, member states.

Paradoxically, critics both overestimate and underestimate the power of IOs. Political realists often dismiss IOs as being ineffectual. These critics have a point insofar as IOs ultimately depend on the consent and on the resources of their member states, and thus cannot replace states in the enforcement of rules or the maintenance of international peace and security. At the same time, however, saying that they are not ultimately the only actors in international relations does not mean that they do not matter at all. IOs do affect the way states behave, do affect the international political agenda, and do succeed at improving cooperation and legitimizing behavior. Criticizing IOs for not being states is missing the point.

At the other extreme, critics of the UN system from the political far right and critics of the international economic institutions from the far left see IOs as potentially undermining state sovereignty. These fears are unfounded. International organizations do not have the power to impose trade rules on unwilling states, let alone invade the United States with black helicopters. They remain ultimately constrained by the states that created them, and therefore cannot undermine the sovereign state system without undermining their own authority and legitimacy. The organizations often come to represent rules that critics oppose, but these rules are nonetheless the result of negotiations and agreements among states. The place to look for the source of these rules, therefore, is with states themselves.

Sovereignty and Globalization

This observation brings us to the broadest of the four distinctions with which this book started, that between sovereignty and globalization. Chapter 1 discusses three traditions of looking at IOs: the realist, the internationalist, and the universalist. The evidence from Chapters 6–13 suggests that the international political system as it is currently constituted falls primarily within the internationalist tradition. There is a trend toward globalization, toward the creation of rules and norms that affect all countries, which states are increasingly hard-pressed to ignore. And IOs play an active role in this trend. But they do so largely as agents of states, not as replacements for states.

There are certainly elements of contemporary global governance that are better described by the realist or universalist traditions. States still play power politics, only partially mediated by cooperative institutions. And there are universalist market and social forces that drive patterns of global governance that do not fall within the direct control of states operating either individually or in concert with each other. The UN system is increasingly attempting to access these universalist forces through the co-optation of NGOs (as representatives of global civil society) and through such initiatives as the "Global Compact," a mechanism for co-opting transnational corporations (as the operatives of the international market system).[2] But the evidence from this book suggests that the core of the contemporary international system is best described by the internationalist tradition.

Having said this, the internationalist tradition is focused on a specific category of actors, states. Network theory provides an interesting alternative viewpoint from which to survey global governance. From this perspective, governance is increasingly being provided by networks of professionals and activists. Officials from various governments in charge of a specific issue deal with other such officials, and with representatives of interested companies and NGOs, more than with other members of their own government. This perspective serves as a useful reminder that states are not individual actors, and that even in an internationalist world issue-specific network connections across state and other actors can matter as much as, but in a different way than, connections within individual governments.

The discussion of the internationalist tradition in Chapter 1 argues that the ideological basis for contemporary IOs is the norm of multilateralism. This norm suggests that IOs are agents of globalization, but of a particular form of globalization that changes rather than undermines sovereignty. In multilateralist globalization, states do lose much of their ability to act independently, to do what they want within their own borders. In return, they get to be the primary participants in the cooperative making of global rules. State sovereignty comes to be less about domestic autonomy and more about participatory decision making at the international level. The processes described in this book, which reveal a proliferation both of IOs and of issue-areas subject to multilateral rules, bear out the view of the internationalist tradition. This empirical support in turn leads to two questions.

The first, and most straightforward, question is this: To the extent that the internationalist tradition accurately explains how international politics works, how do we make the multilateral system work more effectively? At the level of organizational specifics, this question can be addressed by regime and institutional theory, as has been done above. At a broader, systemic level, it seems likely that the system would be at its most effective the more the participant states believe in it. From this perspective, the varying level of enthusiasm for multilateralism from the United States, the most powerful state in the system, which has traditionally been one of the system's greatest proponents, is worrying. It should be noted, however, that while the United States began the twenty-first century by indicating an unwillingness to play by multilateralist rules in a few specific issue-areas, it has remained throughout an active participant in most aspects of the system. China has less of a history of international institution-building, and is yet to find a place in the multilateral system that matches its increasing economic and military power. How these developments in great power politics will affect the system as a whole is unclear.

The second question is: To what extent do those who are ultimately affected by its rules—the world's people—see the multilateralist system as legitimate? The participants in the system are states, not individuals; thus, multilateralist politics risks leaving populations feeling disenfranchised. As noted in Chapter 1, the phenomenon of perceived disenfranchisement is most visible in the politics of the EU, and in the various protests against the role of the international economic institutions in globalization. The EU, over the past decade and more, has tried to deal with the problem by expanding the powers and the visibility of the European Parliament, the EU institution directly elected by EU citizens. This strategy, in terms of alleviating the perception of a democratic deficit, has had only limited success to this point.

Other IOs have less ability, in fact usually no ability, to create direct representation for citizens in their decision-making. With most IOs this is not a problem—no one really cares about the representativeness of the Universal Postal Union (UPU) as long as its job gets done well. But with a few IOs, particularly the international economic institutions such as the WTO, IMF, and World Bank, it does seem to be a real problem. Oddly enough, it seems to be less of a problem with international security institutions such as the Security Council, perhaps because of a stronger assumption that issues of war and peace will be discussed among states rather than among populations. The international economic institutions, and other IOs working in the public eye, have to this point responded by trying to make their inner workings more transparent, and by trying to work more closely and intimately with NGOs as representatives of global civil society. These strategies, like the strategy of empowering the European Parliament, ameliorate the problem without getting to its core. The issue of direct representation of people in decision-making at the multilateral level is going to remain one of the key obstacles facing the multilateralist international system in the foreseeable future.

Notes

Introduction: The State and International Organizations

1. For a discussion of the frequency of emanations, see Cheryl Shanks, Harold Jacobson, and Jeffrey Kaplan, "Inertia and Change in the Constellation of International Governmental Organizations, 1981–1992," *International Organization* 50 (1996): 593–628.
2. The phrase "governance without government" was popularized in the international relations literature in James N. Rosenau and Ernst-Otto Czempiel, eds., *Governance Without Government: Order and Change in World Politics* (Cambridge: Cambridge University Press, 1992).

1 Sovereignty and Globalization

1. The Rhine Commission, which claims to be the first IO, first met in 1816. Renamed the Central Commission for Navigation on the Rhine, it continues to fulfill the function for which it was originally designed. See Central Commission for Navigation on the Rhine, "History," http://www.ccr-zkr.org/ 11010100-en .html. On fur seal fishery cooperation, see the *Convention between the United States, Great Britain, Russia and Japan for the Preservation and Protection of Fur Seals (1911)*, accessible online at http://fletcher.archive.tusm-oit.org/multilaterals /sealtreaty.html. International postal cooperation is discussed in Chapter 10.
2. International Labour Organization, *Constitution* (Geneva: ILO, 2001 [1919]).
3. The role of the UN in the maintenance of international peace and security is discussed in more detail in Chapters 6 and 7.
4. The UN's structure is discussed in detail in Chapter 5.
5. Union of International Organizations, *Yearbook of International Organizations*, 48th ed. (Munchen: K.G. Saur, 2011), pp. 33–35.
6. On this distinction, see Janice Thomson, "State Sovereignty in International Relations: Bridging the Gap between Theory and Empirical Research," *International Studies Quarterly* 39 (1995): 213–234.
7. For a broader discussion of the practical limits of sovereignty in Africa, see Robert Jackson, *Quasi-States: Sovereignty, International Relations, and the Third World* (Cambridge: Cambridge University Press, 1990).
8. On Westphalia as metaphor versus Westphalia as history, see Andreas Osiander, "Sovereignty, International Relations, and the Westphalian Myth," *International Organization* 55 (2001): 251–287.

9. J. Samuel Barkin, "The Evolution of the Constitution of Sovereignty and the Emergence of Human Rights Norms," *Millennium* 27 (1998): 229–252.

10. For a good general introduction to the globalization literature, see Jan Aart Scholte, *Globalization: A Critical Introduction*, 2nd ed. (Houndmills, HA: Palgrave, 2005).

11. On multilateralism, see John Gerard Ruggie, "Multilateralism: The Anatomy of an Institution," *International Organization* 46 (1992): 561–598.

12. For a discussion of the mechanics of this process, and an example of it in the realm of financial regulation, see Beth Simmons, "The International Politics of Harmonization: The Case of Capital Market Regulation," *International Organization* 55 (2001): 589–620.

13. For a discussion of regulatory races to the bottom, see H. Jeffrey Leonard, *Pollution and the Struggle for World Product: Multinational Corporations, Environment, and International Comparative Advantage* (Cambridge: Cambridge University Press, 1988) and Daniel Drezner, "Globalization and Policy Convergence," *International Studies Review* 3 (2001): 53–78. For a range of arguments against globalization, see Jerry Mander and Edward Goldsmith, eds., *The Case against the Global Economy: And for a Turn toward the Local* (San Francisco: Sierra Club Books, 1996).

14. See, for example, Jennifer Clapp, "Africa, NGOs, and the International Toxic Waste Trade," *Journal of Environment and Development* 3 (1994): 17–46.

15. Examples of both arguments can be found in Kevin Gallagher and Jacob Werksman, eds., *The Earthscan Reader on International Trade & Sustainable Development* (London: Earthscan, 2002).

16. For a discussion of this literature in the context of disarmament, see Klaus Knorr, "Supranational Versus International Models for General and Complete Disarmament," in *The Strategy of World Order, vol. 4, Disarmament and Economic Development*, ed. Richard Falk and Saul Mendlovitz (New York: World Law Fund, 1966), pp. 326–353.

17. Hedley Bull, *The Anarchical Society: A Study of Order in World Politics* (London: Macmillan, 1977).

18. The major exception to the rule that it is states that issue currencies is the Euro, issued by the European Central Bank, which is in turn related to (but not, institutionally, part of) the EU.

19. See, for example, Susan Strange, "Cave, Hic Dragones: A Critique of Regime Analysis," *International Organization* 36 (1982): 479–496; John Mearsheimer, "The False Promise of International Institutions," *International Security* 19 (1994–1995): 5–49; and Lloyd Gruber, *Ruling the World: Power Politics and the Rise of Supranational Institutions* (Princeton, NJ: Princeton University Press, 2000).

20. See, for example, Louis Henkin, *How Nations Behave: Law and Foreign Policy*, 2nd ed. (New York: Columbia University Press, 1979).

21. Bull, *The Anarchical Society*, pp. 24–27.

22. See, for example, Margaret Keck and Kathryn Sikkink, *Activists beyond Borders: Advocacy Networks in International Politics* (Ithaca, NY: Cornell University Press, 1998).

23. On "sovereignty" being more of a convenience for powerful states than being an absolute rule, see Stephen Krasner, *Sovereignty: Organized Hypocrisy* (Princeton, NJ: Princeton University Press, 1999).

24. See, for example, Paul Wapner, *Environmental Activism and World Civic Politics* (Albany: State University of New York Press, 1996).

25. Ruggie, "Multilateralism."

26. Mander and Goldsmith, *The Case against the Global Economy.*
27. See, for example, Desmond Dinan, *Ever Closer Union: An Introduction to European Integration,* 4th ed. (Boulder, CO: Lynne Rienner, 2010) and Andrew Moravcsik, *The Choice for Europe: Social Purpose and State Power from Messina to Maastricht* (Ithaca, NY: Cornell University Press, 1998).
28. This is the same argument made in favor of limiting federal policy-making in the United States, and allowing states to experiment with different approaches to public policy.
29. On the processes through which competitive behavior can lead to war, see Robert Jervis, *Perception and Misperception in International Politics* (Princeton, NJ: Princeton University Press, 1976).
30. See, for example, Shirin Sinnar, "Mixed Blessing: The Growing Influence of NGOs," *Harvard International Review* 18 (1995–1996): 54–57.
31. This criticism is discussed in more detail in Chapter 3.

2 Power and Interdependence

1. See, for example, Robert O. Keohane, "Reciprocity in International Relations," *International Organization* 40 (1986): 1–27.
2. For different positions in the absolute/relative gains debate, see David Baldwin, ed., *Neorealism and Neoliberalism: The Contemporary Debate* (New York: Columbia University Press, 1993).
3. For an example of the trade economist viewpoint on international cooperation, see Jagdish Bhagwati, *In Defense of Globalization* (New York: Oxford University Press, 2004).
4. On the subject of the national interest, see Stephen Krasner, *Defending the National Interest: Raw Materials Investment and U.S. Foreign Policy* (Princeton, NJ: Princeton University Press, 1978) and Martha Finnemore, *National Interests in International Society* (Ithaca, NY: Cornell University Press, 1996).
5. Robert Keohane and Joseph Nye, *Power and Interdependence: World Politics in Transition* (Boston, MA: Little, Brown, 1977). It is now in its fourth (and substantially expanded) edition.
6. Ibid., pp. 23–37.
7. Ibid., p. 11.
8. For an example of a conscious effort to create asymmetrical dependence as a power resource, see Albert O. Hirschman, *National Power and the Structure of Foreign Trade* (Berkeley: University of California Press, 1945).
9. In 2009, trade in goods equaled 424 percent of Singapore's GDP, but only 25 percent of the U.S. GDP. Figures from World Bank, *World Development Indicators 2011* (Washington, DC: World Bank, 2011), p. 224.
10. For an argument that this difference in bargaining power has created a system of IOs that are strongly biased against developing countries, see Lloyd Gruber, *Ruling the World: Power Politics and the Rise of Supranational Institutions* (Princeton, NJ: Princeton University Press, 2000).
11. The term was coined by Peter Bachrach and Morton Baratz in "Two Faces of Power," *American Political Science Review* 56 (1962): 947–952.
12. Looking at his process has in many cases, however, become much easier than it was in the days before widespread use of the Web. Many documents on Kyoto's prenegotiation negotiations can be found on the UNFCCC's website, http://www.unfccc.org/. Other useful reports can be found in various issues of the *Earth Negotiation*

Bulletin, available on the website of the International Institute for Sustainable Development (IISD), http://www.iisd.ca.

13. See, for example, Steven Lukes, *Power: A Radical View* (London: Macmillan, 1974). He speaks of a third dimension of power, rather than a third face.

14. Joseph Nye, *Bound to Lead: The Changing Nature of American Power* (New York: Basic Books, 1990).

15. Michael Barnett and Raymond Duvall, "Power in International Politics," *International Organization* 59 (2005): 52–53.

16. Keohane and Nye, *Power and Interdependence.*

17. For a discussion of why a more immediate need for cooperation undermines negotiating power, see J. Samuel Barkin, "Time Horizons and Multilateral Enforcement in International Cooperation," *International Studies Quarterly* 48 (2004): 363–382.

18. See Stephen Krasner, "Global Communications and National Power: Life on the Pareto Frontier," *World Politics* 43 (1991): 336–366.

19. J. Samuel Barkin and George Shambaugh, eds., *Anarchy and the Environment: The International Relations of Common Pool Resources* (Albany: State University of New York Press, 1999).

20. The UN has since internalized the norm of administrative efficiency, and stresses its efforts at reform. See, for example, the "Process of Renewal" website, at http://www.un.org/en/strengtheningtheun/index.shtml.

21. As of 2009. The complete set of country assessments can be found in *General Assembly Resolution 61/237, Scale of Assessments for the Apportionment of the Expenses of the United Nations* (New York: UN, 2007).

22. International Monetary Fund, *Annual Report 2011: Pursuing Equitable and Balanced Growth* (Washington, DC: IMF, 2011), Appendix IV.

23. One example is the Northwest Atlantic Fisheries Organization (NAFO), in which the EU is a member rather than its individual member countries. If the countries that constitute the EU were all members individually, they would have together half of the votes in NAFO (to complicate the issue, France and Denmark have separate membership to represent their territories in St. Pierre et Miquelon and Greenland, respectively, which are not part of the EU). In other organizations, such as the WTO, both the EU and its constituent countries are separate members.

24. United Nations, *Charter of the United Nations* (New York: UN, 1965), Article 18.

25. CCAMLR, "Rules of Procedure," *Basic Documents* (North Hobart, Australia: CCAMLR, 2004), Rule 4.

26. See J. Samuel Barkin and Elizabeth DeSombre, "Unilateralism and Multilateralism in International Fisheries Management," *Global Governance* 6 (2000): 339–360 and Elizabeth DeSombre and J. Samuel Barkin, "The Turbot War: Canada, Spain, and the Conflict over the North Atlantic Fishery," *PEW Case Studies in International Affairs*, Case Study #226 (Washington, DC: Institute for the Study of Diplomacy, 2000).

27. United Nations Office on Drugs and Crime, "About UNODC," http://www.unodc.org/unodc/en/about-unodc/.

28. See Richard Gardner, *Sterling–Dollar Diplomacy in Current Perspective: The Origins and the Prospects of Our International Economic Order* (New York: Columbia University Press, 1980).

29. The GA first met in London, and the UN's site in New York was not chosen until a private citizen (albeit one of the world's richest people), John D. Rockefeller Jr., donated the money to buy the land.

30. See, for example, Jeffrey Chwieroth, *The IMF and the Rise of Financial Liberalization* (Princeton: Princeton University Press, 2010).

31. See, for example, Stephen Ryan, *The United Nations and International Politics* (New York: St. Martin's Press, 2000), pp. 90–91.

32. Ibid., p. 93.

33. For examples of these criticisms from both perspectives in the context of the inter-action of the international trading system and environmental politics, see Gary P. Sampson and W. Bradnee Chambers, eds., *Trade, Environment, and the Millennium* (Tokyo: United Nations University Press, 1999). From an example in the con-text of international finance, see Chwieroth, *The IMF and the Rise of Financial Liberalization*.

34. Some organizations, such as the North Atlantic Treaty Organization (NATO), do have some military assets. But these assets, and the accompanying personnel, are ulti-mately working for and on loan from a national military force. The EU has discussed the creation of an EU military force, but to this point nothing has come of it.

35. For a discussion of different theoretical approaches to international law, see David Armstrong, ed., *Routledge Handbook of International Law* (New York: Routledge, 2009).

36. On moral authority and power in International Relations, see Rodney Bruce Hall, "Moral Authority as a Power Resource," *International Organization* 51 (1997): 555–589.

37. See, for example, Abram Chayes and Antonia Handler Chayes, *The New Sovereignty: Compliance with International Regulatory Agreements* (Cambridge, MA: Harvard University Press, 1995).

38. Susan Burgerman, *Moral Victories: How Activists Provoke Multilateral Action* (Ithaca, NY: Cornell University Press, 2001).

39. See, for example, Darcy Henton, "Not so Picture Perfect," *Toronto Star*, June 4, 1998.

40. World Health Organization, *World Health Report 2001—Mental Health: New Understanding, New Hope* (Geneva: WHO, 2001).

41. Peter Haas, "Introduction: Epistemic Communities and International Policy Coordination," *International Organization* 46 (1992): 3.

42. Peter Haas, *Saving the Mediterranean: The Politics of International Environmental Cooperation* (New York: Columbia University Press, 1990).

43. See World Commission on Environment and Development, *Our Common Future* (Oxford: Oxford University Press, 1987), and Steven Bernstein, *The Compromise of Liberal Environmentalism* (New York: Columbia University Press, 2001).

3   Regimes and Institutions

1. Stephen Krasner, "Structural Causes and Regime Consequences: Regimes as Intervening Variables," in *International Regimes*, ed. Stephen Krasner (Ithaca, NY: Cornell University Press, 1983), p. 1.

2. For a discussion of the black box model and its limitations with respect to domestic politics in the United States, see Roger Hilsman, with Laura Gaughran and Patricia Weitsman, *The Politics of Policy-Making in Defense and Foreign Affairs: Conceptual Models and Bureaucratic Politics*, 3rd ed. (Englewood Cliffs, NJ: Prentice Hall, 1993).

3. An example of this approach is Robert Dahl, *Who Governs? Democracy and Power in an American City* (New Haven, CT: Yale University Press, 1961).

4. The history of IO theory presented here follows that provided in Friedrich Kratochwil and John Gerard Ruggie, "International Organization: A State of the Art on an Art of the State," *International Organization* 40 (1986): 753–775.

5. See, for example, Lawrence Susskind, *Environmental Diplomacy: Negotiating More Effective Global Agreements* (New York: Oxford University Press, 1994), pp. 28–29. He provides a list of the "elements of a typical global environmental convention," but these elements are in fact typical of most treaties that create IOs.

6. Christopher Joyner, "Managing Common-Pool Marine Living Resources: Lessons from the Southern Ocean Experience," in *Anarchy and the Environment: The International Relations of Common Pool Resources*, ed. Samuel Barkin and George Shambaugh (Albany: State University of New York Press, 1999), pp. 70–96.

7. See, for example, Robert Cox and Harold Jacobson, eds., *The Anatomy of Influence: Decision-Making in International Organization* (New Haven, CT: Yale University Press, 1973).

8. International Monetary Fund, "The IMF at a Glance," http://www.imf.org/external /np/exr/facts/glance.htm.

9. See, for example, "Monaco Agreement on the Conservation of Cetaceans in the Black Sea, Mediterranean Sea and Contiguous Atlantic Areas," *ACCOBAMS Bulletin #3* (Monaco: Interim ACCOBAMS Secretariat, 2000).

10. See, for example, Susskind, *Environmental Diplomacy*.

11. The fourth and most recent report, published in 2007 and running to more than 2,800 pages, is available in four volumes: Intergovernmental Panel on Climate Change, *Climate Change 2007: The Physical Basis*; *Climate Change 2007: Impacts, Adaptation and Vulnerability*; *Climate Change 2007: Mitigation of Climate Change*; and *Climate Change 2007: Synthesis Report* (Geneva: IPCC, 2008).

12. For a more thorough discussion of the role of science and knowledge in international environmental cooperation, see Elizabeth DeSombre, *The Global Environment and World Politics*, 2nd ed. (London: Continuum, 2007), esp. ch. 4.

13. International Civil Aviation Organization, "Making an ICAO Standard," http:// legacy.icao.int/icao/en/anb/mais/index.html.

14. International Civil Aviation Organization, "Legal Affairs and External Relations Bureau," http://www.icao.int/secretariat/legal/Pages/default.aspx.

15. The main distinction between the ICJ and the ICC is that the former adjudicates disputes between states, and the latter tries individuals for crimes. Another related distinction is that states can legally decline to accept the jurisdiction of the ICJ if they so choose, whereas individuals cannot decline to accept the jurisdiction of the ICC.

16. United Nations High Commission for Refugees, *UNHCR Global Report 2011* (Geneva: UNHCR, 2011).

17. International Civil Aviation Organization, "Technical Co-operation Bureau," http://www.icao.int/secretariat/TechnicalCooperation/Pages/default.aspx.

18. Information on the World Maritime University can be found at its website, http:// www.wmu.se/.

19. As of 2009. The complete set of country assessments can be found in General Assembly Resolution 61/237, *Scale of Assessments for the Apportionment of the Expenses of the United Nations* (New York: UN, 2007).

20. David Rohde, "Ted Turner Plans a $1 Billion Gift for U.N. Agencies," *New York Times*, September 19, 1997, A1.

21. United Nations Children's Fund, *2010 UNICEF Annual Report* (New York: UNICEF, 2010), p. 33.

22. Ernst Haas, *Beyond the Nation-State: Functionalism and International Organization* (Stanford, CA: Stanford University Press, 1964).

23. See, for example, Ernst Haas, "Is There a Hole in the Whole? Knowledge, Technology, Interdependence, and the Construction of International Regimes," *International Organization* 29 (1975): 827–876.

24. Philippe Schmitter, "Three Neo-Functionalist Hypotheses about International Integration," *International Organization* 23 (1969): 161–166.

25. See, for example, Leon Lindberg and Stuart Scheingold, *Europe's Would-Be Polity: Patterns of Change in the European Community* (Englewood Cliffs, NJ: Prentice Hall, 1970).

26. See, for example, Stanley Hoffmann, "International Organization and the International System," *International Organization* 24 (1970): 389–413.

27. Kratochwil and Ruggie, "International Organization."

28. See, for example, Michael Barnett and Martha Finnemore, *Rules for the World: International Organizations in World Politics* (Ithaca, NY: Cornell University Press, 2004).

29. Interestingly, one of the first voices in this trend was that of Ernst Haas, who had earlier been a pioneer both of functionalism and neofunctionalism. See Haas, *When Knowledge Is Power* (Berkeley: University of California Press, 1990).

30. On IOs as being in the general good, see Harold Jacobson, *Networks of Interdependence* (New York: Alfred A. Knopf, 1979).

31. Barnett and Finnemore, *Rules for the World*.

32. James March, *Decisions and Organizations* (Boston, MA: Basil Blackwell, 1988) and James March and Johan Olsen, *Rediscovering Institutions: The Organizational Basis of Politics* (New York: Free Press, 1989).

33. On bureaucratic politics see Graham Allison, *Essence of Decision: Explaining the Cuban Missile Crisis* (Boston, MA: Little, Brown, 1971); on sociological institutionalism see Paul DiMaggio and Walter Powell, "The Iron Cage Revisited: Institutional Isomorphism and Collective Rationality in Organizational Fields," *American Sociological Review* 48 (1983): 147–160.

34. James March and Johan Olsen, "The Institutional Dynamics of International Political Orders," *International Organization* 52 (1998): 943–969.

35. International Monetary Fund, "About the IMF," http://www.imf.org/external/about .htm. This statement is an abridgement of Article 1 of the *Articles of Agreement of the International Monetary Fund* (Washington: IMF, 1945).

36. Michael Barnett and Martha Finnemore, "The Power, Politics, and Pathologies of International Organizations," *International Organization* 53 (1999): 699–732.

37. Ibid. This term has been applied to the same sort of behavior when undertaken by states as well, for example, James Fearon, "Rationalist Explanations for War," *International Organization* 49 (1995): 379–414.

38. See, inter alia, Bruce Rich, *Mortgaging the Earth: The World Bank, Environmental Impoverishment, and the Crisis of Development* (Boston, MA: Beacon Press, 1994). To be fair, the Bank is trying to address this problem.

39. Example taken from Barnett and Finnemore, "Pathologies of International Organizations." See also David Kennedy, "International Refugee Protection," *Human Rights Quarterly* 8 (1986): 1–9.

40. See, for example, United Nations Security Council Resolutions 1368 and 1373 (New York: UN, 2001).

41. Conditionality refers to a process in which the IMF sets policy conditions, usually involving policy liberalization, that developing countries must meet in

order to gain access to IMF loans. This process is discussed in more detail in Chapter 10.

42. These IOs are called "emanations." Cheryl Shanks, Harold Jacobson, and Jeffrey Kaplan, "Inertia and Change in the Constellation of International Governmental Organizations, 1981–1992," *International Organization* 50 (1996): 593–628.

43. See, for example, Darren Hawkins, David Lake, Daniel Nielson, and Michael Tierney, eds., *Delegation and Agency in International Organization* (Cambridge: Cambridge University Press, 2006).

44. See, for example, Kratochwil and Ruggie, "International Organization."

45. On network analysis in the study of IO generally, see Emilie M. Hafner-Burton, Miles Kahler, and Alexander H. Montgomery, "Network Analysis for International Relations," *International Organization* 63 (2009): 559–592.

46. The term "reflectivism" was introduced into the IO discourse by Robert Keohane in "International Institutions: Two Approaches," *International Studies Quarterly* 32 (1988): 379–396.

4   Efficiency and Ideas

1. See, for example, Stephen Krasner, ed., *International Regimes* (Ithaca, NY: Cornell University Press, 1983). The "rationalist" and "reflectivist" terminology is from Robert Keohane, "International Institutions: Two Approaches," *International Studies Quarterly* 32 (1988): 379–396. The term "neo-liberal institutionalism" was introduced by Joseph Grieco in "Anarchy and the Limits of Cooperation: A Realist Critique of the Newest Liberal Institutionalism," *International Organization* 42 (1988): 485–507. The term "constructivism" was introduced into the international relations discourse by Nicholas Onuf in *World of Our Making: Rules and Rule in Social Theory and International Relations* (Columbia: University of South Carolina Press, 1989).

2. See, inter alia, Kenneth Oye, ed., *Cooperation under Anarchy* (Princeton, NJ: Princeton University Press, 1986), and James Fearon, "Bargaining, Enforcement, and International Cooperation," *International Organization* 52 (1998): 269–306.

3. The seminal work on collective action problems, which uses the union membership example, is Mancur Olson's *The Logic of Collective Action: Public Goods and the Theory of Groups* (Cambridge, MA: Harvard University Press, 1965).

4. Joanne Gowa, "Rational Hegemons, Excludable Goods, and Small Groups: An Epitaph for Hegemonic Stability Theory?" *World Politics* 41 (1989): 307–324.

5. On PD, and on the use of this sort of 2 x 2 game in the study of international relations more generally, see Glenn Snyder and Paul Diesing, *Conflict among Nations: Bargaining, Decision Making, and System Structure in International Crises* (Princeton, NJ: Princeton University Press, 1977).

6. Douglass North and Robert Paul Thomas, *The Rise of the Western World: A New Economic History* (Cambridge: Cambridge University Press, 1973), and Douglass North, *Structure and Change in Economic History* (New York: Norton, 1981) go so far as to claim that economic history as a whole can be written through the story of governments improving markets.

7. Robert Keohane, *After Hegemony: Cooperation and Discord in the World Political Economy* (Princeton, NJ: Princeton University Press, 1984).

8. Robert Keohane, "The Demand for International Regimes," *International Organization* 36 (1982): 325–356.

9. Friedrich Kratochwil and John Gerard Ruggie, "International Organization: A State of the Art on an Art of the State," *International Organization* 40 (1986): 753–775, and Ronald Mitchell, "Sources of Transparency: Information Systems in International Regimes," *International Studies Quarterly* 42 (1998): 109–130.

10. A discussion of the origin and task of the IPCC can be found on its website, http://www.ipcc.ch/.

11. They are then, in practice, often ignored. See, for example, William Aron, "Science and the IWC," in *Toward a Sustainable Whaling Regime*, ed. Robert Friedheim (Seattle: University of Washington Press, 2001), pp. 105–122.

12. Both the IMF and the ISO will be discussed in more detail below, in Chapters 9 and 14, respectively.

13. The administrative functions are provided by the Secretariat (the internal structure of the UN will be discussed in more detail in the next chapter). The rules and procedures of the Security Council are published as chapter 1 of the *Repertoire of the Practice of the Security Council* (New York: UN, serial).

14. GATT, *General Agreement on Tariffs and Trade: Text of the General Agreement* (Geneva: GATT, 1994), Articles I and III.

15. Joseph Kahn, "Nations Back Freer Trade, Hoping to Aid Global Growth," *New York Times*, November 15, 2001, A12.

16. Oran Young, ed., *The Effectiveness of International Environmental Agreements* (Cambridge, MA: MIT Press, 1999), and Edward Miles, Arild Underdal, Steinar Andresen, Jorgen Wettestad, Tora Skodvin, and Elaine Carlin, *Environmental Regime Effectiveness* (Cambridge, MA: MIT Press, 2001).

17. For a complete discussion of the problems of the international whaling regime, see Robert Friedheim, ed., *Toward a Sustainable Whaling Regime* (Seattle: University of Washington Press, 2001).

18. Peter Haas, Robert Keohane, and Marc Levy, eds., *Institutions for the Earth: Sources of Effective International Environmental Protection* (Cambridge, MA: MIT Press, 1993).

19. Bureau of Arms Control, *Fact Sheet: The Biological Weapons Convention* (Washington, D.C.: U.S. Department of State, released May 22, 2002), viewed at http://www.state.gov/t/ac/rls/fs/10401.htm.

20. See, for example, Elizabeth DeSombre and J. Samuel Barkin, "Turbot and Tempers in the North Atlantic," in *Conserving the Peace: Resources, Livelihoods, and Security*, ed. Richard Matthew, Mark Halle, and Jason Switzer (Winnipeg: International Institute for Sustainable Development, 2002).

21. Ronald Mitchell, *Intentional Oil Pollution at Sea: Environmental Policy and Treaty Compliance* (Cambridge, MA: MIT Press, 1994).

22. On the debate about the relationship between regime compliance and regime effectiveness, see Abram Chayes and Antonia Handler Chayes, "On Compliance," *International Organization* 47 (1993): 175–205, and George Downs, David Rocke, and Peter Barsoom, "Is the Good News about Compliance Good News about Cooperation?" *International Organization* 50 (1996): 379–406.

23. For a discussion of international law and adjudication that both discusses and argues against the realist position, see Louis Henkin, *How Nations Behave: Law and Foreign Policy* (New York: Praeger, 1968).

24. Elizabeth R. DeSombre and Joanne Kauffman, "The Montreal Protocol Multilateral Fund: Partial Success Story," in *Institutions for Environmental Aid: Pitfalls and Promise*, ed. Robert Keohane and Marc Levy (Cambridge, MA: MIT Press, 1996).

25. GATT, *General Agreement on Tariffs and Trade*, Article XXIII.

26. For a more complete discussion of constitutive rules in international relations, see Alexander Wendt, *Social Theory of International Politics* (Cambridge, MA: Cambridge University Press, 1999). See also Nicholas Greenwood Onuf, *World of Our Making: Rules and Rule in Social Theory and International Relations* (Columbia: University of South Carolina Press, 1989).

27. WTO, "A Summary of the Final Act of the Uruguay Round," http://www.wto.org /english/docs_e/legal_e/ursum_e.htm.

28. For example, in the period between World Wars I and II, the U.S. approach to international trade was based on bilateral concessions, while British trade policy before World War I was based on unilateral free trade.

29. *Convention (IV) Relative to the Protection of Civilian Persons in Time of War*, United Nations Treaty Series No. 973, vol. 75, p. 287 (Geneva: UN, 1949).

30. For an argument that these ideas are gendered and can be biased in favor of some actors in international relations at the expense of others, see, respectively, Laura Sjoberg, "Gendered Realities of the Immunity Principle: Why Gender Analysis Needs Feminism," *International Studies Quarterly* 50 (2006): 889–910; and Thomas W. Smith, "The New Law of War: Legitimizing Hi-Tech and Infrastructural Violence," *International Studies Quarterly* 46 (2002): 355–374.

31. The seminal work on the role of legitimacy in the study of international organizations is Inis Claude, Jr., "Collective Legitimization as a Political Function of the United Nations," *International Organization* 20 (1966): 367–379. See also Ian Hurd, "Legitimacy and Authority in International Politics," *International Organization* 53 (1999): 379–408.

32. On the relationship between law and legitimacy in international relations, see Judith Goldstein, Miles Kahler, Robert Keohane, and Anne-Marie Slaughter, eds., *Legalization and World Politics* (Cambridge, MA: MIT Press, 2001) and Henkin, *How Nations Behave*.

33. J. Samuel Barkin and Bruce Cronin, "The State and the Nation: Changing Norms and Rules of Sovereignty in International Relations," *International Organization* 48 (1994): 107–130, and Thomas Biersteker and Cynthia Weber, eds., *State Sovereignty as a Social Construct* (Cambridge, MA: Cambridge University Press, 1996).

34. J. Samuel Barkin, "The Evolution of the Constitution of Sovereignty and the Emergence of Human Rights Norms," *Millennium* 27 (1998): 229–252.

35. For a discussion of the history and current state of international human rights agreements, see Jack Donnelly, *International Human Rights* (Boulder, CO: Westview, 1998).

36. See, for example, Rosemary Foot, *Rights beyond Borders: The Global Community and the Struggle over Human Rights in China* (Oxford: Oxford University Press, 2000).

37. Beth Simmons, *Mobilizing for Human Rights: International Law in Domestic Politics* (Cambridge: Cambridge University Press, 2009).

38. Robert Jackson, *Quasi-States: Sovereignty. International Relations, and the Third World* (Cambridge: Cambridge University Press, 1990).

39. World Trade Organization, "China to Join on 11 December, Chinese Taipei's Membership Also Approved," Doha WTO Ministerial 2001: Summary of 11 November 2001, http://www.wto.org/english/thewto_e/minist_e/min01_e/min01 _11nov_e.htm.

40. See, for example, Michael N. Barnett, *Eyewitness to a Genocide: The United Nations and Rwanda* (Ithaca, NY: Cornell University Press, 2002).

41. Jennifer Milliken, "The Study of Discourse in International Relations: A Critique of Research and Methods," *European Journal of International Relations* 5 (1999): 225–254.

42. See, for example, Peter Katzenstein, Robert Keohane, and Stephen Krasner, eds., *Exploration and Contestation in the Study of World Politics* (Cambridge, MA: MIT Press, 1999).

5 The United Nations and Its System

1. To complicate matters further, there are agencies jointly administered by subsidiary agencies and autonomous agencies. For example, the WFP is overseen jointly by ECOSOC and the FAO, and the Global Environment Facility (GEF) projects are created and managed jointly by (among other IOs) the World Bank, UNEP, and the UNDP, the latter two of which are themselves subsidiary agencies to both the GA and ECOSOC.

2. For an extreme example of the latter, see Jim Keith, *Black Helicopters over America: Strikeforce for the New World Order* (Lilburn, GA: IllumiNet Press, 1994).

3. For a more thorough discussion of multilateralism, see John Gerrard Ruggie, ed., *Multilateralism Matters: The Theory and Praxis of an Institutional Form* (New York: Columbia University Press, 1993).

4. United Nations, *Charter of the United Nations* (New York: UN, 1965), Article 18 (2).

5. The caucus got its name because it had seventy-seven members when it was founded in 1964. It currently has 131 members. More information on the organization can be found at its website, www.g77.org.

6. The Secretary-General's High-level Panel on Threats, Challenges and Change, *A More Secure World: Our Shared Responsibility* (New York: UN, 2004), p. 78.

7. Ibid.

8. Officially, the *1997 Convention on the Prohibition of the Use, Stockpiling, Production and Transfer of Antipersonnel Mines and Their Destruction*. The text can be found at International Campaign to Ban Landmines, "Text of the Mine Ban Treaty," http://www.icbl.org/treaty/text.

9. The designers of the Security Council did not use these terms, but the focus on these issues is implicit in the design of the institution.

10. The membership was originally eleven states, but was expanded in 1965 to allow for greater geographic representation as the process of decolonization increased numbers of states in much of the global South.

11. See, for example, Inis Claude Jr., *Swords into Plowshares*, 4th ed. (New York: Random House, 1984), pp. 157–158.

12. Membership in the UN "will be effected by a decision of the GA upon the recommendation of the Security Council." This means in effect that more than a third of the UN's members need to oppose a state's admission in the GA, but one of the permanent members can effectively veto admission in the Security Council. *UN Charter*, Article 4 (2).

13. The system of rotation of Security Council presidents is alphabetic, so all members of the Council will serve as president at least once during their tenure on the Council.

14. *UN Charter*, Article 97.

15. *UN Charter*, Article 99. Gendered language in the original.

16. *UN Charter*, Article 100, paragraph 2. The entire staff of the Secretariat is similarly supposed to be politically neutral, in other words to work for the UN, not for member states.

17. Historically, thus far always a he.
18. For a political history of Secretaries-General, see Stanley Meisler, *United Nations: A History*, rev. ed. (New York: Grove Press, 2011).
19. A complete list of these representatives can be found at http://www.un.org/News /ossg/srsg/.
20. Depending on how one counts. This figure includes staff directly answerable to the Secretary General, including regional commissions and tribunals but not including peacekeeping and related operations. The number of staff at UN headquarters in New York and Geneva number just under 10,000. United Nations Secretary General, *Composition of the Secretariat: Staff Demographics* (UN General Assembly Document A/65/350. New York: UN, 2010).
21. See, for example, two reports of the Secretary-General, *Renewing the United Nations: A Programme for Reform* (New York: United Nations General Assembly A/51/950, 1997) and *Strengthening the United Nations: An Agenda for Further Change* (New York: United Nations General Assembly A/57/387, 2002).
22. A list of these countries, and the declarations by which they have committed themselves, can be found at http://www.icj-cij.org/icjwww/ibasicdocuments/ibasictext /ibasicdeclarations.htm.
23. *UN Charter*, Article 73, chapeau.

6 From International to Human Security

1. See, for example, Robert Jervis, "Security Regimes," *International Organization* 36 (1982): 357–378 and John Mearsheimer, "The False Promise of International Institutions," *International Security* 19 (1994–1995): 5–49.
2. On which see, for example, Paul Diehl, *International Peacekeeping* (Baltimore, MD: Johns Hopkins University Press, 1994).
3. All of the quotations in this paragraph are from United Nations, *Charter of the United Nations* (New York: UN, 1965).
4. United Nations, "Year in Review: United Nations Peacekeeping Operations, 2011," United Nations Department of Public Information (DPI/2579/Rev. 1, March 2012), p. 74.
5. United Nations General Assembly, *Resolution 60/1: 2005 World Summit Outcome* (New York: UN, 2005), p. 30.
6. The wording of the UN Charter suggests that a resolution needs all five permanent members to vote in favor if it is to pass. But in actual practice, abstentions by permanent members do not prevent a resolution from passing, only votes against it do. See the *UN Charter*, Article 27.
7. The USSR was an original permanent member of the Security Council. When the Soviet Union broke up in 1990, Russia adopted both the international prerogatives and the international responsibilities of the USSR, including the permanent seat.
8. See, for example, David Pilling, "Japan Urged to Cut Payments to UN," *Financial Times*, January 17, 2003.
9. See, for example, Kofi Annan, "Secretary-General's Address to the General Assembly, New York, 23 September 2003," http://www.un.org/apps/sg/sgstats.asp? nid=517.
10. "2005 World Summit Outcome," United Nations General Assembly Resolution A/60/L1 (New York: UN, 2005), Article 153.
11. This approval was forthcoming in "Security Council Resolution 1483," United Nations Security Council S/RES/1031, 22 May, 2003.

7 The Institutions of Collective Security

1. More information on the DPKO can be found at the organization's website, http:// www.un.org/Depts/dpko/dpko/index.asp.
2. There are exceptions to this rule; for example, the Secretary-General's Special Representative for Kosovo is also head of the UN's Interim Administration Mission in Kosovo (UNMIK). But the Representative's authority over the mission comes from a Security Council resolution (resolution 1244), not from the Secretary-General.
3. Cf. Chapter 5, note 19, in this book.
4. United Nations Secretary-General, *Implementing the Responsibility to Protect: Report of the Secretary-General* (UN General Assembly Document A/63/677. New York: UN, 2009), and United Nations General Assembly, *The Responsibility to Protect* (UN General Assembly Resolution 63/308. New York: UN, 2009), respectively.
5. The AU was created in 2002, amalgamating the Organization of African Unity (OAU), an organization that dealt with regional collective security issues, and the African Economic Community.
6. Technically, the Organ on Politics, Defence and Security Co-operation of the SADC. See the Protocol on Politics, Defence and Security Co-operation to the Declaration and Treaty of SADC (2001), http://www.sadc.int/english/key -documents/protocols/protocol-on-politics-defence-and-security-cooperation/.
7. A map of member and partner countries can be found at http://www.nato.int /icons/map/b-worldmap.jpg.
8. The peace treaty did call on the Security Council to legitimize the peace treaty through a resolution, which it did. See "Security Council Resolution 1031 (1995) on implementation of the Peace Agreement for Bosnia and Herzegovina and the transfer of authority from the UN Protection Force to the multinational Implementation Force (IFOR)," United Nations Security Council S/RES/1031, December 15, 1995.
9. Formally the *Convention on the Prohibition of the Use, Stockpiling, Production and Transfer of Anti-Personnel Mines and on Their Destruction*, also known as the Ottawa Treaty.
10. United Nations Office for Disarmament Affairs, *Treaty on the Non-Proliferation of Nuclear Weapons*, Article III, http://disarmament.un.org/treaties/t/npt/text.
11. International Atomic Energy Agency, "Member States of the IAEA," http://iaea .org/About/Policy/MemberStates/.
12. International Atomic Energy Agency, *IAEA Annual Report 2010* (Vienna: IAEA, 2011), p. v.
13. On the history of war crimes tribunals, see Gary Jonathan Bass, *Stay the Hand of Vengeance: The Politics of War-Crimes Tribunals* (Princeton, NJ: Princeton University Press, 2000).
14. See the International Criminal Court, *Rome Statute of the International Criminal Court* (The Hague: ICC, 1998), Articles 11 and 12, and International Criminal Court, *Resolution RC/Res.6: The Crime of Aggression* (The Hague: ICC, 2010).
15. International Criminal Court, *Rome Statute of the International Criminal Court*. (The Hague: ICC, 1998), Article 36, 3a.
16. The International Criminal Court, *The Court Today*, updated: April 11, 2012 (The Hague: ICC, 2012).
17. United Nations Security Council, *Security Council Resolution 1593* (New York: UN, 2005).

18. For a brief statement on the U.S. government's position on the ICC, see United States Department of State, "International Criminal Court," Office of Global Criminal Justice, Washington, D.C, http://www.state.gov/j/gcj/icc/.

19. Security Council Resolution 1031. The OSCE is mentioned by name in Article 6. In Article 14, NATO is referred to as "the organization referred to in annex 1-A of the Peace Agreement," which is a rather unwieldy way of saying NATO.

20. On the various aspects of NATO's new mission, and its reorganization to achieve that mission, see NATO Office of Information and Press, *NATO Handbook* (Brussels: NATO, 2001).

8 Human Rights and Humanitarian Aid

1. A fairly comprehensive list of these treaties can be found on the website of the Fletcher Multilaterals Project, a service of Tufts University's Fletcher School, at http://fletcher.archive.tusm-oit.org/multilaterals/humanRights.html. For good general discussions of international human rights issues, see Jack Donnelly, *International Human Rights*, 3rd ed. (Boulder, CO: Westview Press, 2006) and David P. Forsythe, *Human Rights in International Relations*, 2nd ed. (Cambridge: Cambridge University Press, 2006).

2. See, for example, *Convention against Torture and Other Cruel, Inhuman or Degrading Treatment or Punishment,* UN General Assembly RES 39/46 Annex (New York: UN, 1984), Articles 17 and 18, and the *International Convention on the Elimination of All Forms of Racial Discrimination*, 60 UNTS 195 (New York: UN, 1966), Article 8.

3. There are currently ten of these bodies created by treaties covering economic, social, and cultural rights; human rights; torture; enforced disappearances; racial discrimination; discrimination against women; discrimination against people with disabilities; the rights of migrant workers; and the rights of the child.

4. See, for example, Barry James, "Libya to Lead UN Human Rights Body; Tripoli Easily Wins Vote US Demanded," *International Herald Tribune*, January 21, 2003, p. 1.

5. The Secretary-General's High-level Panel on Threats, Challenges and Change, *A More Secure World: Our Shared Responsibility* (New York: UN, 2004), p. 89 (quotation) and pp. 88–90 (recommendations).

6. Office of the High Commissioner for Human Rights, "United Nations Human Rights Council," http://www.ohchr.org/EN/HRBodies/HRC/Pages/AboutCouncil .aspx.

7. United Nations General Assembly, *Resolution 48/141: High Commissioner for the Promotion and Protection of All Human Rights* (New York: UN, 1994).

8. On the role of NGO groups, or "advocacy networks," in the international politics of human rights, see Margaret E. Keck and Kathryn Sikkink, *Activists beyond Borders: Advocacy Networks in International Politics* (Ithaca, NY: Cornell University Press, 1998).

9. Kosovo is also not a member, but it is not recognized by the United Nations as a sovereign state.

10. The text of the European Convention on Human Rights can be found at http://conventions.coe.int/treaty/en/Treaties/html/005.htm.

11. See, for example, Council of Europe, "Execution of Judgments of the European Court of Human Rights," http://www.coe.int/t/dghl/monitoring/execution/default _EN.asp.

12. This argument is made in J. Samuel Barkin, "The Evolution of the Constitution of Sovereignty and the Emergence of Human Rights Norms," *Millennium* 27 (1998): 229–252.

13. See Daniel C. Thomas, *The Helsinki Effect: International Norms, Human Rights, and the Demise of Communism* (Princeton, NJ: Princeton University Press, 2001).

14. The WFP does engage in what it calls development aid. This is still food aid, but it is targeted at long-term malnutrition rather than crisis starvation. In any case, this development aid accounted, as of 2001, for only 13 percent of expenditures. See World Food Programme, *WFP in Statistics—2001* (Rome: WFP, 2003), table 1.

15. In a total budget of about $1.8 billion for 2009, the UNHCR was expecting $40 million from the UN regular budget. Office of the United Nations High Commissioner for Refugees, Contri*butions to UNHCR Programmes for Budget Year 2009: As at 31 December 2009* (Geneva: UNHCR, 2010).

16. Even then, the idea was not a new one. The League of Nations had named a High Commissioner for Refugees, Fritjof Nansen, in 1921.

17. The major exception to this rule is activities relating to Palestinian Refugees, which are undertaken by UNRWA, the United Nations Relief and Works Agency for Palestinian Refugees in the Near East.

18. United Nations High Commission for Refugees, "Staff Figures," http://www .unhcr.org/pages/49c3646c17.html.

19. Figures for the breakdown of funding sources are for 2010, and are from United Nations High Commission for Refugees, *UNHCR Global Report 2010* (Geneva: UNHCR, 2011), pp. 85–88.

20. At the "Donate Online" link on the WFP's homepage at www.wfp.org. There is a similar "donor button" on the UNHCR's homepage at www.unhcr.org.

21. Figures on amounts donated for the last several years can be found at World Food Programme, "Government Donors," http://www.wfp.org/government-donors.

22. The WFP figure is from World Food Programme, "WFP in Numbers," http:// www.wfp.org/wfp-numbers. The UNHCR figure is from UNHCR, "What We Do," http://www.unhcr.org/pages/49c3646cbf.html. "Helped" can mean anything from providing food and shelter to providing legal advice.

23. This critique is made, among other places, in Michael Barnett and Martha Finnemore, *Rules for the World: International Organizations in Global Politics* (Ithaca, NY: Cornell University Press, 2004).

24. See, for example, Adamantia Pollis, "Liberal, Socialist, and Third World Perspectives on Human Rights," in *Human Rights in the World Community*, ed. Richard Claude and Burns Weston, 2nd ed. (Philadelphia: University of Pennsylvania Press, 1992).

25. For an argument that the promotion of human rights internationally is in the U.S. national interest, see William F. Schultz, *In Our Own Best Interest: How Defending Human Rights Benefits Us All* (Boston, MA: Beacon Press, 2001).

9 Economic Institutions and Trade

1. And seen as well at meetings of other related international regimes, particularly meetings of the G-8, which will be discussed in the next chapter.

2. See, for example, Jeffrey Chwieroth, *Capital Ideas: The IMF and the Rise of Financial Liberalization* (Princeton: Princeton University Press, 2010).

3. See, for example, Joseph Stiglitz, *Globalization and Its Discontents* (New York: Norton, 2002).

4. See World Trade Organization, *10 Common Misunderstandings about the WTO* (Geneva: WTO, 2008).

5. A good discussion of the negotiations that led to the creation of the GATT, as well as the IMF and World Bank, during and immediately after World War II can be found in Richard Gardner, *Sterling-Dollar Diplomacy: Anglo-American Collaboration in the Reconstruction of Multilateral Trade* (Oxford: Clarendon Press, 1956).

6. These include agreements on Sanitary and Phytosanitary Measures (SPS), Technical Barriers to Trade (TBT), and Trade-Related Investment Measures (TRIMs). A complete list of these agreements can be found at http://www.wto.org/english/docs _e/legal_e/legal_e.htm.

7. There are some exceptions to this rule, but these are either committees/councils that are strictly advisory in nature or that deal with rules that do not apply to all of the WTO's member countries. An example is the Committee on Trade in Civil Aircraft. A complete organizational chart of the WTO can be found at http://www .wto.org/english/thewto_e/whatis_e/tif_e/org2_e.htm.

8. Organizationally, it reports both to the General Council and to the Director-General.

9. This process worked smoothly in choosing the current Director-General, Pascal Lamy (currently serving his second term in the position). In the previous attempt to choose a Director-General, developed and developing countries could not agree. The compromise reached was that the standard term would be split in half, the first half of which would be served by a New Zealander, Mike Moore, and the second half by a Thai, Supachai Panitchpakdi.

10. The member states of the EU have formally ceded control over tariff policy to the Union. As such, it is the EU that is the formal negotiating party at the WTO, rather than its member countries.

11. These commitments currently run to 30,000 pages (because existing members have made new commitments, and new members have joined the WTO), and can be found at http://www.wto.org/english/docs_e/legal_e/legal_e.htm.

12. Recall from Chapter 4 that in a perfect market, with perfectly specified property rights, the market will always produce the most efficient outcome, but different sets of property rights will result in different allocations of the wealth from that outcome. "Better" in this sense refers only to the efficiency of the outcome, and not to the appropriateness or fairness of the allocation of the benefits from this efficiency.

13. See, for example, Jagdish Bhagwati, *Termites in the Trading System: How Preferential Agreements Undermine Free Trade* (New York: Oxford University Press, 2008).

14. Figures from World Intellectual Property Organization, *Annual Report 2011* (Geneva: WIPO, 2011).

15. More information on WIPO can be found at the organization's website, http:// www.wipo.int.

16. For discussions of the Marshall Plan, see Michael Hogan, *The Marshall Plan: America, Britain, and the Reconstruction of Europe, 1947–1952* (Cambridge: Cambridge University Press, 1987) and Alan Milward, *The Reconstruction of Western Europe, 1945–51* (Berkeley: University of California Press, 1984).

17. This was not the OECD's first venture in this issue-area. It also sponsored the Convention on the Protection of Foreign Property in 1967.

18. On forum-shopping see, for example, Kal Raustiala and David Victor, "The Regime Complex for Plant Genetic Resources," *International Organization* 58 (2004): 277–309.

10 International Finance

1. In 2011, for example, the Fund ran a profit of about $1,260 million, up from $340 million the year before. See International Monetary Fund, *Annual Report 2011: Pursuing Equitable and Balanced Growth* (Washington, DC: IMF, 2011), appendix VI, pp. 6 and 9. The IMF has its own internal accounting currency, the Special Drawing Right (SDR), but for convenience figures here are translated into U.S. dollars.

2. The current distribution of votes can be found at http://www.imf.org/external/np/sec/memdir/members.aspx.

3. Italy and Canada are larger shareholders than Russia, and Italy is a larger shareholder than Saudi Arabia, yet neither country has its own Executive Director.

4. For example, the Netherlands has 46 percent of the vote in its group, and the Director from this group is Dutch. The alternate is from the Ukraine, which holds the second largest bloc of votes in the group.

5. Figures are for fiscal year 2011, and are from IMF, *Annual Report 2011*, p. 53.

6. An organizational chart for the IMF can be found at http://www.imf.org/external/np/obp/orgcht.htm.

7. As of April, 2011. From IMF, *Annual Report 2011*, Appendix II.

8. IMF, "Factsheet: IMF Surveillance—March 2012," http://www.imf.org/external/np/exr/facts/surv.htm.

9. Specific conditions agreed to between various countries and the IMF can be found at the "Country Information" gateway on the IMF's website, at http://www.imf.org/external/country/index.htm.

10. An explanation of conditionality by the IMF can be found in "Factsheet: IMF Conditionality," available at http://www.imf.org/external/np/exr/facts/conditio.htm.

11. For a general overview of criticisms of conditionality from the perspective of an international economist, see Joseph Stiglitz, *Globalization and Its Discontents* (New York: Norton, 2002).

12. Although, as is discussed below, the IMF has indeed been criticized on occasion for making lending decisions on political criteria when these loans did not really make economic sense.

13. On both of these arguments, see Manuel Guitián, *The Unique Nature of the Responsibilities of the International Monetary Fund*, Pamphlet Series #46 (Washington, DC: IMF, 1992).

14. International Monetary Fund, *Annual Report 2007: Making the Global Economy Work for All* (Washington, DC: IMF, 2007), Appendix VI, p. 4.

15. International Monetary Fund, "IMF Executive Board Considers Use of Windfall Gold Sales Profit," IMF Public Information Notice 11/121, September 16, 2011. The IMF is now planning to use much of the money raised to fund concessional lending (i.e., at less than market rates) to the poorest countries.

16. Leo Van Houtven, *Governance of the IMF: Decision-Making, Institutional Oversight, Transparency, and Accountability*, Pamphlet Series #53 (Washington, DC: IMF, 2002).

17. IMF, *Annual Report 2011*, pp. 36–38.

18. For a discussion of the role of international lender of last resort, see Charles Kindleberger, *Manias, Panics, and Crashes: A History of Financial Crises* (New York: Basic Books, 1978).

19. Criticism of the IMF on this point was particularly acute with respect to loans to Russia in the 1990s. See, for example, Zanny Minton Beddoes, "Why the IMF Needs Reform," *Foreign Affairs* 74 (May–June 1995): 123–133.

20. The ECB is not discussed here because it is part of the EU, and is therefore covered by the broader decision not to examine the EU in this book.
21. Bank for International Settlements, "About BIS," http://www.bis.org/about/index.htm?ql=1.
22. Bank for International Settlements, *81st Annual Report* (Basel: BIS, 2011).

11 Development

1. There were discussions about a regional equivalent of the IMF for Asia in the wake of the East Asian financial crisis of 1997. While this has not resulted in a new IO, it has resulted in a multilateral agreement by several East and Southeast Asian countries, called the Chiang Mai Initiative, to support each other's currencies in monetary crises.
2. The United States and Japan are tied at first place in the Asian Development Bank, with roughly 13 percent of the vote each (shares of the vote can be found at Asian Development Bank, "Members," http://www.adb.org/about/members).
3. World Bank Group, *The World Bank Annual Report 2011: Year in Review* (Washington, DC: World Bank, 2011).
4. The Bank itself uses "World Bank" to refer to the IBRD and IDA, and "World Bank Group" to refer to all five institutions.
5. The best-known result of the World Bank's efforts to collect and disseminate information is its annual *World Development Reports.*
6. See, for example, Martha Finnemore, *National Interests in International Society* (Ithaca, NY: Cornell University Press, 1996).
7. Ibid.
8. On the Bank's efforts on the environment, see Tamar L. Gutner, *Banking on the Environment: Multilateral Development Banks and Their Environmental Performance in Central and Eastern Europe* (Cambridge, MA: MIT Press, 2002).
9. See, for example, World Bank, *Making Sustainable Commitments: An Environment Strategy for the World Bank* (Washington, DC: World Bank, 2001). On the mixed success of these efforts, see Gutner, *Banking on the Environment.*
10. An example of this change can be seen in the film *Our Friends at the Bank* (New York: First Run/Icarus Films, 1997), in which Ugandan officials tell Bank officials that they need money for roads, and the Bank officials respond that they prefer to loan money for education and social development programs.
11. For an example of this criticism from an environmental perspective, see Bruce Rich, *Mortgaging the Earth: The World Bank, Environmental Impoverishment, and the Crisis of Development* (Boston, MA: Beacon Press, 1994).
12. See, for example, Finnemore, *National Interests,* and Daniel Nielson and Michael Tierney, "Delegation to International Organizations: Agency Theory and World Bank Environmental Reform," *International Organization* 57 (2003): 241–276.
13. This terminology is not universally used—"development assistance" is sometimes used to cover both aid-granting institutions and the development lenders.
14. Specifically, the Technical Assistance Board and the United Nations Special Fund. For a complete history of the UNDP, see Craig Murphy, *The United Nations Development Programme: A Better Way?* (Cambridge: Cambridge University Press, 2006).
15. See, for example, United Nations Development Programme, *UNDP in Action— Annual Report 2010/2011* (New York: UNDP, 2011).
16. Ibid., p. 38.
17. Ibid., p. 39.

18. See, for example, Murphy, *The United Nations Development Programme*.
19. For details of the various UNCTAD technical cooperation programs, see the "Technical Cooperation" section of UNCTAD's website at http://www.unctad.org.
20. The G-77 in fact grew out of the first UNCTAD meeting in 1964, and some G-77 projects, such as the Global System of Trade Preferences among Developing Countries (GSTP), are run through the UNCTAD Secretariat. Information on the GSTP can be found at its website, http://www.g77.org/gstp/index.htm.
21. For a discussion of the rise and fall of the NIEO, see Stephen Krasner, *Structural Conflict: The Third World against Global Liberalism* (Berkeley: University of California Press, 1985).
22. The primary process for doing this is through the United Nations Development Assistance Framework (UNDAF). For details about this program, see United Nations Development Assistance Framework, *UNDAF Guidelines* (New York: United Nations, 1999).
23. The multilateral development community has also recently been coalescing around the idea of good governance, but it is not clear at this point to what extent this idea has been promoted independently by the IOs, and to what extent it reflects the policies of the major donor countries.
24. As of 2011. The five countries are Denmark, the Netherlands, Sweden, Norway, and Luxembourg. Organization for Economic Cooperation and Development, "Net ODA in 2011," http://webnet.oecd.org/oda2011/.
25. United Nations General Assembly, *Resolution 2626 (XXV): International Development Strategy for the Second United Nations Development Decade* (New York: UN, 1970)
26. United Nations General Assembly, *Resolution 55/2: United Nations Millennium Declaration* (New York: UN, 2000).

12 The Environment

1. For a general overview of global environmental governance, see Elizabeth R. DeSombre, *The Global Environment and World Politics*, 2nd ed. (London: Continuum, 2007).
2. See, for example, J. Samuel Barkin and George Shambaugh, eds., *Anarchy and the Environment: The International Relations of Common Pool Resources* (Albany: State University of New York Press, 1999).
3. On sustainable development as understood within the UN system, see World Commission on Environment and Development, *Our Common Future* (Oxford: Oxford University Press, 1987).
4. The document from Rio+20 is United Nations Conference on Sustainable Development, *The Future We Want* (Rio de Janeiro: UNCSD, 2012).
5. On the design goals and features of UNEP, see Maria Ivanova, "Institutional Design and UNEP Reform: Historical Insights on Form, Function, and Financing," *International Affairs* 88 (2012): 565–584.
6. United Nations Environment Programme, "Environment Fund—Top 20 Donor Countries—Trend in Contributions in 2008–2010," http://www.unep.org/rms/en/Financing_of_UNEP/Environment_Fund/pdf/Top%2020%20Donors%202008.2010%2018.2.2011.pdf.
7. For details see United Nations Environment Programme, *Annual Report 2010* (Nairobi: UNEP, 2011), pp. 10–13.
8. Ibid., pp. 8–9.

9. Ivanova, "Institutional Design and UN Reform," p. 568.

10. See, for example, Frank Biermann and Steffen Bauer, eds., *A World Environment Organization: Solution or Threat for Effective International Environmental Governance* (Aldershot, UK: Ashgate, 2005), for both sides of this argument.

11. See, for example, J. Samuel Barkin, "The Environment, Trade, and International Organizations," in *International Handbook of Environmental Politics*, edited by Peter Dauvergne (London: Edward Elgar, 2005).

12. Ivanova, "Institutional Design."

13. UNCSD, *The Future We Want*.

14. Northwest Atlantic Fisheries Organization, *Annual Report 2011* (Dartmouth, NS: NAFO, 2012), p. 3.

15. On the structure of MEAs in the context of IOs generally, and environmental IOs specifically, see Elizabeth R. DeSombre, *Global Environmental Institutions* (New York: Routledge, 2006).

16. Ibid.

17. For more information, see Global Environment Facility, "What Is the GEF," http:// www.thegef.org/gef/whatisgef.

18. For a complete overview of the global fisheries governance system, see J. Samuel Barkin and Elizabeth R. DeSombre, *Saving Global Fisheres: Reducing Fishing Capacity to Promote Sustainability* (Cambridge, MA: MIT Press, 2013).

19. DeSombre, *The Global Environment and World Politics*.

20. Northwest Atlantic Fisheries Organization, "Scientific Council," http://www.nafo .int/science/frames/science.html.

21. For a discussion of this process, see Marc Levy, "European Acid Rain: The Power of Tote-Board Diplomacy," in *Institutions for the Earth: Sources of Effective International Environmental Protection*, edited by Peter M. Haas, Robert O. Keohane, and Marc A. Levy (Cambridge, MA: MIT Press, 1993).

22. For a full discussion of the role of science and scientists in environmental IOs, see DeSombre, *The Global Environment and World Politics*, chapter 4.

23. United Nations General Assembly, *Resolution 43/53: Protection of Global Climate for Present and Future Generations of Mankind* (New York: UN, 1988).

24. The assessment reports are long enough that they are now published in four volumes. The summary assessment of the fourth report can be found in Intergovernmental Panel on Climate Change, *Climate Change 2007: Synthesis Report* (Geneva: IPCC, 2008).

25. Intergovernmental Panel on Climate Change, "Principles Governing IPCC Work," http://www.ipcc.ch/pdf/ipcc-principles/ipcc-principles.pdf.

13 The Technical Details

1. Universal Postal Union, "The UPU," http://www.upu.int/en/the-upu/the-upu.html.

2. Universal Postal Union, "About Terminal Dues and Transit Charges," http://www .upu.int/en/activities/terminal-dues-and-transit-charges/about-terminal-dues-and -transit-charges.html.

3. Universal Postal Union, "About Financial Inclusion," http://www.upu.int/en /activities/financial-inclusion/about-financial-inclusion.html.

4. International Civil Aviation Organization, "How It Works," http://www.icao.int /pages/how-it-works.aspx.

5. For a broader discussion of this topic, see Baldav Raj Nayar, "Regimes, Power, and International Aviation," *International Organization* 49 (1995): 139–170.

6. See, respectively, Article 2, paragraph 2 of the Kyoto Protocol to the United Nations Framework Convention on Climate Change, and International Civil Aviation Organization, *Resolution A37–19: Consolidated Statement of Continuing ICAO Policies and Practices Related to Environmental Protection—Climate Change* (Montreal: ICAO, 2010).

7. World Health Organization, *Constitution of the World Health Organization* (Geneva: WHO, 1994), Article 1.

8. Technically, avian influenza. For more information on the role of the WHO in the bird flu outbreak, see the organization's avian influenza homepage, at http://www.who.int/mediacentre/factsheets/avian_influenza/en/index.html.

9. World Health Organization, *Financial Report and Audited Financial Statements for the Period 1 January 2010–31 December 2011 and Report of the External Auditor to the World Health Assembly* (Geneva: WHO, 2012).

10. *Constitution of the World Health Organization,* Article 24.

11. See, for example, F. Fenner, D. A. Henderson, I. Arita, Z. Jezek, and I. D. Ladnyi, *Smallpox and Its Eradication* (Geneva: WHO, 1988).

12. Eric Stein, "International Integration and Democracy: No Love at First Sight," *American Journal of International Law* 95 (2001): 498–499.

13. See, for example, World Health Organization, *Report of the Director-General, 2001* (Geneva: WHO, 2002).

14. Stein, "International Integration and Democracy."

15. Ibid., p. 497.

16. For more information on the Convention process, and on the WHO's Tobacco Free Initiative more broadly, see http://www.who.int/tobacco/en/.

17. On the distinction between the coordination and PD game, see Duncan Snidal, "Coordination Versus Prisoners' Dilemma: Implications for International Cooperation and Regimes," *American Political Science Review* 79 (1985): 923–942.

18. See, respectively, *Convention on the Marking of Plastic Explosives for the Purpose of Detection,* accessible at http://www.un.org/en/sc/ctc/docs/conventions/Conv10.pdf, and World Health Assembly Resolution WHA55.2, "Health Conditions of, and Assistance to, the Arab Population in the Occupied Arab Territories, Including Palestine," *Fifty-Fifth World Health Assembly,* Document WHA55/2002/REC/1 (Geneva: WHO, 2002).

14   The Fuzzy Borders of Intergovernmentalism

1. Ernst Haas, *Beyond the Nation-State: Functionalism and International Organization* (Stanford: Stanford University Press, 1964).

2. ICPO-Interpol, *Interpol Annual Report 2010* (Lyon: Interpol, 2011), p. 46.

3. For a more detailed version of this story, see Michael Fooner, *A Guide to Interpol: The International Criminal Police Organization in the United States* (Washington, D.C.: US Department of Justice, National Institute of Justice, 1985).

4. ICPO-Interpol, *Constitution* (Lyon: Interpol, 2004), Article 7.

5. Some of these can be found at http://www.interpol.int/INTERPOL-expertise/Notices.

6. International Organization for Standardization, "ISO in Figures for the Year 2011 (at 31 December)," http://www.iso.org/iso/iso-in-figures_2011.pdf.

7. For a complete discussion of ISO, see Craig Murphy and JoAnne Yates, *The International Organization for Standardization (ISO): Global Governance through Voluntary Consensus* (New York: Routledge, 2009).

8. International Organization for Standardization, "ISO Members," http://www.iso .org/iso/iso_members.

9. Steven Levy, "INTELSAT: Technology, Politics, and the Transformation of a Regime," *International Organization* 29 (1975): 655–680.

10. Jonathan Galloway, "Worldwide Corporations and International Integration: The Case of INTELSAT," *International Organization* 24 (1970): 503–519.

11. Levy, "INTELSAT."

12. Ibid.

13. Some of these investor companies are themselves government-owned, but are nonetheless investors in INTELSAT on a purely commercial basis.

14. "Privatization of INTELSAT," *American Journal of International Law* 95 (2001): 893–895.

15. International Union for Conservation of Nature and Natural Resources, *Statutes and Regulations* (Gland, Switzerland: IUCN, 2012), Article 2.

16. For NGOs dues depend on the organizations' operating expenditures. Figures are for dues for 2012, taken from IUCN, *IUCN Membership Dues Guide 2009–2012* (Gland, Switzerland: IUCN, 2010).

17. There are further complications in the voting structure within the categories; for example, national NGOs get one vote while international NGOs get two. For details see IUCN, *Statutes and Regulations*, Articles 30–35.

18. IUCN, *Statutes and Regulations*, Article 38.

19. International Union for Conservation of Nature and Natural Resources, "The IUCN Red List of Threatened Species," http://www.iucnredlist.org/.

20. See, inter alia, Articles 8, 13, and 14 of the treaty, which can be found on the UNESCO website at http://whc.unesco.org/en/conventiontext.

21. At the time of writing, this translated into a U.S. contribution of $300 million, and a Guyanan contribution of $1,500, of a total ICRC budget of 830 million Swiss francs, or $950 million. International Committee of the Red Cross, *Annual Report 2010* (Geneva: ICRC, 2011), pp. 530–532.

22. François Bugnion, "The Composition of the International Committee of the Red Cross," *International Review of the Red Cross* 307 (1995): 427–446.

23. In 1976, a majority of African countries boycotted the Olympics in Montreal to protest the participation of South African teams in some international competitions. In 1980, the United States led a boycott of the Olympics in Moscow to protest the Soviet invasion of Afghanistan. And in 1984, the USSR boycotted the Olympics in Los Angeles in retaliation for the 1980 boycott.

24. For a more detailed discussion of these rules, see International Olympic Committee, *Olympic Charter* (Lausanne: IOC, 2011).

25. International Olympic Committee, *Olympic Marketing Fact File*, 2012 ed. (Lausanne: IOC, 2012).

26. International Committee of the Red Cross, "ICRC 2001 Financial Statements Meet International Accounting Standards—ICRC First Humanitarian Organization to Apply IAS," ICRC Press Release 02/45, August 16, 2002.

15 Conclusions

1. Daniel Drezner, *All Politics Is Global: Explaining International Regulatory Regimes* (Princeton: Princeton University Press, 2007), p. 72.

2. Information on the UN Global Compact can be found at its website, http://www .unglobalcompact.org/.

References

Print Sources

Allison, Graham. *Essence of Decision: Explaining the Cuban Missile Crisis.* Boston, MA: Little, Brown, 1971.

Armstrong, David, ed. *Routledge Handbook of International Law.* New York: Routledge, 2009.

Aron, William. "Science and the IWC." In *Toward a Sustainable Whaling Regime,* edited by Robert Friedheim, pp. 105–122. Seattle: University of Washington Press, 2001.

Bachrach, Peter, and Morton Baratz. "Two Faces of Power." *American Political Science Review* 56 (1962): 947–952.

Baldwin, David, ed. *Neorealism and Neoliberalism: The Contemporary Debate.* New York: Columbia University Press, 1993.

Bank for International Settlements. *81st Annual Report.* Basel: BIS, 2011.

Barkin, J. Samuel. "The Evolution of the Constitution of Sovereignty and the Emergence of Human Rights Norms." *Millennium* 27 (1998): 229–252.

———. "Time Horizons and Multilateral Enforcement in International Cooperation." *International Studies Quarterly* 48 (2004): 363–382.

———. "The Environment, Trade, and International Organizations." In *International Handbook of Environmental Politics,* edited by Peter Dauvergne. London: Edward Elgar, 2005.

Barkin, J. Samuel, and Bruce Cronin. "The State and the Nation: Changing Norms and Rules of Sovereignty in International Relations." *International Organization* 48 (1994): 107–130.

Barkin, J. Samuel, and Elizabeth R. DeSombre. "Unilateralism and Multilateralism in International Fisheries Management." *Global Governance* 6 (2000): 339–360.

———. *Saving Global Fisheres: Reducing Fishing Capacity to Promote Sustainability.* Cambridge, MA: MIT Press, 2013.

Barkin, J. Samuel, and George Shambaugh, eds. *Anarchy and the Environment: The International Relations of Common Pool Resources.* Albany: State University of New York Press, 1999.

Barnett, Michael. *Eyewitness to a Genocide: The United Nations and Rwanda.* Ithaca, NY: Cornell University Press, 2002.

Barnett, Michael, and Raymond Duvall. "Power in International Politics." *International Organization* 59 (2005): 39–75.

Barnett, Michael, and Martha Finnemore. "The Power, Politics, and Pathologies of International Organizations." *International Organization* 53 (1999): 699–732.

———. *Rules for the World: International Organizations in Global Politics.* Ithaca, NY: Cornell University Press, 2004.

Bass, Gary Jonathan. *Stay the Hand of Vengeance: The Politics of War-Crimes Tribunals.* Princeton, NJ: Princeton University Press, 2000.

"Battling over Racism: The UN Racism Conference." *The Economist*, August 24, 2001.

Beddoes, Zanny Minton. "Why the IMF Needs Reform." *Foreign Affairs* 74 (May–June 1995): 123–133.

Bernstein, Steven. *The Compromise of Liberal Environmentalism.* New York: Columbia University Press, 2001.

Bhagwati, Jagdish. *In Defense of Globalization.* New York: Oxford University Press, 2004.

———. *Termites in the Trading System: How Preferential Agreements Undermine Free Trade.* New York: Oxford University Press, 2008.

Biermann, Frank, and Steffen Bauer. *A World Environmental Organization: Solution or Threat for Effective International Environmental Governance?* Aldershot: Ashgate, 2005.

Biersteker, Thomas, and Cynthia Weber, eds. St*ate Sovereignty as a Social Construct.* Cambridge: Cambridge University Press, 1996.

Bugnion, François. "The Composition of the International Committee of the Red Cross." *International Review of the Red Cross* 307 (1995): 427–446.

Bull, Hedley. The *Anarchical Society: A Study of Order in World Politics.* London: Macmillan, 1977.

Burgerman, Susan. *Moral Victories: How Activists Provoke Multilateral Action.* Ithaca, NY: Cornell University Press, 2001.

Chayes, Abram, and Antonia Handler Chayes. "On Compliance." *International Organization* 47 (1993): 175–205.

———. *The New Sovereignty: Compliance with International Regulatory Agreements.* Cambridge, MA: Harvard University Press, 1995.

Chwieroth, Jeffrey. *The IMF and the Rise of Financial Liberalization.* Princeton: Princeton University Press, 2010.

Clapp, Jennifer. "Africa, NGOs, and the International Toxic Waste Trade." *Journal of Environment and Development* 3 (1994): 17–46.

Claude, Inis Jr. "Collective Legitimation as a Political Function of the United Nations." *International Organization* 20 (1966): 367–379.

———. *Swords into Plowshares*, 4th ed. New York: Random House, 1984.

Convention for the Conservation of Antarctic Marine Living Resources. *Basic Documents.* North Hobart, Australia: CCAMLR, 2004.

Cox, Robert, and Harold Jacobson, eds. *The Anatomy of Influence: Decision-Making in International Organization.* New Haven, CT: Yale University Press, 1973.

Dahl, Robert. *Who Governs? Democracy and Power in an American City.* New Haven, CT: Yale University Press, 1961.

DeSombre, Elizabeth R. *Global Environmental Institutions.* New York: Routledge, 2006.

———. *The Global Environment and World Politics*, 2nd ed. London: Continuum, 2007.

DeSombre, Elizabeth R., and J. Samuel Barkin. "The Turbot War: Canada, Spain, and the Conflict over the North Atlantic Fishery." *PEW Case Studies in International Affairs*, Case Study #226. Washington, DC: Institute for the Study of Diplomacy, 2000.

———. "Turbot and Tempers in the North Atlantic." In *Conserving the Peace: Resources, Livelihoods, and Security*, edited by Richard Matthew, Mark Halle, and Jason Switzer. Winnipeg: International Institute for Sustainable Development, 2002.

DeSombre, Elizabeth R., and Joanne Kauffman. "The Montreal Protocol Multilateral Fund: Partial Success Story." In *Institutions for Environmental Aid: Pitfalls and Promise*, edited by Robert Keohane and Marc Levy. Cambridge, MA: MIT Press, 1996.

Diehl, Paul. *International Peacekeeping*. Baltimore: Johns Hopkins University Press, 1994.

DiMaggio, Paul, and Walter Powell. "The Iron Cage Revisited: Institutional Isomorphism and Collective Rationality in Organizational Fields." *American Sociological Review* 48 (1983): 147–160.

Dinan, Desmond. *Ever Closer Union: An Introduction to European Integration*, 4th ed. Boulder, CO: Lynne Rienner, 2010.

Donnelly, Jack. *International Human Rights*, 3rd ed. Boulder, CO: Westview Press, 2006.

Downs, George, David Rocke, and Peter Barsoom. "Is the Good News about Compliance Good News about Cooperation?" *International Organization* 50 (1996): 379–406.

Drezner, Daniel. "Globalization and Policy Convergence." *International Studies Review* 3 (2001): 53–78.

———. *All Politics Is Global: Explaining International Regulatory Regimes*. Princeton: Princeton University Press, 2007.

Fearon, James. "Rationalist Explanations for War." *International Organization* 49 (1995): 379–414.

———. "Bargaining, Enforcement, and International Cooperation." *International Organization* 52 (1998): 269–306.

Fenner, F., D.A. Henderson, 1. Arita, Z. Jezek, and I.D. Ladnyi. *Smallpox and Its Eradication*. Geneva: WHO, 1988.

Finnemore, Martha. *National Interests in International Society*. Ithaca, NY: Cornell University Press, 1996.

Fooner, Michael. *A Guide to Interpol: The International Criminal Police Organization in the United States*. Washington, DC: U.S. Department of Justice, National Institute of Justice, 1985.

Foot, Rosemary. *Rights beyond Borders: The Global Community and the Struggle over Human Rights in China*. Oxford: Oxford University Press, 2000.

Forsythe, David P. *Human Rights in International Relations*, 2nd ed. Cambridge: Cambridge University Press, 2006.

Friedheim, Robert, ed. *Toward a Sustainable Whaling Regime*. Seattle: University of Washington Press, 2001.

Gallagher, Kevin, and Jacob Werksman, eds. *The Earthscan Reader on International Trade & Sustainable Development*. London: Earthscan, 2002.

Galloway, Jonathan. "Worldwide Corporations and International Integration: The Case of INTELSAT." *International Organization* 24 (1970): 503–519.

Gardner, Richard. *Sterling–Dollar Diplomacy: Anglo-American Collaboration in the Reconstruction of Multilateral Trade*. Oxford: Clarendon Press, 1956.

———. *Sterling–Dollar Diplomacy in Current Perspective: The Origins and the Prospects of Our International Economic Order*. New York: Columbia University Press, 1980.

General Agreement on Tariffs and Trade. *General Agreement on Tariffs and Trade: Text of the General Agreement*. Geneva: GATT, 1994.

Goldstein, Judith, Miles Kahler, Robert Keohane, and Anne-Marie Slaughter, eds. *Legalization and World Politics*. Cambridge, MA: MIT Press, 2001.

Gowa, Joanne. "Rational Hegemons, Excludable Goods, and Small Groups: An Epitaph for Hegemonic Stability Theory?" *World Politics* 41 (1989): 307–324.

Grieco, Joseph. "Anarchy and the Limits of Cooperation: A Realist Critique of the Newest Liberal Institutionalism." *International Organization* 42 (1988): 485–507.

Gruber, Lloyd. *Ruling the World: Power Politics and the Rise of Supranational Institutions.* Princeton, NJ: Princeton University Press, 2000.

Guitián, Manuel. *The Unique Nature of the Responsibilities of the International Monetary Fund.* Pamphlet Series #46. Washington, DC: IMF, 1992.

Gutner, Tamar L. *Banking on the Environment: Multilateral Development Banks and Their Environmental Performance in Central and Eastern Europe.* Cambridge, MA: MIT Press, 2002.

Haas, Ernst. *Beyond the Nation-State: Functionalism and International Organization.* Stanford: Stanford University Press, 1964.

———. "Is There a Hole in the Whole? Knowledge, Technology, Interdependence, and the Construction of International Regimes." *International Organization* 29 (1975): 827–876.

———. *When Knowledge Is Power.* Berkeley: University of California Press, 1990.

Haas, Peter. *Saving the Mediterranean: The Politics of International Environmental Cooperation.* New York: Columbia University Press, 1990.

———. "Introduction: Epistemic Communities and International Policy Coordination." *International Organization* 46 (1992): 1–35.

Haas, Peter, Robert Keohane, and Marc Levy, eds. *Institutions for the Earth: Sources of Effective International Environmental Protection.* Cambridge, MA: MIT Press, 1993.

Hafner-Burton, Emilie, Miles Kahler, and Alexander Montgomery, "Network Analysis for International Relations." *International Organization* 63 (2009): 559–592.

Hall, Rodney Bruce. "Moral Authority as a Power Resource." *International Organization* 51 (1997): 555–589.

Hawkins, Darren, David Lake, Daniel Nielson, and Michael Tierney, eds. *Delegation and Agency in International Organization.* Cambridge: Cambridge University Press, 2006.

Henkin, Louis. *How Nations Behave: Law and Foreign Policy*, 2nd ed. New York: Columbia University Press, 1979.

Henton, Darcy. "Not so Picture Perfect." *Toronto Star*, June 4, 1998.

Hilsman, Roger, with Laura Gaughran and Patricia Weitsman. *The Politics of Policy-Making in Defense and Foreign Affairs: Conceptual Models and Bureaucratic Politics*, 3rd ed. Englewood Cliffs, NJ: Prentice Hall, 1993.

Hirschman, Albert O. *National Power and the Structure of Foreign Trade.* Berkeley: University of California Press, 1945.

Hoffmann, Stanley. "International Organization and the International System." *International Organization* 24 (1970): 389–413.

Hogan, Michael. *The Marshall Plan: America, Britain, and the Reconstruction of Europe, 1947–1952.* Cambridge: Cambridge University Press, 1987.

Hurd, Ian. "Legitimacy and Authority in International Politics." *International Organization* 53 (1999): 379–408.

Intergovernmental Panel on Climate Change. *Climate Change 2007: Impacts, Adaptation and Vulnerability.* Geneva: IPCC, 2008.

———. *Climate Change 2007: Mitigation of Climate Change.* Geneva: IPCC, 2008.

———. *Climate Change 2007: The Physical Basis.* Geneva: IPCC, 2008.

———. *Climate Change 2007: Synthesis Report.* Geneva: IPCC, 2008.

International Atomic Energy Agency. *IAEA Annual Report 2010.* Vienna: IAEA, 2011.

International Civil Aviation Organization. *Resolution A37–19: Consolidated Statement of Continuing ICAO Policies and Practices Related to Environmental Protection—Climate Change.* Montreal: ICAO, 2010.

International Committee of the Red Cross. "ICRC 2001 Financial Statements Meet International Accounting Standards—ICRC First Humanitarian Organization to Apply IAS." ICRC Press Release 02/45, August 16, 2002.

———. *Annual Report 2010.* Geneva: ICRC, 2011.

International Criminal Court. *Rome Statute of the International Criminal Court.* The Hague: ICC, 1998.

———. *Resolution RC/Res.6: The Crime of Aggression.* The Hague: ICC, 2010.

———. *The Court Today,* Updated April 11, 2012. The Hague: ICC, 2012.

International Criminal Police Organization-Interpol. *Constitution.* Lyon: Interpol, 2004.

———. *Interpol Annual Report 2010.* Lyon: Interpol, 2011.

International Labour Organization. *Constitution.* Geneva: ILO, 2001 [1919].

International Monetary Fund. *Articles of Agreement of the International Monetary Fund.* Washington, DC: IMF, 1945.

———. *Annual Report 2007: Making the Global Economy Work for All.* Washington, DC: IMF, 2007.

———. *Annual Report 2011: Pursuing Equitable and Balanced Growth.* Washington, DC: IMF, 2011.

———. "IMF Executive Board Considers Use of Windfall Gold Sales Profit." IMF Public Information Notice 11/121, September 16, 2011.

International Olympic Committee. *Olympic Charter.* Lausanne: IOC, 2011.

———. *Olympic Marketing Fact File,* 2012 ed. Lausanne: IOC, 2012.

International Union for Conservation of Nature and Natural Resources. *IUCN Membership Dues Guide 2009–2012.* Gland, Switzerland: IUCN, 2010.

———. *Statutes and Regulations.* Gland, Switzerland: IUCN, 2012.

IUCN Species Survival Commission. *2004 IUCN Red List of Threatened Species: A Global Species Assessment,* edited by Jonathan E. M. Baillie, Craig Hilton-Taylor, and Simon N. Stuart. Cambridge: IUCN (The World Conservation Union), 2004.

Ivanova, Maria. "Institutional Design and UNEP Reform: Historical Insights on Form, Function, and Financing." *International Affairs* 88 (2012): 565–584.

Jackson, Robert. *Quasi-States: Sovereignty, International Relations, and the Third World.* Cambridge: Cambridge University Press, 1990.

Jacobson, Harold. *Networks of Interdependence.* New York: Alfred A. Knopf, 1979.

James, Barry. "Libya to Lead UN Human Rights Body; Tripoli Easily Wins Vote U.S. Demanded." *International Herald Tribune,* January 21, 2003, p. 1.

Jervis, Robert. *Perception and Misperception in International Politics.* Princeton, NJ: Princeton University Press, 1976.

———. "Security Regimes." *International Organization* 36 (1982): 357–378.

Joyner, Christopher. "Managing Common-Pool Marine Living Resources: Lessons from the Southern Ocean Experience." In *Anarchy and the Environment: The International Relations of Common Pool Resources,* edited by Samuel Barkin and George Shambaugh, pp. 70–96. Albany: State University of New York Press, 1999.

Kahn, Joseph. "Nations Back Freer Trade, Hoping to Aid Global Growth." *New York Times,* November 15, 2001, A12.

Katzenstein, Peter, Robert Keohane, and Stephen Krasner, eds. *Exploration and Contestation in the Study of World Politics.* Cambridge, MA: MIT Press, 1999.

Keck, Margaret, and Kathryn Sikkink. *Activists beyond Borders: Advocacy Networks in International Politics.* Ithaca, NY: Cornell University Press, 1998.

Keith, Jim. *Black Helicopters over America: Strikeforce for the New World Order.* Lilburn, GA: IllumiNet Press, 1994.

Kennedy, David. "International Refugee Protection." *Human Rights Quarterly* 8 (1986): 1–9.

Keohane, Robert. "The Demand for International Regimes." *International Organization* 36 (1982): 325–356.

———. *After Hegemony: Cooperation and Discord in the World Political Economy.* Princeton, NJ: Princeton University Press, 1984.

———. "Reciprocity in International Relations." *International Organization* 40 (1986): 1–27.

———. "International Institutions: Two Approaches." *International Studies Quarterly* 32 (1988): 379–396.

Keohane, Robert, and Joseph Nye. *Power and Interdependence: World Politics in Transition.* Boston, MA: Little, Brown, 1977.

———. Power and Interdependence, 3rd ed. New York: Longman, 2001.

Kindleberger, Charles. *Manias, Panics, and Crashes: A History of Financial Crises.* New York: Basic Books, 1978.

Knorr, Klaus. "Supranational Versus International Models for General and Complete Disarmamant." In *The Strategy of World Order. Vol. IV, Disarmament and Economic Development,* edited by Richard Falk and Saul Mendlovitz, pp. 326–353. New York: World Law Fund, 1966.

Krasner, Stephen. *Defending the National Interest: Raw Materials Investment and U.S. Foreign Policy.* Princeton, NJ: Princeton University Press, 1978.

———, ed. *International Regimes.* Ithaca, NY: Cornell University Press, 1983.

———. "Structural Causes and Regime Consequences: Regimes as Intervening Variables." In *International Regimes,* edited by Stephen Krasner, pp. 1–21. Ithaca, NY: Cornell University Press, 1983.

———. *Structural Conflict: The Third World against Global Liberalism.* Berkeley: University of California Press, 1985.

———. "Global Communications and National Power: Life on the Pareto Frontier." *World Politics* 43 (1991): 336–366.

———. "Westphalia and All That." In *Ideas and Foreign Policy: Beliefs, Institutions, and Political Change,* edited by Judith Goldstein and Robert Keohane, pp. 235–264. Ithaca, NY: Cornell University Press, 1993.

———. *Sovereignty: Organized Hypocrisy.* Princeton, NJ: Princeton University Press, 1999.

Kratochwil, Friedrich, and John Gerard Ruggie. "International Organization: A State of the Art on an Art of the State." *International Organization* 40 (1986): 753–775.

Leonard, H. Jeffrey. *Pollution and the Struggle for World Product: Multinational Corporations, Environment, and International Comparative Advantage.* Cambridge: Cambridge University Press, 1988.

Levy, Marc. "European Acid Rain: The Power of Tote-Board Diplomacy." In *Institutions for the Earth: Sources of Effective International Environmental Protection,* edited by Peter M. Haas, Robert O. Keohane and Marc A. Levy. Cambridge, MA: MIT Press, 1993.

Levy, Steven. "INTELSAT: Technology, Politics, and the Transformation of a Regime." *International Organization* 29 (1975): 655–680.

Lindberg, Leon, and Stuart Scheingold. *Europe's Would-Be Polity: Patterns of Change in the European Community.* Englewood Cliffs, NJ: Prentice Hall, 1970.

Lukes, Steven. *Power: A Radical View.* London: Macmillan, 1974.

Mander, Jerry, and Edward Goldsmith, eds. *The Case against the Global Economy: And for a Turn toward the Local.* San Francisco: Sierra Club Books, 1996.

March, James. *Decisions and Organizations.* Boston, MA: Basil Blackwell, 1988.

March, James, and Johan Olsen. *Rediscovering Institutions: The Organizational Basis of Politics*. New York: Free Press, 1989.

———. "The Institutional Dynamics of International Political Orders." *International Organization* 52 (1998): 943–969.

Mearsheimer, John. "The False Promise of International Institutions." *International Security* 19 (1994–1995): 5–49.

Meisler, Stanley. *United Nations: A History*, rev. ed. New York: Grove Press, 2011.

Miles, Edward, Arild Underdal, Steinar Andresen, Jorgen Wettestad, Tora Skodvin, and Elaine Carlin. *Environmental Regime Effectiveness*. Cambridge, MA: MIT Press, 2001.

Milliken, Jennifer. "The Study of Discourse in International Relations: A Critique of Research and Methods." *European Journal of International Relations* 5 (1999): 225–254.

Milward, Alan. *The Reconstruction of Western Europe, 1945–51*. Berkeley: University of California Press, 1984.

Mitchell, Ronald. *Intentional Oil Pollution at Sea: Environmental Policy and Treaty Compliance*. Cambridge, MA: MIT Press, 1994.

———. "Sources of Transparency: Information Systems in International Regimes." *International Studies Quarterly* 42 (1998): 109–130.

Monaco Agreement on the Conservation of Cetaceans in the Black Sea, Mediterranean Sea and Contiguous Atlantic Areas. *ACCOBAMS Bulletin #3*. Monaco: Interim ACCOBAMS Secretariat, 2000.

Moravcsik, Andrew. *The Choice for Europe: Social Purpose and State Power from Messina to Maastricht*. Ithaca, NY: Cornell University Press, 1998.

Murphy, Craig. *The United Nations Development Programme: A Better Way?* Cambridge: Cambridge University Press, 2006.

Murphy, Craig, and JoAnne Yates. *The International Organization for Standardization (ISO): Global Governance through Voluntary Consensus*. New York: Routledge, 2009.

Najam, Adil. "The Case against a New International Environmental Organization." *Global Governance* 9 (2003): 367–384.

NATO Office of Information and Press. *NATO Handbook*. Brussels: NATO, 2001.

Nayar, Baldav Raj. "Regimes, Power, and International Aviation." *International Organization* 49 (1995): 139–170.

Nielson, Daniel L., and Michael J. Tierney. "Delegation to International Organizations: Agency Theory and World Bank Environmental Reform." *International Organization* 57 (2003): 241–276.

North, Douglass. *Structure and Change in Economic History*. New York: Norton, 1981.

North, Douglass, and Robert Paul Thomas. *The Rise of the Western World: A New Economic History*. Cambridge: Cambridge University Press, 1973.

Northwest Atlantic Fisheries Organization. *Annual Report 2011*. Dartmouth, NS: NAFO, 2012.

Nye, Joseph. *Bound to Lead: The Changing Nature of American Power*. New York: Basic Books, 1990.

Olson, Mancur. *The Logic of Collective Action: Public Goods and the Theory of Groups*. Cambridge, MA: Harvard University Press, 1965.

Onuf, Nicholas. *World of Our Making: Rules and Rule in Social Theory and International Relations*. Columbia: University of South Carolina Press, 1989.

Osiander, Andreas. "Sovereignty, International Relations, and the Westphalian Myth." *International Organization* 55 (2001): 251–287.

Oye, Kenneth, ed. *Cooperation under Anarchy*. Princeton, NJ: Princeton University Press, 1986.

Pilling, David. "Japan Urged to Cut Payments to UN." *Financial Times*, January 17, 2003.

Pollis, Adamantia. "Liberal, Socialist, and Third World Perspectives on Human Rights." In *Human Rights in the World Community*, edited by Richard Claude and Burns Weston, 2nd ed. Philadelphia: University of Pennsylvania Press, 1992.

"Privatization of INTELSAT." *American Journal of International Law* 95 (2001): 893–895.

Raustiala, Kal, and David Victor. "The Regime Complex for Plant Genetic Resources." *International Organization* 58 (2004): 277–309.

Rich, Bruce. *Mortgaging the Earth: The World Bank, Environmental Impoverishment, and the Crisis of Development*. Boston, MA: Beacon Press, 1994.

Risse, Thomas, Stephen Ropp, and Kathryn Sikkink, eds. *The Power of Human Rights: International Norms and Domestic Change*. Cambridge: Cambridge University Press, 1999.

Rohde, David. "Ted Turner Plans a $1 Billion Gift for U.N. Agencies." *New York Times*, September 19, 1997, A1.

Rosenau, James N., and Ernst-Otto Czempiel, eds. *Governance without Government: Order and Change in World Politics*. Cambridge: Cambridge University Press, 1992.

Ruggie, John Gerard. "Multilateralism: The Anatomy of an Institution." *International Organization* 46 (1992): 561–598.

———, ed. *Multilateralism Matters: The Theory and Praxis of an Institutional Form*. New York: Columbia University Press, 1993.

Ryan, Stephen. *The United Nations and International Politics*. New York: St. Martin's Press, 2000.

Sampson, Gary P., and W. Bradnee Chambers, eds. *Trade, Environment, and the Millennium*. Tokyo: United Nations University Press, 1999.

Schmitter, Philippe. "Three Neo-Functionalist Hypotheses about International Integration." *International Organization* 23 (1969): 161–166.

Scholte, Jan Aart. *Globalisation: A Critical Introduction*, 2nd ed. Houndmills, Hampshire: Palgrave, 2005.

Schultz, William F. *In Our Own Best Interest: How Defending Human Rights Benefits Us All*. Boston, MA: Beacon Press, 2001.

Secretary-General. *Renewing the United Nations: A Programme for Reform*. New York: United Nations General Assembly A/51/950, 1997.

———. *Strengthening the United Nations: An Agenda for Further Change*. New York: United Nations General Assembly A/57/387, 2002.

Shanks, Cheryl, Harold Jacobson, and Jeffrey Kaplan. "Inertia and Change in the Constellation of International Governmental Organizations, 1981–1992." *International Organization* 50 (1996): 593–628.

Simmons, Beth. "The International Politics of Harmonization: The Case of Capital Market Regulation." *International Organization* 55 (2001): 589–620.

———. *Mobilizing for Human Rights: International Law in Domestic Politics*. Cambridge: Cambridge University Press, 2009.

Sinnar, Shirin. "Mixed Blessing: The Growing Influence of NGOs." *Harvard International Review* 18, no.1 (Winter 1995–1996): 54–57.

Sjoberg, Laura. "Gendered Realities of the Immunity Principle: Why Gender Analysis Needs Feminism," *International Studies Quarterly* 50 (2006): 889–910.

Smith, Thomas W. "The New Law of War: Legitimizing Hi-Tech and Infrastructural Violence." *International Studies Quarterly* 46 (2002): 355–374.

Snidal, Duncan. "Coordination Versus Prisoners' Dilemma: Implications for International Cooperation and Regimes." *American Political Science Review* 79 (1985): 923–942.

Snyder, Glenn, and Paul Diesing. *Conflict among Nations: Bargaining, Decision Making, and System Structure in International Crises.* Princeton, NJ: Princeton University Press, 1977.

Stein, Eric. "International Integration and Democracy: No Love at First Sight." *American Journal of International Law* 95 (2001): 498–499.

Stiglitz, Joseph. *Globalization and Its Discontents.* New York: Norton, 2002.

Strange, Susan. "Cave, Hic Dragones: A Critique of Regime Analysis." *International Organization* 36 (1982): 479–496.

Susskind, Lawrence. *Environmental Diplomacy: Negotiating More Effective Global Agreements.* New York: Oxford University Press, 1994.

Thomas, Daniel C. *The Helsinki Effect: International Norms, Human Rights, and the Demise of Communism.* Princeton, NJ: Princeton University Press, 2001.

Thomson, Janice. "State Sovereignty in International Relations: Bridging the Gap between Theory and Empirical Research." *International Studies Quarterly* 39 (1995): 213–234.

Union of International Organizations. *Yearbook of International Organizations*, 48th ed. Munich: K.G. Saur, 2011.

United Nations. "Convention (IV) Relative to the Protection of Civilian Persons in Time of War." *United Nations Treaty Series No. 973, vol. 75.* Geneva: UN, 1949.

———. *Charter of the United Nations.* New York: UN, 1965.

———. *International Convention on the Elimination of All Forms of Racial Discrimination*, 60 UNTS 195. New York: UN, 1966.

———. "Secretary-General's High-Level Panel on Threats, Challenges and Change." *A More Secure World: Our Shared Responsibility.* New York: UN, 2004.

———. "Year in Review: United Nations Peacekeeping Operations, 2011." United Nations Department of Public Information (DPI/2579/Rev. 1), March 2012.

United Nations Children's Fund. *2010 UNICEF Annual Report.* New York: UNICEF, 2010.

United Nations Conference on Sustainable Development. *The Future We Want.* Rio de Janeiro: UNCSD, 2012.

United Nations Development Assistance Framework. *UNDAF Guidelines.* New York: UN, 1999.

United Nations Development Programme. *Human Development Report 2002: Deepening Democracy in a Fragmented World.* New York: Oxford University Press, 2002.

———. *United Nations Development Programme Annual Report 2003: A World of Development Experience.* New York: UNDP, 2003.

United Nations Environment Programme. *Annual Report 2010.* Nairobi: UNEP, 2011.

United Nations General Assembly. *Resolution 2626 (XXV): International Development Strategy for the Second United Nations Development Decade.* New York: UN, 1970.

———. *Convention against Torture and Other Cruel, Inhuman or Degrading Treatment or Punishment. UN General Assembly Resolution 39/46 Annex.* New York: UN, 1984.

———. *Resolution 43/53: Protection of Global Climate for Present and Future Generations of Mankind.* New York: UN, 1988.

———. *Resolution 48/141: High Commissioner for the Promotion and Protection of All Human Rights.* New York: UN, 1994.

———. *Resolution 55/2: United Nations Millennium Declaration.* New York: UN, 2000.

———. *Resolution 60/1: 2005 World Summit Outcome.* New York: UN, 2005.

———. *Resolution 61/237: Scale of Assessments for the Apportionment of the Expenses of the United Nations.* New York: UN, 2007.

United Nations General Assembly. *Resolution 63/308: The Responsibility to Protect.* New York: UN, 2009.

United Nations High Commission for Refugees. *Contributions to UNHCR Programmes for Budget Year 2009: As at 31 December 2009.* Geneva: UNHCR, 2010.

———. *UNHCR Global Report 2010.* Geneva: UNHCR, 2011.

United Nations Secretary-General. *Implementing the Responsibility to Protect: Report of the Secretary-General.* UN General Assembly Document A/63/677. New York: UN, 2009.

———. *Composition of the Secretariat: Staff Demographics.* UN General Assembly Document A/65/350. New York: UN, 2010.

United Nations Security Council. *Repertoire of the Practice of the Security Council.* Serial. New York: UN, 1946–present,

———. *Security Council Resolution 1031 on Implementation of the Peace Agreement for Bosnia and Herzegovina and the Transfer of Authority from the UN Protection Force to the Multinational Implementation Force (IFOR).* New York: UN, 1995.

———. *Security Council Resolution 1368.* New York: UN, 2001.

———. *Security Council Resolution 1373.* New York: UN, 2001.

———. *Security Council Resolution 1483.* New York: UN, 2003.

———. *Security Council Resolution 1593.* New York: UN, 2005.

Van Houtven, Leo. *Governance of the IMF: Decision-Making, Institutional Oversight, Transparency, and Accountability.* Pamphlet Series #53. Washington, DC: IMF, 2002.

Wapner, Paul. *Environmental Activism and World Civic Politics.* Albany: State University of New York Press, 1996.

Wendt, Alexander. *Social Theory of International Politics.* Cambridge: Cambridge University Press, 1999.

World Bank Group. *Making Sustainable Commitments: An Environment Strategy for the World Bank.* Washington, DC: World Bank, 2001.

———. *The World Bank Annual Report 2011: Year in Review.* Washington, DC: World Bank, 2011.

———. *World Development Indicators 2011.* Washington, DC: World Bank, 2011.

World Commission on Environment and Development. *Our Common Future.* Oxford: Oxford University Press, 1987.

World Food Programme. *Fighting Hunger Worldwide: Annual Report 2010.* Rome: WFP, 2010.

World Health Organization. *Constitution of the World Health Organization.* Geneva: WHO, 1994.

———. *World Health Report 2001—Mental Health: New Understanding, New Hope.* Geneva: WHO, 2001.

———. "Health Conditions of, and Assistance to, the Arab Population in the Occupied Arab Territories, Including Palestine." Fifty-Fifth World Health Assembly. Document WHA55/2002/REC/1. Geneva: WHO, 2002.

———. *Report of the Director-General, 2001.* Geneva: WHO, 2002.

———. *Financial Report and Audited Financial Statements for the Period 1 January 2010–31 December 2011 and Report of the External Auditor to the World Health Assembly.* Geneva: WHO, 2012.

World Intellectual Property Organization. *Annual Report 2011.* Geneva: WIPO, 2011.

World Trade Organization. *10 Common Misunderstandings about the WTO.* Geneva: WTO, 2008.

Young, Oran, ed. *The Effectiveness of International Environmental Agreements.* Cambridge, MA: MIT Press, 1999.

Film Source

Our Friends at the Bank. New York: First Run/Icarus Films, 1997.

Web Sources

All web sources are current as of July 17, 2012.

Annan, Kofi. "Secretary-General's Address to the General Assembly, New York, September 23, 2003." http://www.un.org/apps/sg/sgstats.asp?nid=517.

Asian Development Bank. "Members." http://www.adb.org/about/members.

Bank for International Settlements. "About BIS." http://www.bis.org/about/index .htm?ql=1.

Bureau of Arms Control. *Fact Sheet: The Biological Weapons Convention.* Washington: U.S. Department of State, released on May 22, 2002. http://www.state.govt/ac/rls /fs/10401.htm.

Central Commission for Navigation on the Rhine. "History." http://www.ccr-zkr.org /11010100-en.html

Convention Concerning the Protection of the World Cultural and Natural Heritage. http:// whc.unesco.org/world_he.htm#debut.

Convention on the Marking of Plastic Explosives for the Purpose of Detection. http://www .un.org/en/sc/ctc/docs/conventions/Conv10.pdf.

Convention between the United States, Great Britain, Russia and Japan for the Preservation and Protection of Fur Seals (1911). http://fletcher.archive.tusm-oit.org/multilaterals /sealtreaty.html.

Council of Europe. *Convention for the Protection of Human Rights and Fundamental Freedoms.* http://conventions.coe.int/treaty/en/Treaties/html/005.htm.

———. "Execution of Judgments of the European Court of Human Rights," http://www .coe.int/t/dghl/monitoring/execution/default_EN.asp.

Global Environment Facility, "What Is the GEF." http://www.thegef.org/gef/whatisgef.

Group of 77. www.g77.org.

Intergovernmental Panel on Climate Change. "Principles Governing IPCC Work." http://www.ipcc.ch/pdf/ipcc-principles/ipcc-principles.pdf.

International Atomic Energy Agency. "Member States of the IAEA." http://iaea.org /About/Policy/MemberStates/.

International Campaign to Ban Landmines. "Text of the Mine Ban Treaty." http://www .icbl.org/treaty/text.

International Civil Aviation Organization. "How It Works." http://www.icao.int/pages /how-it-works.aspx.

———. "Legal Affairs and External Relations Bureau." http://www.icao.int/secretariat /legal/Pages/default.aspx.

———. "Making an ICAO Standard." http://legacy.icao.int/icao/en/anb/mais/index .html.

———. "Technical Co-operation Bureau," http://www.icao.int/secretariat/Technical Cooperation/Pages/default.aspx.

International Court of Justice. "Declarations Recognizing as Compulsory the Jurisdiction of the Court." http://www.icj-cij.org/icjwww/ibasicdocuments/ibasic text/ibasicdeclarations.htm.

International Institute for Sustainable Development. *Earth Negotiation Bulletin.* http:// www.iisd.ca.

International Monetary Fund. "About the IMF." http://www.imf.org/external/about.htm.

International Monetary Fund. "Factsheet: IMF Conditionality." http://www.imf.org /external/np/exr/facts/conditio.htm.

———. "Factsheet: IMF Surveillance—March 2012," http://www.imf.org/external/np /exr/facts/surv.htm.

———. "IMF Members' Quotas and Voting Power, and IMF Board of Governors." http://www.imf.org/external/np/sec/memdir/members.aspx.

———. "IMF Organization Chart." http://www.imf.org/external/np/obp/orgcht.htm.

International Organization for Standardization. "ISO in Figures for the Year 2011 (at 31 December)." http://www.iso.org/iso/iso-in-figures_2011.pdf.

———."ISO Members." http://www.iso.org/iso/iso_members.

International Union for Conservation of Nature and Natural Resources. "The IUCN Red List of Threatened Species." http://www.iucnredlist.org/.

Interpol. "Notices." http://www.interpol.int/INTERPOL-expertise/Notices.

Northwest Atlantic Fisheries Organization. "Scientific Council." http://www.nafo.int /science/frames/science.html.

Office of the United Nations High Commissioner for Human Rights. "United Nations Human Rights Council." http://www.ohchr.org/EN/HRBodies/HRC/Pages /AboutCouncil.aspx.

Organization for Economic Cooperation and Development. "Net ODA in 2011." http:// webnet.oecd.org/oda2011/.

South African Development Community. "Protocol on Politics, Defence and Security Co-operation to the Declaration and Treaty of SADC (2001)." http://www.sadc.int /english/key-documents/protocols/protocol-on-politics-defence-and-security-coope ration/.

United Nations. "Process of Renewal." http://www.un.org/en/strengtheningtheun/index .shtml.

United Nations Conference on Trade and Development. "Technical Cooperation." http://www.unctad.org.

United Nations Department of Peacekeeping Operations. "United Nations Peacekeeping." http://www.un.org/Depts/dpko/dpko/index.asp.

United Nations Department of Public Information. "Special and Personal Representatives and Envoys of the Secretary-General." http://www.un.org/News/ossg/srsg/.

———. "The United Nations System." http://www.un.org/aboutun/chart.html.

United Nations Development Programme. "About UNDP: A World of Development Experience." http://www.undp.org/about/.

United Nations Environment Programme. "Environment Fund—Top 20 Donor Countries—Trend in Contributions in 2008–2010." http://www.unep.org/rms/en /Financing_of_UNEP/Environment_Fund/pdf/Top%2020%20Donors%20 2008.2010%2018.2.2011.pdf.

United Nations Global Compact. "The Global Compact." http://www.unglobalcompact .org/.

United Nations High Commission for Refugees. "Contributions to 2001 UNHCR Programs (in United States Dollars): Situation as at 31 December 2001." Geneva: UNHCR. www.unhcr.ch.

———. "UNHCR Headquarters Structure." http://www.unhcr.ch/cgi-bin/texis/vtx /admin.

———. "Staff Figures." http://www.unhcr.org/pages/49c3646c17.html.

———. "What We Do." http://www.unhcr.org/pages/49c3646cbf.html.

United Nations Office for Disarmament Affairs. *Treaty on the Non-Proliferation of Nuclear Weapons.* http://disarmament.un.org/treaties/t/npt/text.

United Nations Office on Drugs and Crime. "About Us." http://www.unodc.org/unodc
/about.html.

United States Department of State. "International Criminal Court," Office of Global
Criminal Justice, Washington, DC. http://www.state.gov/j/gcj/icc/.

Universal Postal Union. "About Financial Inclusion." http://www.upu.int/en/activities
/financial-inclusion/about-financial-inclusion.html.

———. "About Terminal Dues and Transit Charges." http://www.upu.int/en/activities
/terminal-dues-and-transit-charges/about-terminal-dues-and-transit-charges.html.

———. "The UPU." http://www.upu.int/en/the-upu/the-upu.html.

World Conference against Racism. "Basic Information: The World Conference against
Racism, Racial Discrimination, Xenophobia and Related Intolerance." http://www
.un.org/WCAR/e-kit/backgrounder1.htm.

———. *Durban Declaration and Programme of Action.* http://www.unhchr.ch/html/
racism/02-documents-cnt.html.

World Food Programme. "Government Donors." http://www.wfp.org/government
-donors.

World Health Organization. "Avian Influenza." http://www.who.int/mediacentre/fact
sheets/avian_influenza/en/index.html.

———. "WFP in Numbers." http://www.wfp.org/wfp-numbers.

World Trade Organization. "China to Join on 11 December, Chinese Taipei's Membership
also Approved." Doha WTO Ministerial 2001: Summary of November 11, 2001.
http://www.wto.org/english/thewto_e/minist_e/min01_e/min01_11nov_e.htm.

———. "A Summary of the Final Act of the Uruguay Round." http://www.wto.org
/english/docs_e/legal_e/ursum_e.htm.

———. "WTO Legal Texts." http://www.wto.org/english/docs_e/legal_e/legal_e.htm.

———. "WTO Organizational Chart." http://www.wto.org/english/thewto_e/whatis_e
/tif_e/org2_e.htm.

Index